LONDON'S CHURCHES

LONDON'S CHURCHES

ELIZABETH
AND WAYLAND YOUNG

with the assistance of
LOUISA YOUNG

GRAFTON BOOKS
A Division of the Collins Publishing Group

LONDON GLASGOW
TORONTO SYDNEY AUCKLAND

Grafton Books
A Division of the Collins Publishing Group
8 Grafton Street, London W1X 3LA

Published by Grafton Books 1986
in association with the English Tourist Board

British Library Cataloguing in Publication Data
Young, Elizabeth
London's churches.
1. Church architecture—England—London
2. London (England)—Buildings, structures, etc.
I. Title   II. Kennet, Wayland
726'.5'09421   NA5470.A1

ISBN 0–246–12696–5 (Paperback)
ISBN 0–246–12961–1 (Cased)

Typeset by CG Graphic Services, Aylesbury, Bucks
Printed in Great Britain by
Butler & Tanner Ltd, Frome and London

Designed by The Pinpoint Design Company

DEDICATED

TO THE

MEMORY

OF

JOHN BETJEMAN AND NIKOLAUS PEVSNER

AND

'OUR FATHERS THAT BEGAT US'

CONTENTS

PREFACE

London's Churches is intended to encourage the visitor – or the Londoner – to go where he or she might otherwise not go and where fewer visitors have been, but where beauties and curiosities are to be found. The three cathedrals (St Paul's, Westminster and Southwark) and Westminster Abbey are magnificent, but they are well known and well documented: many of the churches are not.

The book bears the following relationship to our *Old London Churches*, which was published in 1956. *Old London Churches* attempted to give an account of every church and chapel in the old London County Council area which, whether still standing or not, was built before 1830 or was on the site of a church built before 1830. That added up to 386 churches. We stopped at 1830 not because what came later was uninteresting but because it was too much: to have gone on with the 'every church and chapel' criterion would have landed us up with at least 1,400 more entries, such was the scale of London's expansion and of church building in the 19th century.

The present book is not an inclusive account of any particular category of London's churches. Seventy-seven of our 101 are from our original 386, and there are 24 new entries on churches built in or after the Victorian age. We have tried to include something at least of every style and period, but much that is interesting has still had to be left out; most of the foreign churches or temples for instance, and most of the Nonconformist churches and chapels.

The Introduction has been fully revised and expanded to cover what came after 1830. The texts about the churches which were in the former book have also been revised, and in some cases rewritten. In this work, and in the church-crawling it entailed, we were very much helped by Louisa Young, and also by Tracey Brett. The 24 new entries on later churches are entirely new.

Our thanks also to many others for unstinted good advice. The choice of churches to include was made by the authors and of course any errors in the book are our responsibility.

How to use the book

The Introduction gives a general account of church building and using in London from the earliest times. The single churches then appear in alphabetical order. The entry for each church is headed by these pieces of information:
1) the street it is in, and the postal district; 2) an indication of its position, e.g. IC4, IIE3, on one of the two maps on pages xii–xv; 3) the nearest

underground ('U') or railway station ('BR'). Each church is also numbered: to find a given church look for its number on the maps. To plan a church-crawl, look at the map and see how the numbered dots group themselves. Alternatively, look at the charts on pp. 205–9 and choose a handful of Wren churches, or of Hawksmoor's, or of Victorian ones. To find the precise location of a church you will need to use a London street map or atlas. When the name of a church is printed in small capital letters (in the Introduction or under another church in the main text), it will be found to have its own entry in the alphabetical sequence.

  ° Indicates a church no longer standing.

Opening times

As in other cities throughout Christendom, thefts and vandalism have made it no longer possible for London churches to be open all the time. The most likely time to find them open is of course Sunday, and particularly Sunday morning. Weekday lunchtimes are also likely, particularly in the City. In several of the finer churches, there are also sometimes concerts or organ recitals.

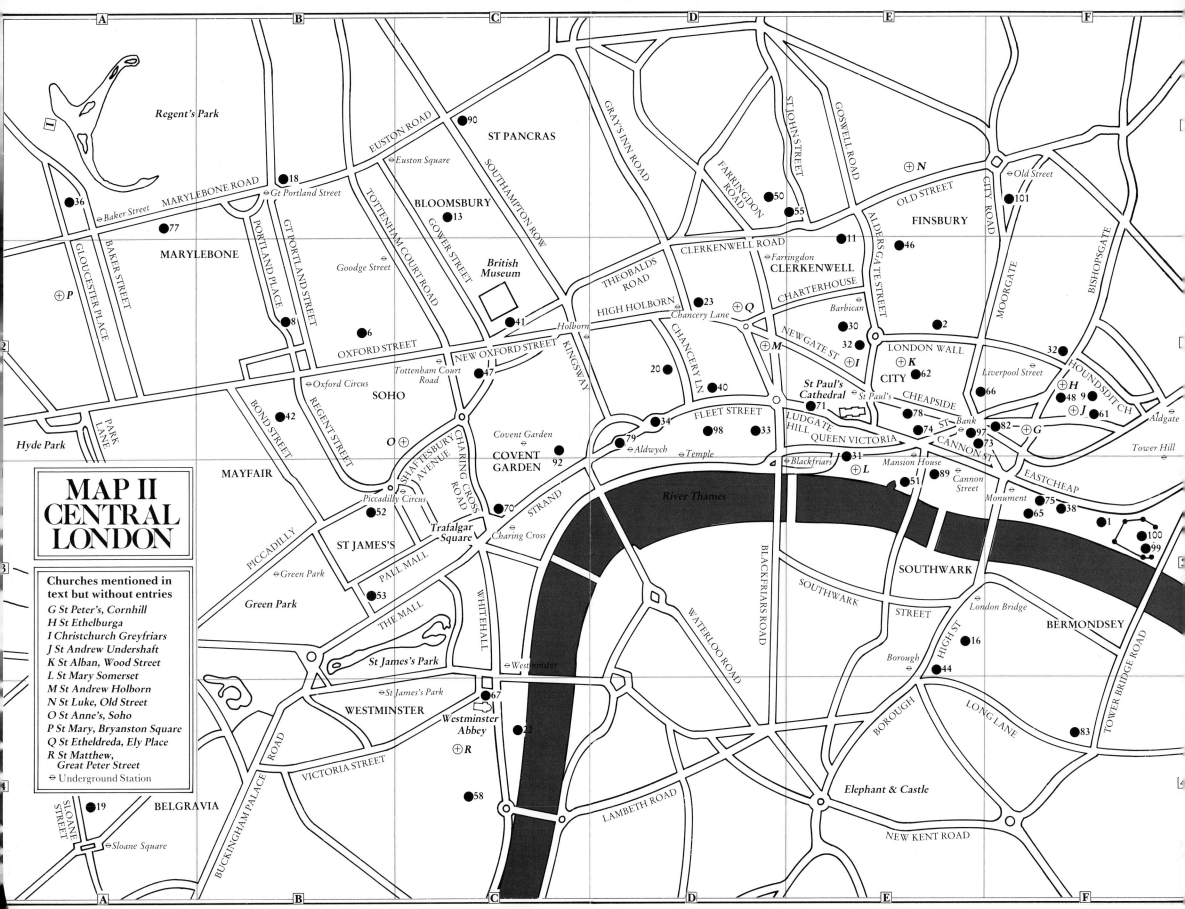

MAP II CENTRAL LONDON

Churches mentioned in text but without entries

G St Peter's, Cornhill
H St Ethelburga
I Christchurch Greyfriars
J St Andrew Undershaft
K St Alban, Wood Street
L St Mary Somerset
M St Andrew Holborn
N St Luke, Old Street
O St Anne's, Soho
P St Mary, Bryanston Square
Q St Etheldreda, Ely Place
R St Matthew, Great Peter Street

⊖ Underground Station

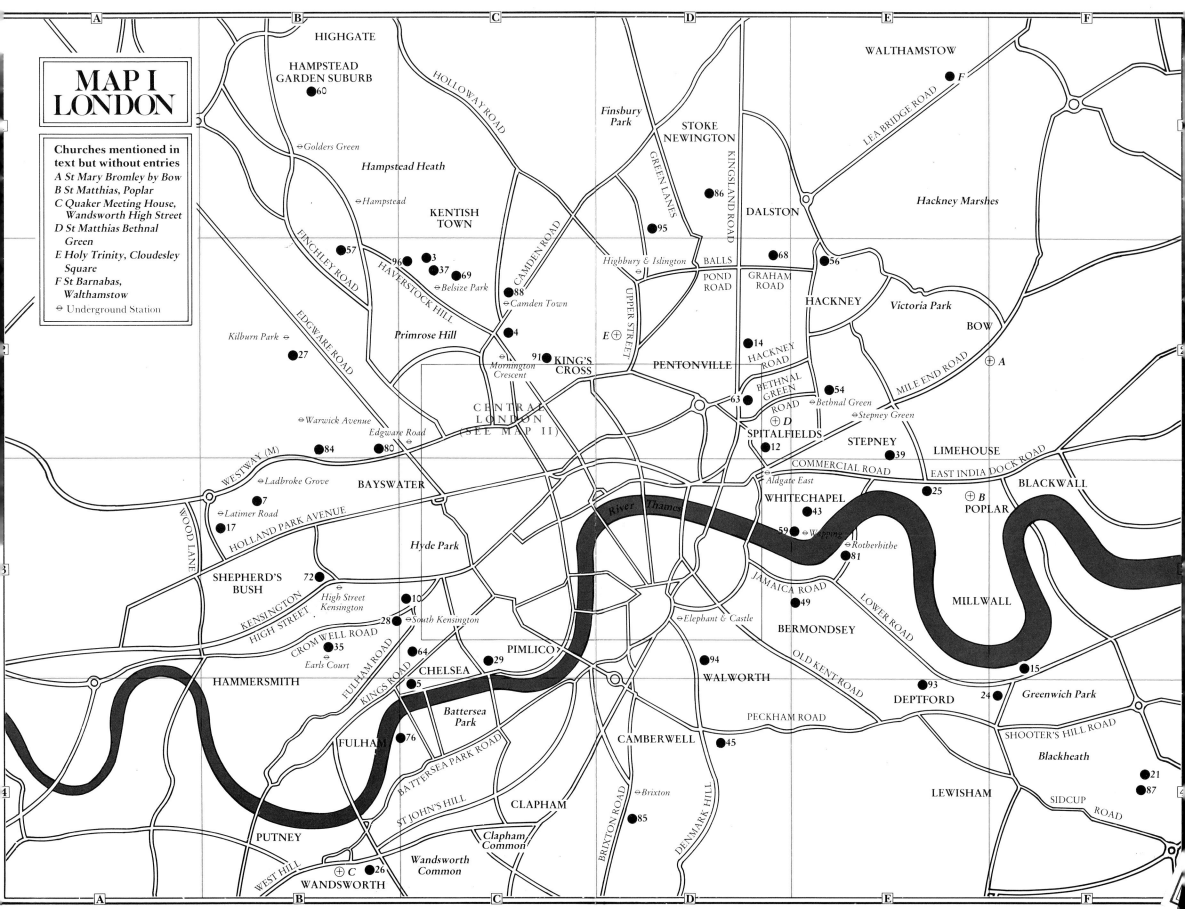

MAP I
LONDON

Churches mentioned in text but without entries

A St Mary Bromley by Bow
B St Matthias, Poplar
C Quaker Meeting House, Wandsworth High Street
D St Matthias Bethnal Green
E Holy Trinity, Cloudesley Square
F St Barnabas, Walthamstow

⊕ Underground Station

INTRODUCTION

'The great test of architectural beauty is the fitness of the Design to the purpose for which it is intended.' Thus wrote Augustus Welby Pugin, one of the inventors of the Gothic Revival.[1] It is an acceptable statement of practice, if not of theory, and can account very well for the divergent views different generations hold of their predecessors' church architecture. The logic is clear: God has been and continues to be worshipped in churches. As there is nothing more fundamental than God, and birth, marriage and death, the purposes for which churches are built do not change. Therefore a church should look like . . . this. If it is not like this, it cannot be a true church; it should be pulled down or altered, or used for something else altogether, and a true church put up in its stead. Also, in fact if not in intention, its builders were ungodly. This argument holds water only if one believes that human attitudes to fundamentals do not change, which is a matter of history, or ought not to change, which is a matter of something else. Historically it is clear that they do. Birth, marriage and death are now consulting-room stuff much of the time, which they have not been before. The priest is sometimes thought to be God's deputy, and sometimes the people's leader; sometimes he is done without.

Churches have been built as they were wanted and neglected or pulled down as they were not. We must take their existence as evidence of our ancestors' serious and respectable purpose (and their destruction as signs of absence of mind). Few church builders in London were frivolous – perhaps the earl who instructed Inigo Jones to build no more than a barn at ST PAUL'S, COVENT GARDEN; and few ungodly – one known as the 'Obelisk Parson' perhaps, who was a transvestite. Churches must be accepted either as spilt milk there is no crying over, or as buildings where the past is alive and where our present will join it when we too are dead.

The Romans had built a wall round their London, parts of which remain visible, and drained land. Londoners lived and built churches inside the wall and out. As time passed inner suburbs amalgamated. The two medieval cities, London and Westminster, joined along 'the strand'; spread across the single bridge over the Thames and along 'the Surrey side'; reached and overtook towns and villages in the countryside, whose old parish churches today still tenaciously flag their continuing existence.

St Paul's,[2] a college of secular priests, the Benedictine Abbey of St Peter's at Westminster,[3] and that of St Mary Overy[4] at Southwark, have histories dwindling back into the very dark ages. Some of the parish churches also run back a faint thin line: a legend as at St Peter's, Cornhill,

---

[1] A. W. Pugin, *Contrasts*, London 1841, p. 1.   [2] Now St Paul's Cathedral.
[3] Now Westminster Abbey.   [4] Now Southwark Cathedral.

1

a carved stone as at ST DUNSTAN, STEPNEY, a name as at St Ethelburga, a mention in a document as at St Gregory by Paul's.° By the end of the 12th century there were some 120 churches in the city of London. The previous void is due to lack of information: there is no Domesday Book for London.

A Bishop of London called Restitutus appeared at the Council of Arles in 314, but after St Augustine brought St Benedict's rule to England (he reached Canterbury in 597), religious life was practically confined to the monasteries. At first these were places where whoever wished to follow Christ could do so, and only later did they become centres of learning and of, as it were, official intercession. During the 8th century they flourished particularly; by the end of the 9th their vitality was flickering. Parishes there certainly were, more or less demarcated from the 8th century, but parish life was inefficient, the clergy was ignorant, and almost all the churches were someone's private property, to build, to derive revenue from and to bequeath, like any other. This was not a field that could be irrigated by the great waves of vitality which refreshed and altered monasticism.

In the 10th century St Dunstan (see ST DUNSTAN, STEPNEY), in a movement analagous to and derived from the great revival at the Benedictine Abbey of Cluny, refurbished the whole of monastic life in England. By the 11th century the force of this revival was spent, and the next influx came from Normandy: first Norman ideas and then, with the Conqueror, Normans. Till then London had been neither ecclesiastically eminent nor politically pre-eminent, but now the city's economic supremacy attracted both Church and State. The Tower of London, the Palace at Westminster, and a great number of monasteries were all established at the periphery, and various old establishments were renewed. English building was never uninfluenced by the Continent, but now all influences, political, economic, artistic and religious, coincided. Norman architecture flowered overnight and for a hundred years.

The Chapel of St John in the White Tower (see TOWER OF LONDON) has passed almost intact into our century from the 11th: Caen stone brought by water from Normandy, Norman design, Norman workmanship. A stone and some hinges bear scanty witness to the great Cluniac Abbey of Bermondsey, one of the most gorgeous in England, which was founded in 1084 (see ST MARY MAGADALENE, BERMONDSEY). Augustinian priories (that is, houses of secular priests living a regular life according to St Augustine's revision of St Benedict's rule) were founded at St Mary Overy (whose successor building is now Southwark Cathedral), at Holy Trinity Aldgate (see ST KATHERINE CREE), and at St Bartholomew, West Smithfield (see ST BARTHOLOMEW THE GREAT). The Knights Hospitaller of St John of Jerusalem (see ST JOHN'S, CLERKENWELL) and the Knights Templar (see TEMPLE CHURCH) built their principal English houses up against the City walls. Of these much remains of substance or of form. The 12th-century wave of monasticism left splendid wrack on the London scene: the great estropiated hulk of St Bartholomew, the buried crypt at St John's, Clerkenwell, the form of the much-renewed Temple Church. The

Cistercians, who were at this time taking their valiant purity of life to the wilds of Rievaulx and Fountains and Tintern, by rule avoided London. Only in 1350, when the purity was stained by property, was the Cistercian Abbey of St Mary Graces,° Eastminster, founded in London.

In the 12th century the papal policy of removing churches and priests from lay hands was at last beginning to succeed: ownership of churches and the right to appoint priests were more and more passing to bishops or to monasteries, both English and foreign (see ST HELEN'S, BISHOPSGATE), and new-built churches passed immediately under their control. Priests were better educated, less often married, more often stipendiary. By 1291, the year of the Taxatio of Pope Nicholas IV which listed all the churches, parish life begins to appear decent and well enough regulated, though still poor.

The king was the feudal lord of all monastic lands – the Abbess of Barking held hers by barony and properly provided her men and took precedence – but gradually the popes established their claim to direct authority over all monasteries, by-passing the national hierarchies of bishops. The monasteries claimed full authority over the parish churches they provided for the lay inhabitants of their precincts: ST MARGARET'S was such a church to Westminster Abbey, St Mary Magdalene to Bermondsey. Indeed St Mary Bromley by Bow managed to keep until the 19th century the independence of the Bishops of London which it inherited from the Convent of St Leonard; in perfect decency moreover, which is more than can be said of some others.

The monasteries accumulated riches and, along with riches, power; also suspicion and unpopularity. In the 1220s the friars arrived. As mendicant preachers they were greeted enthusiastically by everyone but the monks. First and most important came the Dominicans and the Franciscans, then the Carmelites, the Augustinian Friars and the dim little orders of the Crutched Friars and the Friars of the Sac.

At first they built little or nothing; but, in spite of the humility of their early ambitions, the Dominicans and the Franciscans were soon caught up into the great world by the ways of scholarship, diplomacy and a reputation for leniency in the confessional. They too became rich, built big, and acquired enemies. In 1309 some London curates petitioned against the friars, who, they claimed, were taking away their remunerative deathbed business. And about the same time some of the London clergy formed themselves into a 'confederation' to safeguard their interests, probably against the friars.

One can begin to visualise London Church life at the turn of the 14th century. There were St Paul's and the great abbeys, huge and splendid, where worship was at its most sumptuous and most processional. The services were carried on by priests and monks, the public was either excluded, or at any rate not liturgically essential, required only to make a feast day more festive. There were the friary churches, large and with great chancels for the regular saying of mass, but also with huge unencumbered naves specifically intended for preaching. Of these there now remains nothing but the dimensions of the Grey Friars' church in the combined church and graveyard of Christchurch Greyfriars. (Even that now is stamped on by a giant traffic roundabout.) There were also the churches of the smaller houses: at St Helen's, Bishopsgate, convent church and parish church were almost exactly alike in size, two equal naves under a double roof, separated by a screen. There were the parish churches, very numerous, mostly tiny, providing for the day-to-day sacramental needs of their parishioners and used for many secular parochial purposes too. There were the chapels of ease which provided services but not sacraments in the outposts of a parish; there were the private chapels in the royal and episcopal palaces; there were hermitages and anker-holes; there were Paul's Cross and the Spital Cross where outdoor sermons and services took place.

Until the 12th century a church had been a piece of property: in the 12th century, its private owners tended to hand it over to a monastery or a prelate. Throughout, the parishioner's only right, or duty, had been that of going to church. As the feudal system disintegrated, as a wider variety of loyalties offered itself to the common man, and particularly as a middle class became rich, self-conscious and suspicious, the relationship of parishioner to parish altered. In practice, the priest, or rather his patron, was responsible for the chancel and sanctuary, and the parishioners looked after the nave, repairing, enlarging, furnishing. At St Stephen Coleman° they even maintained a parish privy. Sometimes they were helped by papal indulgences to pilgrims.

During the 14th and 15th centuries the monasteries' growth was halted. They were no longer relied on to ease the progress of souls from purgatory to heaven: better to leave specific money for specific masses. The chantry and the chantry priest flourished: the payer was concerning himself with the piper's tune – a whiff of the Reformation. Certainly at some monasteries behaviour was riotous, and they found themselves in debt (see ST HELEN'S, BISHOPSGATE). New foundations tended to have a definite purpose; Bethlem Hospital was the first of these: it became in time Bedlam, the madhouse whose name is now a language word. Alien connections and allegiances were forcibly severed and even papal support was no longer certain (see TEMPLE CHURCH). Instead, small colleges of priests were instituted by rich men, as by Mayor Whittington at ST MICHAEL PATERNOSTER ROYAL, and supported by poor men. The three chaplains at St Peter ad Vincula were supported by the contributions of all who worked in the Tower of London, workmen paying a penny a week, the Constable a pound a year. Or 'many of the parishioners . . . being laymen and women, did sundry tymes meete together and did make good cheere togither and contribute their monies towardes the mayntenaunce and repayringe of the churche, which meetinges were termed amongst them brotherhoodes.'[1] And churches were sometimes surnamed after those who

---

[1] Exchequer Depositions, 31 Eliz. No. 18, q. in *London Survey*, vol 7. Shoreditch, 1922. p. 94. This was an old man remembering the time before the Reformation.

paid for rebuilding them (e.g. St Lawrence Pountney° and St Leonard Milkchurch°), who thus achieved an immortality.

The earliest churches had probably been built in any material that came to hand. Some were stone, like the first St Paul's of 604, but this was unusual, and even Stow in the late 16th century still thought it worth mentioning when a church was built all in stone. Until the loss of Normandy, Caen stone was used for grand work and rubble, plastered and lime-washed, for modest. Chalk was sometimes included. To a plain nave and sanctuary would be added an aisle, or two, or even three, or a transept, or some chantry chapels. Some churches always had a tower, like ST MARY LE BOW: some got them later, some never had one at all, like St Helen's, Bishopsgate. Sometimes there were crypts, big as at St Mary le Bow, or small. Usually there was a chancel screen, but in the big, spacious Perpendicular churches like St Andrew Undershaft there was no structural division between nave and sanctuary. Chantry chapels could be built anywhere in or on to a church (see ST HELEN'S, BISHOPSGATE). Some churches had a grammar school, some a cloister, like ST MARY WOOLNOTH. In the 13th century private pews had been allowed only to noblemen and patrons, but by the 15th century pew-rents were going towards the upkeep of the church. So private a thing was a pew that a parishioner was sometimes buried at his pew door. At St Bartholomew the Great a chamber and privy were let off in the triforium arcade: the Temple Church was probably used for the safe-keeping of treasure and later as a rendezvous for lawyers and their clients.

The sublime symbolism and purity of worship, which Pugin and the Ecclesiologists came in the 19th century to detect in Gothic architecture and the medieval church, were – one cannot, in the face of variety, say never there – but seldom, anyway.

The practical effects of the Reformation on London churches were three: it made some of the monastic churches available for parish use, it confined Italian influence on English architecture to books, and, much the most important, it altered the purpose of the liturgy. The Counter-Reformation, with its emphasis on the Real Presence, on the altar, shows by contrast the way in which the Reformation in England moved: that is, to the Word of God historically spoken, the Word as understood Truth and as opposed to the Presence as an immediately sensed Vision.

Books, with the impetus given by the invention of printing, provided the 16th century, at least in England, with its key to understanding:

> Nor shall Death brag thou wander'st in his shade,
> When in immortal lines to time thou grow'st:
> So long as men can breathe, or eyes can see,
> So long lives this, and this gives life to thee.[1]

Words confer immortality: words escape the clutch of decay, the limits of age and distance. In words, the Greeks and Romans live on: in the Bible, God and Christ declare themselves; in the Prayer Book, the Church of

---

[1] William Shakespeare, Sonnet 18 ('Shall I compare thee to a summer's day?').

England takes shape. The plays, the poems, the songs; the schools and grammar books; the afternoon lectures and the sermons; the epitaphs, the Tables of the Law and the texts on church walls: words were the fuel of the century.

Chantries were now, like the Mass, abolished, but one could still have written on one's monument:

> I humbly do require all which do pass this way
> For Henry Webb Esq., his soul devoutly to pray.[1]

And although his monument of 1552 in St Katherine Coleman° has vanished, the name of Henry Webb has not.

Appointment was again in lay hands, sometimes even the parishioners' own. The problem, which was not theoretically solved until the Restoration, was what to do with, or rather how to behave in, churches built for the Mass. In practice the priest said the service where he could be seen and understood, and a reading-desk was provided there. The altar was a table, and the chancel was where the communicants could most conveniently and privately commemorate their Saviour. Steps, rails, chancel screens, the exact position of the table – these were questions passionately argued. Some parishes panicked and did all that authority bade them: others, perhaps keeping one parson throughout all the changes, took everything in their stride and continued to have communion administered at the altar-rails because it was more convenient, or refused to take down a chancel-screen because it kept out the dogs. In one sense the Reformation was no more than a significant milestone. The processes went on: the parish still increased in importance and became the unit of local government; the useful functions of the monasteries continued in schools and hospitals, while private charity built almshouses and more schools in the suburbs. Stepney, Greenwich and Camberwell were filling up with them.

Of actual church building there was very little in the second half of the 16th century. The churches of the suppressed monasteries were put to many, often inappropriate, uses, or were allowed to fall gradually down, or were made over to enlarged parishes. There had been a good deal of stone building in the 15th and early 16th centuries, and the parish churches either continued adequate or had their accommodation increased in the usual way with aisles, and then, so as not to send any of the congregation beyond the preacher's voice, with galleries.

There was not for over a hundred years a parish ambitious to have an entire building in the new and fashionable Italian style. Monuments, yes, and an occasional porch (see ST HELEN'S, BISHOPSGATE); no more. And after all, this style, which arrived in illustrated books, was inevitably understood to be, like the illustrations, two-dimensional; rather small, rather fiddly, flat; concerning parts of buildings rather than buildings, and of course subject to authority and so to be copied rather than invented. Some of the books were Italian but more were Flemish, themselves

---

[1] Maitland, *History and Survey of London*, London 1754, p. 1113.

reporting the Renaissance at one remove. Most strapwork decoration has this bookish, out-of-the-blue look, and one even finds designs described in words in a contract, instead of being annexed as drawings. The contract for the building of Dulwich College (1613) reads in part: 'and that the said Chappell and Scholehouse shall be bewtifyed with six Doricke pillasters with pettystalls, bases, capitalls and cornishe ... and twoe pillasters to bewtifie the same porche, and the said six foote of fynishinge worke on the hedd or top before mentioned, to rise and be made with a small pillaster on the heade of every greate pillaster, with three kind of tafferells on the forefront ... and in the same forefront fower half roundes for the bewtifyinge and between every tafferell and halfe rounde one piramides'.[1]

It was Inigo Jones who, by a combination of opportunity, genius, and knowledge, put life into this curious fashion. His first profession, that of court stage-designer, faced him with the precise problem of making two-dimensional sets appear three-dimensional. This training and his travels in Italy made him able, evidently, to read books of architecture in the same way that a good musician can 'read' a full score: an accomplishment which was to be a godsend also to Wren and Hawksmoor. Jones was not, as the great Italian theorists Alberti and Palladio had been, a fundamentally serious man, or even an original architect: his genius was for using and adapting the fashionable architectural idioms 'according to the rules'. He was 'one of these Puritans, or rather people without religion'[2] and able to build a rich Roman Catholic chapel for the Queen at Somerset House,° to accept the Earl of Bedford's commission for a barn-like church in Covent Garden, St Paul's, Covent Garden, and to cover Old St Paul's in a classical skin of Portland stone. Later he was accepted as a great Palladian, but Palladio's church architecture seems to have passed him by and only reached England with Hawksmoor and Archer two generations later.

The use of Portland stone ('the finest building stone in England'[3]) spread fast with the introduction of new cutting techniques, but Jones's Italian style, being a court style, remained effectively in suspense until after the Restoration. Of the churches built in London during his heyday, St James, Dukes Place, and even St Katherine Cree were influenced only in detail by the Italian style, and the rest not at all.

During the Commonwealth only the tower of ALL HALLOWS-BY-THE-TOWER was built and the East India Company's private chapel at Poplar (which later became St Matthias, Poplar) with seven of its eight columns cut from the masts of ships.

Argument had moved on from liturgy to theology and personalities. Different parishes reacted differently, as always. Suburban parishes off the main roads, like St Mary Magdalen, Battersea, and ST MARY'S, ROTHERHITHE, were nearly able to ignore the whole thing. Clapham was

---

[1] Contract between Edward Alleyn and John Benson, quoted in W. H. Blanch, *Ye Parish of Camerwell* (sic), London, 1875, p. xxxvi.

[2] Jean-Marie de Trélon, Superior of the Queen's Capuchins, quoted by Professor R. Wittkower in the *Burlington Magazine*, Feb. 1948, p. 51.

[3] Alec Clifton-Taylor, *The Pattern of English Building*, London 1962, p. 90.

quietly concerned. At ST JAMES GARLICKHYTHE they pensioned their vicar when he was expelled. The parish of St Stephen Coleman° was a little theocracy on the Geneva model. At ST JAMES, CLERKENWELL, the parishioners bought the church and forever after elected their rectors.

In the 1660s and 1670s, as the tensions of the Reformation and the Commonwealth relaxed, the atomisation of religious life was carried a step further. Up to this time diversity within the national church had been either ignored or suppressed as heresy: a tolerable cleavage had never been contemplated. But now, as official attempts at wholesale control succeeded fruitless attempts at suppression, the cleavage had to be admitted. A fundamental nonconformity existed alongside conformity: control softened, except of Roman Catholicism (and was maintained there partly because of the political implications).

Many still-existing Nonconformist congregations, in Bermondsey, in Peckham, in Deptford and Camberwell, in Bethnal Green, even in Mayfair, trace their history back to the 1660s, when parties of parishioners chose to leave their parish churches, following the parsons ejected under the Act of Uniformity, and set up in rooms and houses as inconspicuously as possible. These early-founded Nonconformist congregations show in their history little continuity of affiliation. There were splits and mergers. The Baptists split into the Particular (or Calvinistic) Baptists and the General Baptists; the latter split into the New and the Old Connexions; and some of the Old Connexion later became Unitarian. Unitarianism also absorbed many Presbyterian congregations, while other Presbyterians and Independents of Commonwealth vintage passed to Congregationalism. Between all these, chapels changed hands rapidly. Only the Quakers remained unaffectedly Quakers, uninterested in the forms of denominational organisation.

Of all this ferment little, in the material sense, remains. Dimness was the quality the Dissenters most required in their buildings, fearing renewed suppression: it survives for instance in two little Quaker meeting houses, one in Church Street, Deptford, another in Wandsworth High Street.[1] The Church of England, on the other hand, reached a self-confidence and maturity which are displayed in, and partly formed by, the sudden explosion of the church architecture of Sir Christopher Wren.

In 1666, God's judgement had fallen on the City:

Righteous art thou, O Lord: and just are thy Judgements . . .

Therefore didst thou make us like a fiery oven in time of thy wrath: the Lord did destroy us in his displeasure and the fire did consume us . . .

It was of thy goodness that we were not consumed: that when we had provoked thee to give us all up to utter ruine and desolation, and thy hand was stretched out to do thy whole displeasure upon us: yet

---

[1] See illustration on p. 9 of the Friends' Meeting House in Wandsworth High Street. It is now almost overwhelmed by neighbouring buildings.

Friends' Meeting House, Wandsworth

didst thou preserve a remnant, and pluck us a brand out of the fire, that we should not utterly perish in our sins.[1]

Eighty-seven churches were burnt, and in the next 30 years 51 of them were rebuilt. Their rebuilding and that of St Paul's Cathedral was financed by a tax on coals. Over a million tons of Portland stone was used, supplemented with brick lest the quarries run out. Wren had a monopoly of its use and his workmen's tallies can still be seen in the quarries.

Many of the citizens driven beyond the walls by the Great Fire did not return within them afterwards. The Strand was already thick with houses along to Westminster, and there the town was spreading up through St James's and Soho. Moorfields was gradually drained. It was in these parts to the west that the well-off settled. In Stepney to the east, shipbuilding was filling up the Tower Hamlets: ST JOHN, WAPPING, was among the new churches. In Spitalfields great numbers of Huguenot weavers settled after the repeal of the Edict of Nantes (see CHRIST CHURCH SPITALFIELDS). There

---

[1] From the *Special prayers to be used yearly on 22nd September for the Dreadful Fire of London*, issued in 1666 by the Archbishop of Canterbury. These prayers can be compared with a broadsheet of 1850 referring to the recent fire at ST ANNE'S, LIMEHOUSE:

> And may not our dear old Church have fall'n
> 'neath God's avenging hand
> For some continuous crying sin
> Of its large and numerous band?

were other foreign Protestants, some refugees, some traders, with their churches and chapels, in Wandsworth, in Westminster, and in the City itself. Jews were again allowed to settle in England, and the BEVIS MARKS SYNAGOGUE was built at this time. The south bank of the river was also thickening up with wharves and shipyards and ropeyards right down to Woolwich.

A taste for the new architecture had by now permeated society. In the City, only at ST MARY ALDERMARY and at St Alban, Wood Street, was unambiguous Gothic demanded. The altarpiece of St Michael, Queenhithe,° was a 'painted perspective of the Gothic order' on canvas.[1] Wren, Hawksmoor, John James and others all worked in Gothic at Westminster Abbey and in various repair jobs, as at St Margaret's, Westminster. Elsewhere, even where Wren himself was not concerned, as in the synagogues, the suburban parishes, and the almshouses, Wren-like churches and chapels went up. There were a whole lot of them, new-founded or new-built. Some of the down-river ones (St Nicholas, Deptford, St Mary Magdalene, Bermondsey) seem to have been modelled, internally at least, and fairly roughly, on Wren's ST MAGNUS THE MARTYR of 1676. Bermondsey and Rotherhithe churches showed all the new idioms with something of a Cockney accent. Many of these riverside churches have towers outlined with stone: perhaps to make a pattern recognisable to boatmen through the mists of the unembanked Thames. (See illustrations of ST JOHN, WAPPING, ST BENET, PAUL'S WHARF, ST MARY, BATTERSEA.)

The word 'Wren' is used now as much to describe a style as to denote something actually designed by Christopher Wren. He was a prolific designer of buildings, his official position as Surveyor of the King's Works made him control and supervise the designing of many more, and some of the great army of workmen employed in rebuilding the City returned to their country homes with a knowledge of his style and of no other.[2] This style, particularly in the City churches, was a synthetic response to many requirements. Seldom can an architect have had so many masters to please: the King, whose servant he was; the Church, whose buildings he was making; the parishioners, who were going to use them; the City, whose guest he was; the architectural authors whom he read and respected; and himself. Often the shape of the site, or even a remnant of the burned-down church, constricted him still further. Luckily his genius was practical and empirical. Like the great Gothic builders before him he was able to make a virtue of necessity and to adapt his first ideas good-humouredly when they did not suit. His skill with an odd-shaped site is always astonishing, as at ST MARTIN LUDGATE, or at any of those slightly irregular ones which he firmly orders by a centralised pattern, depending not on the walls but on the columns or the ceiling, or even the decoration. The extent to which he actually designed the churches varies enormously: some, like ST STEPHEN WALBROOK, are all his, others much less so.[3] The

---

[1] *Parentalia*, quoted in *Wren Society*, vol. x.
[2] Of this style Boone's Chapel (1680) in Lee High Road, Lewisham, is a pretty and stylish example. It is all that remains of a set of almshouses, replaced in 1877. See photo on p. 11.
[3] See Appendix I, for a complete list of Wren's London churches.

*Boone's Chapel,
Lewisham (see p. 10)*

furniture, woodwork, font, organ and so on, were in any case the responsibility of the parishes. The towers and spires and lanterns are much more completely his, and they have a clear and studied relationship with the dome of St Paul's. It is this huge concept, this panoramic balancing of the shape, texture, colour and distances of the dome and the steeples of London which makes Wren one of the supreme artists. Here the professor of astronomy built his own solar system of white stone, black lead and sometimes crystal air. The overall pattern is now gone, destroyed by German bombs and civil and ecclesiastical vandals. Something of the original debonair energy can be glimpsed in the tower which is all that remains of St Mary Somerset: its top bursts into a great pulsing crop of obelisks and blazing urns, 20 feet high: a sermon in stone on Pentecost.

In 1802, William Wordsworth could still write:

> Earth has not anything to show more fair,
> Dull would he be of soul who could pass by
> A sight so touching in its majesty:
> This City now doth, like a garment, wear
> The beauty of the morning: silent, bare,
> Ships, towers, domes, theatres, and temples lie
> Open unto the fields, and to the sky;
> All bright and glittering in the smokeless air.[1]

---

[1] *Sonnet: Composed upon Westminster Bridge.*

This London, which Canaletto recorded, was the one Wren put in hand. Although it used coal, wind and rain could still scrub it silky and translucent as Wordsworth saw it.

The need to rebuild all these churches, coming so soon after the Restoration settlement, called forth a vigorous new interest in the externals of religion. Church decoration was anything but sombre or austere.[1] Rumbustious font-covers, sprightly reredoses and organs, jolly churchwardens' pews, paintings, odd carvings, fake candlesticks, even dog-kennels, broke out in solid profusion. 'There prevailed in those days an indecent custom: when the preacher touched any favourite topic in a manner that delighted his audiences, their approbation was expressed by a loud hum, continued in proportion to their zeal and pleasure. When Burnet preached, part of his congregation hummed so loudly that he sat down to enjoy it, and rubbed his face in his handkerchief.'[2] The font-cover at St Swithin's, London Stone,° was 'thoroughly pagan in its symbolism, the cherubs' heads being meaningless from a doctrinal point of view'.[3] On the clock at St Magnus the Martyr were Hercules and Atlas as well as St Magnus and St Margaret. More usual heroes were Moses and Aaron: in paintings or statues they appeared almost as often as not, either as part of the reredos, between the inevitable Paternoster, Decalogue and Creed, or somewhere else on the east wall, a vogue which endured well into the 19th century. Even the synagogue at Bevis Marks had them; perhaps to emphasise the Jewish religion's common origin with the Christianity which, in England, had so recently offered it a home.

This was the first great age of British science and philosophy and the intellectual religion of the Church of England now achieved a state of unprecedented self-confidence.

Among the fruits of the triumphant Tory reaction which followed the accession of Queen Anne was the scheme of 1711 for the Fifty Churches. Partly it was a celebration of the fall of the Whigs after 22 years. Another reason for it was that law and order in the suburbs were seen to be suffering for want of churches, and the conventicles were snapping up likely churchmen. The catalyst was the collapse of ST ALFEGE, GREENWICH.

The Act required the building of 'fifty new churches of Stone and other proper materials, with Towers or Steeples to each of them'[4] and of course churchyards, burying-places and houses for ministers. A Commission was appointed to put all this into effect. To it Wren wrote: '. . . in our reformed

---

[1] At St Andrew Holborn the woodwork included:
    Lace at 2/– a foot
    Foliages at 12/– a pair
    Truss Scrowls at 5/–
    Cherubine's heads with festoones at 15/– each
    Rapehild leaves with a codd in the hipp at 4/– a foot
    Small leaves at 4d. a foot
and Eggs about ye Capitalls at 6d. a foot
                          (*Wren Society*, vol. x, p. 103)
[2] Dr Johnson, quoted in T. F. Bumpus, *London Churches*, London 1908, vol. i, p. 181.
[3] B. R. Leftwich, *A Short History and Guide to St Swithin London Stone*, London 1934, p. 14.
[4] Quoted in H. Colvin, 'Fifty New Churches', *Architectural Review*, vol. cvii, no. 639, p. 189.

Religion, it should seem vain to make a Parish Church larger than that all who are present can both see and hear. The Romanists, indeed, may build larger churches, it is enough if they hear the Murmur of the Mass, and see the Elevation of the Host, but ours are to be fitted as Auditories.'[1] This difference between the Roman and the Anglican requirements was as important to Wren and his successors from the architectural point of view as from the doctrinal.

Italy continued to provide the most impressive architectural inspiration. France and the Low Countries were also significant, but rather as fellow-interpreters of a common source. Both James Gibbs and Thomas Archer, whom the Commission employed respectively on ST MARY-LE-STRAND, and on ST PAUL'S, DEPTFORD, and ST JOHN'S, SMITH SQUARE, had travelled in Italy, and to both Wren and Nicholas Hawksmoor (who built six of the Commission churches) the works of Palladio and the baroque architects were well known through illustrations.[2] But the actual problems the Italians faced were, as Wren so clearly saw, different. One was how to put a classically appropriate façade on to a church with a high nave and lower side aisles. This did not worry the English architects, because the auditory church was almost bound to have galleries, and therefore high aisle ceilings. The Italians hardly concerned themselves with towers and steeples, which were a specific requirement of the 1711 Act. Moreover, for a variety of local reasons, the Italians did not often build a free-standing church; most of the Commission's new-built churches were free-standing, and for ideas about these the Englishmen had to turn back to Roman temples.[3] And the Italian interiors were usually either directed on to one supremely emphatic altar or, round or oval, implied a series of altars.

Sixteenth-century England had used Italianate detail, copied flatly from the page. Inigo Jones also copied Italian architecture, using it to provide direct solutions to actual problems: the Queen's House at Greenwich and the Banqueting Hall are Italian rather than Italianate. Wren and his immediate successors, Hawksmoor and Vanbrugh, Gibbs and Archer, particularly in the churches they built, were solving un-Italian problems while still holding fast to Italian experience.

Wren has always been revered as a national institution, but uncomfortably, and his works have not received particularly reverent treatment. Vanbrugh has been admired and disliked in turn; and Hawksmoor was, until recently, ignored. But the searchlight of taste, which in the last 30 years lit up with sudden brilliance Caravaggio and Borromini, has also picked out the unexpected virtues and grandeur of the short-lived English baroque.[4]

---

[1] Quoted in *Wren Society*, vol. ix, p. 15.
[2] Christ Church Spitalfields is singularly close in feeling to Palladio's Redentore in Venice.
[3] Hawksmoor provided austerely fanciful plans and elevations of one of the Roman temples at Baalbek, comparing it to St Paul's, Covent Garden, as illustrations for the third and later editions of Henry Maundrell's *A Journey from Aleppo to Jerusalem at Easter, AD 1697*.
[4] The television series *Brideshead Revisited* brought Castle Howard and its Mausoleum, by Vanbrugh and Hawksmoor, into the world's living-room.

Wren's own buildings are seldom thoroughly baroque, that is to say, the parts are usually intelligible by themselves as well as in relation to the whole; one is delighted, but seldom in doubt; fascinated, but not struck ambiguously dumb. Baroque is in fact a romantic form of Renaissance architecture, and Wren was too practical a man, too well aware of the needs and the likings of people he was building for, to indulge in romancings. ST JAMES, PICCADILLY, was the church he felt most suited to 'our reformed Religion.' Only at St Stephen Walbrook (and perhaps even more at the destroyed St Benet Fink° or St Antholin°) is there the delight and doubt, the intellectual ambiguity of the best Italian baroque. St Stephen, moreover, thoroughly pleased its parishioners, and was perfectly appropriate to the form of their worship.

Vanbrugh built no churches. Hawksmoor built six for the Commission and they are much the most 'architectural' of all London's churches until we come to some of the great Victorians. In them one is not aware of the parishioners, nor very much of the Church of England. They are heroic, monumental and unconstricted; utterly without meanness or gaudy pride; occasionally with a soaring certainty.

This very monumental quality in Hawksmoor's churches was a sign of something new. After the Fire had destroyed most of the City churches, it was obvious that the parishes would not have the financial resources to rebuild, and the Government had stepped in. This was not unprecedented, for until 1629 if a church fell down the parish could apply to the Common Purse for money to rebuild it. The initiative was with the parish itself, and this was also more or less true of the rebuilding after the Fire. For instance during the rebuilding of ST BRIDE'S, FLEET STREET, a committee from the parish went to view the galleries at St Paul's, Covent Garden; and always delegations were 'going to Sir Christopher, to put him in mind of building the church'. The 1711 scheme on the other hand was imposed, admittedly on thankful people. Indeed more parishes than would be accommodated asked for one of the new churches for their swelling populations.

Nevertheless, the idea came from above: architects and funds were provided, and needs assessed, by those who knew best for those who by themselves might not have chosen the Church of England. The Church of England in short was becoming the church of the ruling class. (This did not become completely true for another hundred years when the Waterloo churches were scattered wholesale throughout the country, and certainly the matter was not yet generally considered.)

The scheme never came to fifty churches. Hawksmoor's six, two fine ones by Archer, and Gibbs's ST MARY-LE-STRAND make up the splendour of its achievement. From these it rather tailed off, with John James's ST GEORGE'S, HANOVER SQUARE, the purchase of a number of second-hand churches like ST JOHN'S, CLERKENWELL, and a certain amount of assistance to suburban parishes re-building, like Woolwich and ST GEORGE THE MARTYR, SOUTHWARK. Also those two flights of logic, St Luke, Old Street, and St John Horsleydown,° one with a huge obelisk for its spire, and the other with a gigantic Ionic column. (The former is still there to astonish us.) Models, which were made and preserved of ten other churches, were destroyed in the mid-19th century.

Of these architects, James Gibbs was the most successful. With the arrival of the Hanover dynasty, that crowning of the Glorious Bloodless Revolution, emerged a taste for glorious bloodless architecture. Just as the king's powers were now curbed by constitutional government so the architect's imagination was curbed by an anaemic interpretation of the laws of Vitruvius and Palladio. Borromini, who had 'endeavoured to debauch Mankind with his odd and chimerical beauties', and the 'licentious' Bernini and Fontana[1] were execrated and abandoned. Wren was looked on with regretful reserve; Vanbrugh and Hawksmoor were disliked or forgotten; and Inigo Jones was raised to unrivalled eminence. Gibbs, in this tergiversation of taste, never having gone far into 'odd and chimerical beauties', and having derived his style from what was most sensible in Wren and Rome, suffered little in his reputation or employment. Indeed his designs, published with comments in his *Book of Architecture* of 1728, became something of a best-seller and were very influential both in England and in North America. Thomas Archer, the other traveller to Italy, who was neither a prolific nor even a professional architect, was much more uncompromising than Gibbs, and as a church builder much more truly Palladian. He and Gibbs both suffer, in their churches, from a certain faintness about the Anglican parts: there is about their east ends a sense of anticlimax; about their steeples, something unconvinced.

The important architecture of the previous hundred years had mostly issued from the Office of Works. But the position of Surveyor now became a fruit of office; taste became quietly oligarchic: private rather than public building was required. In the previous fifty years or so, so many churches had been built in London that new ones were needed only to replace those which fell down. A few burial-ground chapels were built, and a large number of proprietary chapels in Westminster and Marylebone where the town was leaping up, estate after estate.

Preaching and religious music were now both highly thought of. At the Foundling Hospital Chapel £7,000 was taken at performances of the *Messiah* conducted by Handel himself. These were as much a social 'must' as attendance at the Chapel Royal in ST JAMES'S PALACE, where the pews were heightened to prevent ogling. Thus among the fashionable and respectable. There was also another side to it. 'It would be to no Purpose to send servants to keep our pews clear for us . . . To disencumber the Passage and free it from the Crowd, it would require half a regiment of soldiers with their Bayonets fixed.'[2]

'The Crowd' in fact was taking to preachings, particularly to Methodist preachings. Just as the itinerant friars had been suspected and disliked by the clergy of the 13th century, so were the Wesleys and their fellow-preachers by the established clergy of the 18th. 'When I mention

---

[1] Colen Campbell, *Vitruvius Britannicus*, 1717, vol. i, p. 3.
[2] From a pamphet published by the parishioners of ST DUNSTANS IN THE WEST in 1759, urging the dismissal of a lecturer.

that the late well-known methodist Mr Gunn was a preacher in it [St Mary Somerset] on certain days, the trampled and dirty state of the church will not be wondered at.'[1] Enthusiasm permeated all of Nonconformity and part of the Church of England itself. At first there was no question of the Methodists leaving the Church of England, but eventually they did, splitting into two parts: the Countess of Huntingdon's Connexion, who were Calvinistic Methodists, and the Wesleyan Methodists proper. The Establishment disapproved. (The Gordon Riots of 1780, in the suppression of which 210 people died, were in objection to the extension of tolerance to Catholics.)

The tradition of Anglican church building was certainly flagging. The Palladian movement had given London no specifically Palladian churches, even in the English, or Burlingtonian, sense: still less in the sense of Palladio's own powerful churches in Venice.

London churches in the second half of the 18th century fall roughly into four classes. Lord Burlington's protégé Henry Flitcroft designed ST GILES-IN-THE-FIELDS and St Olave, Tooley Street,° dull churches continuing the Wren–Gibbs tradition. William Newton, the *de facto* designer of the GREENWICH ROYAL HOSPITAL CHAPEL, presented plans for rebuilding St Mary, Battersea, very Palladian, but they were rejected. At a lower social level a little solid but uninspired church building went on. George Dance the Elder's St Matthew, Bethnal Green, was the tail-end of the 1711 scheme. ST MARY, BATTERSEA, was home-made in the same line, ST JAMES, CLERKENWELL, just a little more interesting, and Dance's ST LEONARD'S, SHOREDITCH, rather more ambitious.

The second class was that of the whimsical odd-shaped churches which were more common in the country: ST MARY, PADDINGTON, neat and charming, is a good example. Although a Gothic church might well be repaired in its own style (ST MARGARET'S, WESTMINSTER, often was), or something Gothic might be retained as at ST MARY, BATTERSEA, where the old east window was re-inserted in the new church, or a Gothic porch or tower top might be put on as at St Mary Magdalene, Bermondsey, yet there was little true Georgian Gothic in London.

The third class arose from the fact that the Reformation was reaching its ultimate objective. The religious enthusiasm of the age – and enthusiasm had reappeared – had turned inward, focusing on the relationship of the individual soul to God, and this required no particular architectural setting, nor anything much in the way of clergy, or church organisation, or ecclesiastical conviction. A drab and undistinguished little chapel, or an old building made over, sufficed a good preacher, whether he was one of the Countess of Huntingdon's Methodist chaplains, William Huntington the coal-heaver, or a Church of England parson turning an honest penny in Mayfair or Holborn. Even so, many of these chapels, Nonconformist or of the established Church, had the unpretentious merits of Georgian street architecture.

There was also a succession of seriously built churches, bigger or better

---

[1] J. P. Malcolm, *Londinium Redivivum*, 1807, vol. iv, p. 428.

than the chapels, which adumbrate what might have been the style of late Georgian pre-Regency church building in London had there been more of it. They were domestically plain outside, in stock brick like other street architecture, of good proportions and simple plans, with flat decoration inside; when there is a steeple, it is conspicuous, idiosyncratic and not at all derivative. ST JOHN AT HACKNEY is the grandest of these, St Anne's, Soho, is the oddest, and George Dance the Younger's ALL HALLOWS ON THE WALL is much the best. Soane's rather later churches (ST JOHN ON BETHNAL GREEN, HOLY TRINITY, MARYLEBONE, and ST PETER'S, WALWORTH) have a real if not very obvious resemblance of manner to them. These architects are the nearest England produced to the French rationalist architects Ledoux and Boullée.

Part of the reason why church building in the second half of the 18th century did not keep up with the spread of the town was the difficulty of financing not only the building, but also the minister's stipend and the upkeep of the church in a new parish without endowments. A church rate, pew rents, burial fees, might be tied up to repay a loan. Bonds might be raised for the stipend. If Flitcroft's proposal to rebuild ST JOHN'S, HAMPSTEAD had been accepted, he would have been paid by a fixed proportion of the pew-rents for himself and his heirs. At ST JOHN AT HACKNEY, recently become a rich suburb, there was a church rate; £8,000 at 8½% was raised on the security of burial fees for rebuilding ST LEONARD'S, SHOREDITCH; Lady Huntingdon bought the Clerkenwell Pantheon° for her chaplains; £40,000 was raised by subscription for ST LUKE'S, CHELSEA. When St Mary, Hammersmith Road, was sold, the auctioneer's bill claimed that 'a VERY CONSIDERABLE INCOME' could, by a clever man, be derived from it.

By about 1800 it was found that not enough churches had been built to keep the lower classes in order. Religious enthusiasm had in parts gone sour, and produced extravagances like the Obelisk Chapel,° where homosexual marriages were performed; religious mania was so usual that the inmates of Bedlam were allowed no religious services; even the more respectable enthusiasms of Methodism were disapproved of by the governing classes. Disapproved of, but not feared, until the French Revolution showed up the dangerous potentialities of 'the Crowd'. The question how to tame 'the Crowd' was answered in many minds by the thought: 'more churches'. In 1818, partly in commemoration of victory, partly in hope of a return of moral efficacy to the established church, a million pounds was set aside by Parliament for what came to be called the Waterloo Commission to build as many churches as possible in the big cities of England. The eventual figure was 214.

The flood of building this released did not confine itself within the Act of 1818. A trickle had already begun of churches built by those parishes which could afford them for themselves: NEW ST PANCRAS, one of the plums of the Greek Revival, had been proposed in 1813, and new ST MARYLEBONE in the same year. ALL SOULS, LANGHAM PLACE, and other Regent Street churches were part of Nash's great Regent Scheme; and a few suburban churches were built or rebuilt, for instance St Mary,

Bryanston Square, by Robert Smirke, the architect of the British Museum. But the main stream of the flood in the 1820s and early 1830s in greater London was the churches built by the 1818 Commissioners.

Referring to this time, and particularly to John Nash, whose stagy achievements seemed limitless, John Summerson wrote 'In this universal, hasty, slick eclecticism we recognise, unmistakably, the end of an epoch. When the time has come that everything can be done, quickly and easily, it is time to think again.'[1] Although church architecture was only a drop in this 'everything', thinking again was as urgent there as elsewhere, and the 'Waterloo' million pounds began to be spent well before the thinking had started. When eventually it did start, the result was the great explosion known as the Gothic Revival.

Most of the Commissioners' churches are dull. The 'battle of the styles', which was taking place rather superficially in fashionable architecture, barely affected churches. Liturgical requirements were not supposed to have changed much since the 17th century, and it was a dimly traditional host of churches that sprouted up all over London. Bath stone and stock brick combined, some Grecian, some more or less Gothic. A few like ST JAMES, BERMONDSEY, or ST MATTHEW'S, BRIXTON, are buildings to which their architects gave good thought; Smirke's ST ANNE'S, WANDSWORTH, is respectable if scarcely distinguishable from his Bryanston Square church; some, like all Francis Bedford's, are dreary to distraction.

There was a repetitive dullness about the constantly same materials, the barely distinguishable architects repeating the same building several times over. Nash's St Mary Haggerston,° improper and foolish as its Gothic may have been, was comic relief of a sort: Soane's three curiously skeletal churches, the mausoleum he built at Dulwich and his wife's tomb at OLD ST PANCRAS, all of them with each part just failing to touch the next, display something fleshless and final.

The Gentleman's Magazine, commenting in March 1827 on one of the Commission churches, wrote that the erection and filling of churches such as these 'ought to be hailed as a triumph of intellectual religion and good sense over cant and fanaticism'. An intellectual religion was indeed what Wren had had in mind when he envisaged 'the auditory church' and, between the late 17th century and the 1820s, there had been developments rather than changes in the setting for the Anglican liturgy. This process too was now reaching a logical conclusion.

In Wren's day the pulpit was usually near one of the walls; during the 18th century it came more and more to be placed centrally in the nave, in front of the communion table, and to be a three-decker portmanteau of pulpit, reading-desk and clerk's desk. (At the chapel in the GEFFRYE MUSEUM in Shoreditch there is an unexplained little four-decker.) The font, which had previously been somewhere at the west end of the church, moved eastwards and the three centres of worship, font, pulpit and table, came to be superimposed upon each other, like symbolical Chinese boxes. The little church of St Nicholas, Tooting Graveney,° which was pulled

---

[1] John Summerson, *Architecture in Britain 1530–1830*, London 1953, p. 300.

down in 1832, had three-decker pulpit, font and communion table all huddled together up two steps in the tiny chancel. St Mary, Bryanston Square, one of the 1818 Commission churches, had its font right up under the central three-decker pulpit. At Holy Trinity, Cloudesley Square,[1] the pulpit and reading-desk were placed ambo-like opposite each other; at St Luke's, West Norwood, the pulpit and altar faced each other on the long walls of the church. At St Marylebone, with the organ over the communion table and curtained family pews in two tiers of galleries, the extreme expression of the movement was reached.

By 1830 there was not yet a full coincidence of historical cadences: architecture had stopped moving; liturgical change was obviously due; only philanthropy, itself something new or at least reinvented by the new Bishop of London, Bishop Blomfield, was on its way. The will to build churches even for those who did not want them was not to be halted. Cheap churches went up fast at the expense of the Church Building Society and the Church Building Endowment Fund; the cheaper, the more. Haggerston, Hoxton, Hackney saw them and omitted to use them. In fact, underlying everything else, were the ferocious workings of the industrial revolution: a cauldron of new ideas, new techniques, new ambitions, new problems, about to transmute every aspect of British life.

For the Church the explosion finally came in the 1830s and 1840s with a reaction against the intellectual religion of the establishment, against the fanaticism of the Nonconformists, against the shoddy of the philanthropists, against the plurality of style and emotion that romanticism had legitimised.

'So sacred, so awful, so mysterious is the sacrifice of the mass,' wrote Pugin, 'that if men were seriously to reflect on what it really consists in, so far from advocating mere rooms for its celebration, they would hasten to restore the reverential arrangements of Catholic antiquity.'[2] The 'all-hearing' church, which alone had seemed truly serious to Wren, he deplored. Equally the 'all-seeing' church: 'if religious ceremonies are to be regarded as spectacles, they should be celebrated in regular theatres'.[3] This strong yearning for reverence in architecture and liturgy which he and many like him felt found no satisfaction in the Roman Church. Pugin, himself a Roman Catholic, wrote: 'The consideration of modern degeneracy in the Roman Church tends to alleviate the sorrow we feel at protestant ravages.'[4] Indeed, throughout the 19th century in London, even during the greatest excesses of eclecticism, there was no movement towards contemporary Roman Catholic architectural practice, nor towards the baroque it stemmed from. The yearning was for the 'true Catholic religion' of the Middle Ages, and its architecture, before it was polluted by Reformation, Renaissance or Counter-Reformation.

The reaction was also, and as much, against the individualist fanaticism which still flourished in the 1820s. As feeling for church buildings grew

---

[1] Now the Celestial Church of Christ, belonging to a mainly Yoruba sect.
[2] A. W. Pugin, *A Treatise on Chancel Screens . . .* , London 1851, p. 7.
[3] A. W. Pugin, op. cit., p. 8.
[4] A. W. Pugin, *Contrasts*, edn. 1841, pp. 52–3.

stronger, so did the demand for proprietary chapels dwindle. Dissent was no longer discriminated against under the law, and Nonconformists, now accepted as respectable, became church-conscious and developed characteristic forms of building.[1] Ritualism, reacting against the hideousness of the cheap churches of the philanthropists, represented not only a sense of the splendour and awefulness of the Mass, not only the return of mystery to worship, but also a promotion of the priest from the position of *primus inter pares*, of leader of his flock, to that of God's representative, one more exalted than his congregation, who could, not inappropriately, have his liturgical being in the sanctuary near the altar. The Oxford Tractarian Movement took shape, and Roman Catholicism too reached full legitimacy. (As for the hunting parsons of the English counties, they held out for a decade or two yet.)

Alongside Anglo-Catholic responses to the immediate religious past went an increasingly serious interest in Gothic architecture; an interest which went back to the 18th century, to Horace Walpole and the dilettante antiquarians. Their romantic taste for things Greek and Chinese had been beyond the means of the multitude of educated men, but their taste for Gothic was not, and while some pottered scientifically through nature, others pottered scientifically through medieval architecture. A group of undergraduates formed the Cambridge Camden Society, later the Ecclesiological Society, to study medieval architecture systematically and to evaluate new-built churches. Suddenly they were overwhelmed by the messages they found: about building, about decoration, about the liturgy and ritual; they went on to become uniquely powerful arbiters of taste in church building.

The Evangelicals on the other hand, earnest, Low Church, deeply suspicious of both Tractarians and Ecclesiologists, were considering the social implications of the Christian religion. Clearly the parish church should be the centre of its community with clergy house, church school and various institutes for adults all attached, all part of one religious, architectural and social ensemble. Bishop Blomfield established such a one in Bethnal Green and the model was set. From then on they were built in the East End of London and other poor districts, Pimlico, even Westminster. These were mission churches, with missionary priests and helpers going as energetically into the slums as their brothers and sisters were going into the spiritual wastes of India, Africa and Polynesia. Bishop Blomfield himself consecrated nearly 200 churches.

The revival of classical architecture in 15th-century Italy and the Gothic Revival in 19th-century England had in common a belief in perfect architecture, never perhaps achieved even in the Golden Age, but none the less to be worked for. The chief difference lay in the fact that the classical revivalists had in Vitruvius a Revealed Truth, expressed in words, and thus subject to a freedom of interpretation which the remaining buildings of the ancients did little to constrict, while the 'ecclesiologists' found

---

[1] For instance, the Union Chapel in Islington, by James Cubitt (1876).

buildings galore and at hand but no Word, and therefore had to work out for themselves the laws they believed to be there.

In the 30 years after 1840 these several forces combined and the Gothic Revival, harnessing the Ecclesiological and the Oxford (Tractarian) Movements, burst into such abundant flower that we, a hundred-odd years later, are still reacting to it. It embodied for its proponents their dissatisfaction not only with much recent and contemporary church building, but with the procedures and doctrines of the established Church: within the Church of England the most ferocious doctrinal battles were to be fought out between the bishops and the Anglo-Catholics during the rest of the century. (See ST GEORGE'S IN THE EAST, ST CYPRIAN'S, CLARENCE GATE, and ST BARNABAS, PIMLICO.) The architectural battle was won sooner than the liturgical: by 1840, confidence in the 'Gothic Revival' was established. Architects, said Charles Eastlake, the Revival's first and contemporary historian, could now engage 'the task of uniting the long discovered elements of comeliness and devotion'.[1] In the next 30 years hardly any churches but 'Gothic' were built.[2]

The architectural requirements and the spiritual implications of this limited consensus were several, ambiguous, and not consistent either with each other or with the 14th century, which it came to be agreed was the Golden Age. They included: the symbolism of pointed arches and of the medieval articulation of parts – that is, a deep and specially decorated sanctuary with a dominating altar; a chancel for a surpliced choir to sing in; the font symbolically by the door; a south porch for penitents; and no chancel screen or anything which would impede the sight of the sacred mystery being wrought at the altar; or, alternatively, a screen which, Pugin and many others maintained, was no 'mere question of architectural detail' but involved 'great principles connected with discipline, and even faith'.[3] Overriding everything else was the need for purity of heart – good buildings could only be built by good men – and the avoidance of 'sham'.

Wordsworth, standing on Westminster Bridge that September morning in 1802, had seen Wren's London across the wide waters of the still unembanked Thames 'All bright and glittering in the smokeless air'. He lived on until 1850, by when industry and commerce had exploded and caused a vast sucking in to London not only of workers from the rest of the country and trade from the whole world, but coal, coal, coal, which blackened the buildings and pea-souped the river mists and fogs. London became, in Geoffrey Best's words, a 'City where atmosphere was all, where no light from whatever source came unfiltered or unenriched by steam,

[1] Charles L. Eastlake, *A History of the Gothic Revival*, 2nd edn, Leicester 1978, ed. J. Mordaunt Crook (first edition 1872), p. 208. Eastlake's intention was to record 'one of the most remarkable revolutions in national art that this country has ever seen' (p. 14). He illustrated and discussed 343 neo-Gothic buildings.
[2] A fine 'Italian' Romanesque church, Christ Church, Streatham, was built by J. W. Wild in 1841–2. But the style did not take at the time. It reappeared most conspicuously with J. F. Bentley's Westminster Cathedral at the very end of the century.
[3] A. W. Pugin, *A Treatise on Chancel Screens . . .* , London 1851, p. 1.

mist, haze, smoke or fog'.[1] To Henry James, arriving in London in 1868, 'the low black houses were as inanimate as so many rows of coal-scuttles, save where at frequent corners, from a gin shop, there was a flare of light more brutal still than the darkness.'[2]

Because of the population explosion, large parts of central London were slum and shanty-town,[3] little different from what appals us today at the rim of the capital cities of developing countries: communities dirty, deprived, often criminal, often ill. London was the largest city in the world: in 1841 Greater London contained 2¼ million – 14% of the (itself rapidly expanding) population of England and Wales; in 1861, 3¼ million – 16.6%; in 1881, 4¾ million – 18.4%. (Paris then held some 2 million, New York even less.) Already in 1851 fewer Britons were living in the countryside than in towns, a situation no other country experienced before 1900.[4]

London spread outwards along the old main roads, meeting and blanketing towns and villages as it went. Their parish churches and High Streets and sometimes a few elegant acres of Georgian suburbia survive into our last quarter of the 20th century.

The industrial revolution provided the conditions for the new London. New kinds of transport: local – canal, rail, train, tram, omnibus – which allowed commuting from suburb to centre and back; and distant – canal and rail again, and new shipping and dock techniques which made every kind of material available everywhere from everywhere. The steam engine was allowing mining on a new scale, and steel was encouraging new methods not only for building itself but also for the extraction and transport of building materials.

In the 1840s some now central areas of London – Kensington, Pimlico, Belgravia, Bayswater – were still not built up; by 1870 they were densely packed, as were Paddington, Hampstead, Holloway and Stoke Newington beyond them. 'Kensington Italianate' predominated in terraces and squares but there were garden suburbs too – the Ladbroke Estate, Aberdeen Park, Bedford Park, Hampstead. To the east of the City the riverside was stuffed with docks, and the same was happening on the Surrey side. Churches and their attendant buildings sprang up in the spreading flood in far greater numbers than ever before, usually big, sometimes enormous, intended to dominate their surroundings. The towers of James Brooks's many brick churches then dominated the East End, as Wren's did the City and Hawksmoor's Stepney. Some of these churches are still described in their 'literature' as 'the Cathedral of the East End' (ST MARK, DALSTON) or 'the

---

[1] & [2] Geoffrey Best, *Mid-Victorian Britain 1851–75*, London 1971, p. 27.
[3] See for instance, Gustave Doré and Blanchard Jerrold's *London, A Pilgrimage*, London 1872.
[4] Best, op. cit., p. 24. The City of London, the 'square mile', was already losing its resident population: from nearly 130 000 in 1851, to 113 000 in 1861, to 76 000 in 1871 and 51 000 in 1881: the streets, railways, stations, warehouses and great public buildings of the capital city serving the world's largest and widest-flung political industrial and trading empire required people to move out. By 1984, Greater London's population, which had declined from 7.5 million in 1971 to 6.7 million in 1981, appeared to have stabilised at about 6.75 million.

Cathedral of North London' (ALL HALLOWS, SAVERNAKE ROAD), and the purpose was to impress and influence *non*-churchgoers.

For two or three generations past, Victorian churches have been held in blanket disesteem: gloomy, heavy, depressing, pretending to be medieval when all can see they are not. A generation back John Betjeman opened eyes to the charms of Victorian architecture: charms at first believed to be recondite, bound up with nostalgia, little to do with real architectural quality. (That, for the period, was to be found in the remarkable Victorian stations and office blocks and dock buildings which were the forebears of the Modern Movement.) Yet architectural quality is most certainly present in the churches, and among their builders are some of England's grandest and most original architects. That they should have dubbed themselves 'gothic *revivalists*' has led to confusion and easy misjudgement: it is not in comparison with the architecture of the Middle Ages that their achievements should be set, but rather with the other achievements of their own age. These were genuine Victorian architects, imbued with the same explosive vitality and determination as their great contemporaries in the sciences and in literature, in exploration and administration, in industry and trade, in empire building.[1]

In his history of the Revival, Charles Eastlake wrote as follows about the building of Butterfield's ALL SAINTS, MARGARET STREET (1849–59): 'The truth is that the design was a bold and magnificent endeavour to shake off the trammels of antiquarian precedent, which had long fettered the progress of the Revival, to create not a new style, but a development of previous styles; to carry the enrichment of ecclesiastical Gothic to an extent which even in the Middle Ages had been rare in England; to add the colour of natural material to pictorial decoration; to let marbles and mosaic take the place of stone and plaster; to adorn the walls with surface ornament of an enduring kind; to spare, in short, neither skill, nor pains, nor cost, in making this church the model church of its day – such a building as should take a noticeable position in the history of modern architecture.'[2] All Saints was indeed intended as the model church of the ecclesiological movement, but it outran the prescriptions.

H. S. Goodhart-Rendel, a talented 20th-century architect and a truly catholic observer of his predecessors' work (his eyes were open to Hawksmoor's glories when others were not) saw the situation thus: 'The Gothic Development, because that would really be a better name than Gothic Revival for what resulted in the end from the functionalist theories of Pugin, had no parallel in France nor in any other European country.' Butterfield and others were 'carrying on an experiment Pugin had initiated

---

[1] And in fact many Victorian architects dispatched designs for cathedrals and churches and mission compounds to various parts of the Empire: R. C. Carpenter, architect of Lancing College Chapel, designed three churches for Tasmania and cathedrals for Ceylon and Jamaica; Butterfield designed churches and cathedrals for Port Elizabeth, Cape Town, Poona, Bombay, Adelaide and Melbourne and also the Séminaire de St Paul at Ambatoharanana in the mountains of Central Madagascar (according to his biographer Paul Thompson); Blomfield designed for Copenhagen, Cannes, Demerara and the Falkland Islands.
[2] Eastlake, op. cit., pp. 253–4.

... that of evolving a method of commonsense building free from both Tudor and from post-renaissance conventions, which used the steep roof, the pointed arch and the buttress as what, indeed, they still were at the time, convenient forms of economical construction.'[1]

One of the significant dates for 19th-century architecture is 1840, and 1870 is another. In the 30 years between, Butterfield,[2] Street,[3] Gilbert Scott,[4] Brandon,[5] White,[6] and Teulon[7] set moving a new architecture, fully worthy of the name High Victorian: powerful, disciplined, strenuous, impressively individual, passionately idiosyncratic with Butterfield and Teulon.[8] Butterfield is the genius of the time.

With the next, post-1870, generation, discipline begins to relax, revival 'Gothic' – theoretically English 13th century – is no longer the only desiderated norm: 'Queen Anne'[9] and then 'Arts and Crafts'[10] become acceptable as well as various kinds of continental Gothic and Romanesque. With the BROMPTON ORATORY even Italian mannerist, *le style jésuite* as the French call it, appeared.

Moral fervour subsided, and charm, as an architectural virtue, returned; the passionate search for principle, so characteristic of the Revival's early days had been called off.

Still within the new Gothic tradition, Pearson,[11] Brooks,[12] and Bodley and Garner[13] were giving Londoners buildings altogether more restful, though no less admirable, than their predecessors. Pearson's ST AUGUSTINE is one of London's most exhilarating buildings, and it embodies not only the virtues the Revival had renewed but also the traditional, classical proportions as well.

By the end of the 19th century the fervours, both architectural and liturgico-theological, had worn themselves out and church building had become a mild, genial activity calling on nothing so dangerous as passion or conviction: Sedding's over-relaxed 'bric-à-brac'[14] church in Sloane Street; W. D. Caroe's pleasant brick churches in East London[15] with their nice draughtsmanly detailing; Ninian Comper's comfortable glitter.[16]

---

[1] H. S. Goodhart-Rendel, 'Victorian Conservanda', *Journal of the London Society*, Feb. 1959, p. 10. Hawksmoor of course had built quite unforcedly in 'Gothic': notably the western towers of Westminster Abbey.
[2] See ALL SAINTS, MARGARET STREET, ST MATTHIAS, HACKNEY, and ST AUGUSTINE, QUEEN'S GATE.
[3] See ST MARY MAGDALEN, PADDINGTON.
[4] See ST MARY ABBOTS and ST GILES, CAMBERWELL.   [5] See THE CHURCH OF CHRIST THE KING.
[6] See ST SAVIOUR'S, ABERDEEN PARK.   [7] See ST STEPHEN'S, ROSSLYN HILL.
[8] Among their contemporaries, the idiosyncratic sometimes spilt over into wild eccentricity, as with E. B. Lamb, at ST MARTIN, GOSPEL OAK.
[9] See HOLY TRINITY, LATIMER ROAD.
[10] See HOLY TRINITY, SLOANE STREET.   [11] See ST AUGUSTINE, KILBURN.
[12] See ALL HALLOWS, SAVERNAKE ROAD.   [13] See ST MICHAEL, CAMDEN ROAD.
[14] HOLY TRINITY; the words are Goodhart-Rendel's, op. cit., p. 178.
[15] E.g. St Barnabas, Walthamstow.
[16] See ST CYPRIAN'S, CLARENCE GATE, and the crypt chapel at ST MARY MAGDALEN, PADDINGTON. Perhaps the Horniman Museum (by Harrison Townsend, 1897–1901) should be added to this short list. With its powerful, rounded 'nave'-end and round-pinnacled tower facing London Road in Forest Hill, and its anthropological and natural history collections, it is a kind of secular, or free-thinkers', church. The subject of the mosaic on the south front is 'Humanity in the House of Circumstance'.

Lutyens' great church of ST JUDE ON THE HILL is the last substantial statement to be made in church form in London.

Among the fervours released by the Gothic Revival had been a violent distaste for all immediately preceding architecture and then for virtually all preceding architecture: that of the gimcrack philanthropists, of the Georgian Palladians, of the capricious early 18th-century group (Hawksmoor's Gothic was a travesty), Wren's (his Gothic, too, was intolerable), the Tudors' and the 15th century's. As to the Normans', that was of course too early. Only the 13th and early 14th centuries were really all right. All earlier and later buildings could be improved, and usually were, with a kind of bravura self-confidence as characteristic of Victorian England as the bitter doubts and the obscure passions.[1] Few medieval churches escaped (for instance, St Etheldreda, Ely Place, and ST JOHN IN THE WHITE TOWER). In 1863 Wren's ST LAWRENCE JEWRY narrowly escaped a general 'enrichment' with marble pavements, alabaster tables, majolica dados and stained glass windows proposed, all of which Wren would 'himself have done had the means been within his reach'.[2] Another would-be beautifier of ST LAWRENCE confessed, after submitting proposals in which the words 'pull out' and 'hack down' appear several times, that he had 'had to depend entirely upon my own feeling of reverence and respect for the great architect'.[3]

In 1873 the not very splendid medieval crypt of St James in the Wall,° when the ground over it was sold, was moved to another site and carefully preserved, but of the 18 Wren churches which were demolished only one was ever rebuilt and that, St Bartholomew Exchange, only lasted 50 years on its new site. The earliest to be demolished was St Christopher-le-Stocks in 1782, and reasons did exist for its demolition. The later destructions were motivated by the need for a new bridge, for a new road, for new churches in the suburbs. Wren was believed to be held in general respect, but in fact a conscientious dislike of his architecture and the intellectual religion he built for existed among those most concerned, churchmen and architects, and indifference among most of the rest.

The excessive purification of medieval buildings led to a famous polemic between the forces of 'scrape' and 'anti-scrape': scraping off the additions and ornaments of later ages to achieve as 'authentic' a condition as possible as against letting them be because, after all, they too were part of our history. The champion of anti-scrape was the great socialist moralist and craftsman William Morris, who founded the Society for the Protection of Ancient Buildings, the original of all the voluntary conservation societies in Britain.

Mostly 'scrape' had been for architectural purity, but sometimes for

---

[1] A few people regretted the wholesale alterations. William Rogers, rector of ST BOTOLPH, BISHOPSGATE, wrote: 'I may be succeeded by some desperate character who will want to remove the galleries, and cut down the pews, and supplant our honest fireplace in the middle aisle by some patent hot-water apparatus worked from the vaults.' (William Rogers, *Reminiscences*, London 1888, p. 96.)

[2] Guildhall Additional Manuscripts 305: 'Mr Digby Wyatt, architect; July 16th 1863. First estimates to the Vestry.' These estimates were not accepted.

[3] Francesco Galli, Guildhall Add. Mss 305.

propriety, as at ST BARTHOLOMEW THE GREAT and St Ethelburga (compare the photographs of 1910 and 1955.) Alongside 'scrape' went various kinds of liturgical updatings: the insertion or removal of screens, of chancels, of crosses on or not on the altar, all in a generally High Church direction until the Church of England in the mid-20th century became seized of, or by, the same kind of progressivism as dismantled so much else in Britain in the 1950s and 1960s.

In the 1940s Hitler had taken over from earlier vandals, and after 1945

St Ethelburga,
Bishopsgate, in 1910

the church authorities resumed the work, though no longer in the City of London: the churches there were now safe from demolition if not from overshadowing. Elsewhere in London many fine buildings have been lost by a mixture of genuine poverty, bureaucratic delay on the part of the state and an opinion within the church that holds that its old buildings can hardly be relevant to today's religion.[1] London corner sites are gold-mines for development, and all over England the clergy are on pitifully low pay. The argument continues to rage, but it seems to us that the archdeacons (who are the ecclesiastical authority mainly concerned) have forgotten that the faith of our ancestors still brings many of us to faith now, and so does beauty, as well as truth. The Church's determination to abandon the Book of Common Prayer and the King James Bible coincided with its increasingly mercenary attitude to its old buildings.

St Ethelburga, Bishopsgate, now

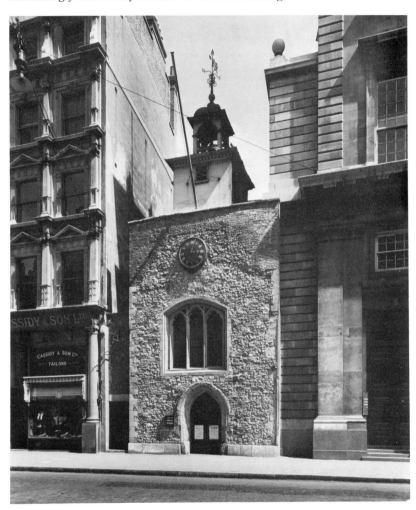

Today's London is the melting pot of both its own long history and the old sea-linked *Pax Britannica*; its huge population has seeped outwards; its slums have been cleaned (and often up-ended); its simple 19th-century class divisions – big houses for the rich, small for the poor – have been

---

[1] The determination of a parish to keep its church can sometimes be successful, as at St Barnabas, Walthamstow, and at St Matthew, Great Peter Street. At St Matthew, after a disastrous fire, the church has been admirably remade within the shell of the Gilbert Scott chancel: architect, Donald Buttress.

blurred by multiple occupancy on the one hand and gentrification on the other. Although its air can again be 'smokeless' as Wordsworth saw it, the mid-20th century's tower blocks have invaded and crowded its middle layers, which once held only Wren's and his successors' 'towers and domes . . . and temples', white and black and brick.

Every day Westminster Abbey is filled with men and women worshipping, looking, resting, and against the walls stand the marble ghosts of the past, soldiers, sailors, rich men, poets. All, living and dead, are enclosed together in Henry Yevele's great nave. It is a fabric built up of architectural grandeur, of traditional worship and of the inescapable and immemorial presence of ourselves and our ancestors. Of this fabric every church is made and in every church, 'each moment's sickle, emulous / Of Time's great scythe,' lays up a little of its harvest.

1. ALL HALLOWS-BY-THE-TOWER
BYWARD STREET, BARKING, EC3

IIF3   U: Tower Hill

Both site and church are of enormous antiquity: beneath the ground
certain ashes represent Boadicea's sack of London; certain worked stones,
a Roman building; an arch in a wall laid bare by the bombing represents
Saxon building of the late 7th century. Bits of a Saxon cross have turned
up, and the name Barking Church appearing in the 12th century connects
the church with the 7th-century Abbey of Barking to which it no longer
belonged.

In the churchyard to the north of the church was a chapel which
Richard Coeur de Lion was alleged to have founded, containing a
miraculous image of the Virgin which Edward I was alleged to have given.
Whether these stories were true or not, the chapel certainly did have royal
connections: Edward IV made it a royal chantry and Richard III planned to
make it into a deanery. In it the Court of Chancery sometimes sat and in
it, too, some of the Templars were examined before their Order was
suppressed (see TEMPLE CHURCH). Official use and royal interest were
probably due to the nearness of the Tower. Even nearer was Tower Hill,
and All Hallows' graveyard temporarily harboured many headless bodies
(Bishop Fisher's, the Earl of Surrey's, Archbishop Laud's, among them)
which were later moved elsewhere. The royal chapel was completely
destroyed at the Dissolution and its site was forgotten except in the name
of Chapel Alley.

During the 16th and 17th centuries the parishioners of All Hallows were
divided fairly equally between High Churchmen and Puritans: in 1587 an
alderman left money for sermons to be preached in his memory instead of
for the usual masses; in 1583 an Italian called Benalius was allowed a
monument in the church although he was a Roman Catholic. During the
Commonwealth the Covenant was hung up in the chancel, but the Royal
Arms remained as well. And at the Restoration exactly half the vestry
resigned while the other half joyfully welcomed back the vicar who had
been expelled in 1643. Disagreement continued, particularly over a figure
moved from the clock to the reredos, and known as St Michael. A
churchwarden, Mr Sherman, reproved for allowing the presence of an
image in the church answered: 'It stood there so many years, and had done
no miracle, therefore we conceived it could not be a saint.'[1] But he took it
away and burned it in the vestry grate, only to be pounced on at once by
another faction who had liked it. He was a sensible man, so he proposed:
'Now . . . let's go to the Tavern, and merrily discourse what all of us can
say farther upon this matter.'[2]

The church narrowly escaped the Great Fire, but it was badly damaged
and burnt by high explosives and incendiary bombs in World War II. The

---

[1] E. Sherman, *The Birth and Burning of the IMAGE called St Michael*, London 1681, p. 5.
[2] op. cit., p. 7.

tall plain brick tower of 1659 remained intact. It was built after the
medieval tower was shaken and weakened by a gunpowder explosion in
Tower Street. It is set crooked to the church in a way which surprises
one's sense of perspective. Until the war the much-altered 13th-century
nave arcade survived, also the 14th-century east window. There was a
pulpit of 1613; a grey marble font of perhaps 1645, with a particularly
lovely cover of the end of the century (which survived the bombing), a pile
of cherubs and fruit with a dove on top by Gibbons, which now lies, sadly,
behind an iron grille. Brass communion rails of 1741, no mere tubes but
properly formed balusters, were damaged, but restored, and three fine
sword-rests, formally flowered, of the 18th century also survived. There are
many brasses (one of the London Brass Rubbing Centres has been set up
here); and some good monuments. Expensive repairs were carried out
between 1813 and 1815 in a 'sort of attempt in the Tudor style'.[1] A
proposal to put the pulpit in the centre of the nave, 'a modern and
unaccountable practice, prevailing in too many of our London places of
Divine worship',[2] was not accepted. Another thorough restoration by J. L.
Pearson in the 1880s, and later restorations in the same spirit, took away
some of the character of the church. It has now been rebuilt with curved
steel girders and concrete to simulate a medieval church.

Lancelot Andrewes was born in the parish, and William Penn was
baptised here.

2. ALL HALLOWS ON THE WALL
LONDON WALL, AT BROAD STREET, CITY, EC2
IIE2   U: Liverpool Street

GEORGE DANCE THE
YOUNGER
1765–7

The medieval church survived the Great Fire, a low building with a nave
and south aisle only and weather-boarded tower. Before the Reformation
anchorites lived there in an 'Anker-Hole', one of whom, in the early 16th
century, had a servant. The younger Dance rebuilt the church in 1765,
when he was only 24 and fire-new from his travels in Italy. John
Summerson analysed the interior in his book on Sir John Soane:[3] a barrel
vault pierced by ample semi-circular windows rests directly on attached
Ionic columns without the mediation of frieze or cornice. This suppression
of frieze and cornice marks the beginning in England of a rationalising
movement, since the cornice, being only a formalisation of an eaves, has
really no place on the inside of a building. The apse has a half-dome
coffered in a fine intellectual pattern provided by the hypothetical
intersection of this sphere by segments of other spheres. The whole
interior is the work of the most pleasing exactitude and grace.

[1] *Gentleman's Magazine*, vol. 85, pt. 1, London 1815, p. 36.
[2] loc. cit.
[3] John Summerson, *Sir John Soane*, London 1952, p. 21.

The exterior is plain brick except for a miniature stone frontispiece and turret at the west end. This, raised quite high above the street, has a light, thoroughbred look among the sprawling offices all round. The church has been restored. It is now a Guild Church and houses the Council for the Care of Churches.

JAMES BROOKS
1892

3. ALL HALLOWS, SAVERNAKE ROAD
CAMDEN, NW3

IC2 | BR: Gospel Oak

James Brooks was a prolific church architect in London from the 1860s to the 1890s, particularly in the East End, where it is said that his towers and spires dominated the skyline as Wren's did the City. No longer. But his

*All Hallows,
Savernake Road*

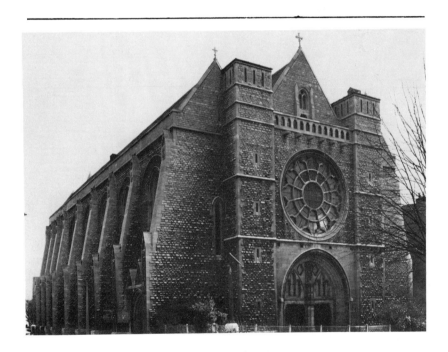

quality can still be seen south of the Thames at the Church of the Ascension, Lavender Hill, at St John the Baptist, Holland Road, and at All Hallows. The church was never finished. Brooks intended high stone vaults, but a domestic wooden ceiling now cuts off his enormously tall, water-smooth columns just as they begin to spread. Sir Giles Gilbert Scott completed the chancel in 1913. This is a hall church, aisles as tall as nave, and all is very light, very airy, but not for that unmysterious: a calm shadowlessness and cool grey stone. On Savernake Road a regiment of buttresses along the north side of the church and its west end are in turn defensive and shield-like.

Among Brooks's other churches, St Columba in the Kingsland Road was, until its recent dilapidation, one of the most coherent of the 'Holy Villages': red brick, something of a happy fortress.

All Hallows,
Savernake Road

4. ALL SAINTS, CAMDEN TOWN
CAMDEN STREET, CAMDEN ROAD, NW1

IC2

U: Camden Town

WILLIAM INWOOD
and WILLIAM HENRY
INWOOD
1822–4

When the Inwoods had finished NEW ST PANCRAS, they put up three chapels of ease in the parish. This one was paid for entirely by the vestry. It was called at first the Camden Chapel then, unofficially, St Stephen's, and since 1920, officially, All Saints. Since 1948 it has been lent to the Greek Orthodox Church.

Like St Pancras it is Ionic, but it only cost a quarter as much. It has a cheap look, in spite of a bold semicircular portico answered at the other end by a bold semicircular apse which has an impressively funereal dual staircase down to the vaults round its outside. In accordance with the orthodox rite the apse is entirely occluded within. The tower is rather papery, and all is made delicately queer by the squiggly decoration on the capitals which Henry Inwood adapted from some fragments he brought back from Greece. The same capitals reappear under the galleries where they bear a strangely abrupt entablature.

All Saints, Camden Town

VARIOUS DATES

5. ALL SAINTS, CHELSEA OLD CHURCH
OLD CHURCH STREET, AT CHEYNE WALK, SW3

IC4   U: Sloane Square, then buses

Chelsea Old Church, which was almost entirely destroyed in World War II, was a building with a pretty riverside setting but no architectural interest: it had on the other hand a magnificent collection of monuments. Symbolically, the very church itself stood on a monument; at a repair of

1784 there was so little room for anything but monuments that the great triumphal arch of the Jervoise family (1563) was made to serve as one side of a structural arch. Thirty-five years later the altar tomb which stood within it was removed and pews were run right through.

The oldest part of the church was the 15th-century chancel and two chantry chapels to the north and south of it. That on the south was fitted up by Sir, or St, Thomas More in 1528 to contain his tomb. The tomb is now in the chancel, as is the inscription he wrote, recut in the 19th century, but it is doubtful if More was in fact buried here after his execution, or martyrdom. There also survive two wide low capitals of More's time on the responds of the arch which led to the chancel: they show an interesting and graceful grafting of classical cherubs and foliage on to the medieval tradition. The More Chapel and the one opposite were freeholds passing through various hands, until in 1874 and 1894 R. H. Davies, then rector of Chelsea, bought them and gave them to the church; the More Chapel cost him £100, the Lawrence Chapel £250.

The nave and tower, which were knocked down, were built between 1667 and 1674. The tower bore a small cupola until 1815. They were plain and substantial in brick, and the nave was wider than it was long. The nave roof was the gift of Lady Jane Cheyne, the Lady of the Manor, whose name is perpetuated in Cheyne Walk. She died of epilepsy in 1669 and her monument by Pietro Bernini, a baroque edicule with recumbent figure which would go unnoticed in Rome as a routine work from the studio of Bernini, is striking enough in London. The Jervoise and the Cheyne monuments were both preserved. Two other great monuments can also be seen; that of Lord Dacre of the South, 1594, a magnificent firework display of strapwork with obelisks above, and that of Sir Robert Stanley, 1632, a quite unusual open composition of figures and urns unenclosed by any arch. It is now in the Lawrence Chapel. An inscription to the novelist Henry James, 1916, includes the happy phrase: 'lover and interpreter of the fine amenities of brave decisions'.

The church was rebuilt after the war, and reconsecrated in 1958; it now houses again a run of monuments unique in the village churches which have been absorbed in London.

In 1819 the population had increased so much that Chelsea Old Church was demoted to be a chapel of ease to the new ST LUKE'S, but after surviving the bombing, holding out for being rebuilt, and spending the nine interim years in a borrowed hospital room, the congregation were rewarded by reinstatement as a parish. The graveyard in the King's Road was given to the parish by Sir Hans Sloane the physician in 1736. He had bought the Manor of Chelsea, and was himself buried in the old churchyard under the monument which is now so much more conspicuous than what remains of the Old Church.

WILLIAM
BUTTERFIELD
1849–59

IIB2

6. ALL SAINTS, MARGARET STREET
WESTMINSTER, W1
U: Oxford Circus

Charles Eastlake had this to say about All Saints, Margaret Street: '. . . the building itself, as it was gradually raised, and still more when it came to be decorated, revealed a tendency to depart from ancient precedent in many important particulars. In the first place, the use of red brick for the external walls was a novelty, brick having been hitherto only used for the cheap churches, while in this case the very quality of the brick used made it more expensive than stone. Again, the tower and spire were of a shape and proportions which puzzled the antiquaries, scandalised the architects, and sent unprofessional critics to their wit's end with amazement. Passers-by gazed at the iron-work of the entrance gateway, at the gables and dormers of the parsonage, at the black brick voussoirs and stringcourses, and asked what manner of architecture this might be, which was neither Early English, Decorated, nor Tudor, and which could be properly referred to no century except the nineteenth.'[1]

William Butterfield, like all great men, is a conundrum. He has been adored, reviled, and dismissed. If your star is the classical one, you revile him. If it is ruggedness and strength, you adore him. If you seek calm and grace, you dismiss him instantly. And here lies the conundrum, since Butterfield himself sought calm, the calm of objectivity. 'Not our feelings', he wrote, 'but our faith must sustain us.' And 'The highest function of art is I think an objective one. It succeeds in a Creed, perhaps because it is in its nature a fixed and unchanging thing, better than it can do in a sermon.' Throughout his life he thought and worked in accordance with Pugin's famous maxim: 'It is the devotion, majesty and repose of Christian art, for which we are contending: it is not a *style*, but a *principle*.'[2]

Social harmony was to match inner calm. Throughout his life Butterfield also campaigned against box pews, owned and paid for by single families; and many a fine churchful of them he destroyed. His reason was a political one: 'The working men have never been heartily welcome in our cities', he wrote. Calm, and equality. Living and working in Bedford Square, he could have rubbed shoulders with Karl Marx on his way to the British Museum reading room.

And yet, when you walk into any of his best buildings, and especially All Saints, Margaret Street, you are undoubtedly assailed by the clamour of a soul in pain. The noble steeple[3] springs and soars above a dense and jostling courtyard (choir school, clergy house and church had all to be got into a 100-foot square); the inside certainly *includes* a Gothic revival nave, reredos etc., but the hunched and jarring forms, the insistent clamour of decoration, some from alternating materials, some from later

---

[1] Charles Eastlake, *A History of the Gothic Revival*, 1872, 2nd edn, Leicester 1978, p. 252.
[2] See Paul Thompson, *William Butterfield*, London 1971, *passim*.
[3] A descendant of one in Lübeck, op. cit., p. 93.

All Saints, Margaret Street

superimposition, above all an ornate but insistent curtness, all override any possible recourse to the spiritual certainty of the Middle Ages. If Butterfield's internal tensions sprang from the tension in society between simple faith and scientific doubt, as is very likely (though perhaps his celibacy contributed) then All Saints more than any other London church affirms the exaltation of faith and the suppression of rebellious doubt. Magnificently prolific in architecture and trenchantly communicative in letters, this highly intellectual man never wrote a book or an article.

The famous half-arches which articulate the nave and chancel aisles under their lean-to roof drew this comment at the time from *The Ecclesiologist* magazine: 'Mr Butterfield is so strongly convinced that every gable implies an altar that, as is well-known, he will not even build gabled chancel aisles, and that in cases like the communication between the nave aisles and chancel aisles of All Saints Margaret Street he has designed a half-arch, still further to emphasise the fact. This is to carry a principle to extremes.' Indeed, *The Ecclesiologist* might have gone further and pointed out how adhering to this principle – one altar and one only – led to the cutting in half of one of the main elements of another great principle, 'the repose of Christian art'. When principles conflict, then all must flow. Butterfield's architecture is sometimes frozen turmoil, and that, through the added force of his completely assured use of the new materials and techniques which were just ready in time for his genius, is another contradiction which disturbs us as much as it delights us today.

The church has a strong musical tradition. Sir Laurence Olivier started his career here in choir-school Shakespeare.

All Saints, Margaret Street

7. ALL SAINTS, TALBOT ROAD
(NOW POWYS SQUARE), W11

WILLIAM WHITE
1852–5

IB3

U: Ladbroke Grove

This large church was damaged in World War II and has only recently been repaired and restored. The roadway in front of it has been pedestrianised and new development to the north makes much of it. It is a pleasing airy building; short marble piers support a generous arcade. Many altars, much new glass, including a satisfying rose window to the north.

8. ALL SOULS, LANGHAM PLACE
REGENT STREET, W1

JOHN NASH
1822–4

IIB2

U: Oxford Circus

This church is one of the most conspicuous objects in all London. Nash was a backstairs politician as well as an architect and it was this which, in a country where the monarchy traditionally allowed the capital to grow undirected, enabled him to assemble and push through under George IV the great piece of town planning which still gives the West End of London its shape – the Mall, Regent Street, Portland Place (with the Adam houses taken in his stride) and the surroundings of Regent's Park; all these Nash laid out and built. His buildings have been destroyed everywhere but in the Mall and the Regent's Park Terraces. The plan remains.

Twice in its course, owing to tenacious landowners, Nash's triumphal way had to swerve to the west. The first wobble he punctuated with Piccadilly Circus, now entirely rebuilt, and entirely philistinely (the question of possible further rebuilding remains a national hobby). The second he punctuated with All Souls Church. The body of the church he laid out to the north-east, diagonal to the bend, and at the road end of it he put a 290° peristyle porch with a very tall, sharp, fluted steeple. If you look up from Oxford Circus you can still see the intention of the layout: the eye is made to chassé to the left round Broadcasting House.

In the peristyle and steeple Nash finally blew up the laborious search after propriety which was deadening the Grecian movement. To begin with, nothing could be less Greek than a spire, and not even in the Gothic North had a spire ever been so sharp before: it is finished with a metal spike. To go on with, nothing could be more Greek than a peristyle, and consequently nothing could be more improper than a spire rising from within a peristyle, and showing through it. Naturally it was violently attacked in the press and even in Parliament; cartoons showed fat old Nash impaled on the top, and so on. To them an outrage, to us it is a joke; but a very graceful and imaginative joke.

The interior used to be fine in a perfectly serious way. The galleries were shallow and high, giving an admirable spaciousness, and the pedestals of the columns which rise from them, always a tricky articulation, showed through the wooden fronting like limbs through wet drapery: a true Hellenic touch. They went round all four sides and were only broken over the altar.

All Souls, Langham Place. An old photograph, before it was dwarfed by slab buildings behind

But in the 1970s a disastrous remodelling took place which, though it kept much of the detail, destroyed the essence of this once beautiful space. In order to accommodate a new hall in the basement, the floor of Nash's church was raised, an apsidal platform was raised again, and another step raised yet again within that. The space is now squat and claustrophobic. The revelation of the inverted brick foundation arches between the new hall and the canteen ('refectory'), which were never meant to be revealed, is of course no recompense.

There are also a new metal altar, pulpit and lectern, which are grossly incompatible with Nash, and black plastic chairs which would be incompatible with anything. The porch has been turned into a sort of reception area with things for sale and a little window like a ticket office. All the same, the place is humming with life.

9. BEVIS MARKS SYNAGOGUE
HENEAGE LANE, OFF BEVIS MARKS, CITY, EC3

IIF2   U: Aldgate

JOSEPH AVIS
1701

In the centuries while the Jews were being driven round the world from pillar to post they became divided into two observances; the Sephardim, who lived mainly round the Mediterranean and in the Low Countries, and the Ashkenazim, who lived in Central and Eastern Europe. The difference is mainly in the pronunciation of the Hebrew of the Scriptures and in certain other ritual matters. Historically in England (unlike in modern Israel) the Sephardim have been socially and economically superior to the Ashkenazim, who arrived as poor refugees from Eastern Europe in the late 19th century (see CHRIST CHURCH SPITALFIELDS).

Bevis Marks Synagogue

Unofficially under the Commonwealth and officially under Charles II Sephardic Jews, many of them coming from the Canary Islands whither they had been chased by the government of Spain, obtained leave to settle in London for the first time since the medieval expulsion. They had their first synagogue in Creechurch Lane, but in 1700 the present building was begun. The builder – a carpenter who worked at ST BRIDE'S, FLEET STREET – was a Quaker and he exceeded his contract time because he had not realised he would not be able to work on Saturdays. Legend has it that he returned much of the money he was paid, as he would not make a profit from building a house of God. The exterior of the building is very plain, although the west front, facing on to a courtyard, has charm. But the inside is better preserved and more magnificent than the inside of most

City churches. The air is full of brass candelabra – branches is the old word – holding candles still, and aflame even by day with a swirl of dull gold. The woodwork, carved by the same craftsmen as carved for Wren's churches,[1] has for a Christian all the fascination of a familiar style devoted to unfamiliar purposes. The Ark is like any altarpiece of 1700 but instead of backing an altar it opens in the middle to show where the scrolls of the Law are stacked at a tilt, each covered in a mantle and topped with a little silver peal of bells, or rimmon. Many of these pretty ornaments are English and Dutch of the 17th and 18th centuries. The congregation sits in rows facing inwards, and at the west end is the great raised reading-desk with twisted balusters and heavy brasswork. There is a wealth of interesting equipment: old wrought silver pointers for pointing out the place when reading the Law, and, in the Vestry Room, a high graceful chair of the late 18th century for sitting little boys up in to be circumcised. The godfather sits in the chair and holds the child between his knees on a pull-out shelf. Disraeli was circumcised at Bevis Marks by his uncle, David Abarbanel Lindo. There is a picture of 1674, from the former synagogue, of Moses and Aaron holding up the Decalogue in Hebrew and Portuguese: '. . . No forniques . . . no hurtes . . .' Moses and Aaron appeared in many churches in the 17th century, but their presence in a synagogue is not usual.

Until the 1880s, there was an orphanage, almshouses and so on surrounding the synagogue. But there are not many practising Sephardim left now. The services at Bevis Marks are of course in Hebrew throughout (with some announcements in Portuguese still), unlike those of the Reformed synagogues, or indeed of many middle-of-the-road synagogues, and since some Jewish observances cannot take place without a quorum, or minyan, Bevis Marks has at times been forced to rely on paid minyanistas.

HERBERT GRIBBLE
1880–4

10. THE BROMPTON ORATORY
(The Oratory of St Philip Neri)
BROMPTON ROAD, AT THURLOE PLACE, SW3
IC3   U: South Kensington

This striking and conspicuous church is an English version of the sort of large mannerist (not baroque, as is often said) church which can be seen all over northern Italy. It is an affirmation of the ultramontane link which English Catholicism had not long been free to affirm, and antedates Westminster Cathedral by 20 years.

St Philip Neri in the 16th century led a life of prayer and good works in Rome, and many, especially young men, gathered round him. The first Oratory was and still is in Corso Vittorio Emmanuele, and it includes the

---

[1] It is not unreasonable to imagine Wren may have had a hand in the building in his old age. He wrote of 'the obstinate valour of the Jews'.

*The Brompton
Oratory*

saint's own church, the Chiesa Nuova, the New Church. It also includes
the later Oratory Church and the Library, two interiors by Francesco
Borromini, the greatest architect of the Italian baroque.

The cult of St Philip became an especially urban apostolate all over
Europe, and thus it was that this very large Catholic church was built by
the Oratorian Order at a time of rapid growth and change in London.

An open competition was won by the little-known young architect
Gribble. He did not seek a model in either the Chiesa Nuova or the
baroque Oratory beside it. His domed church has, or even rises out of, a
severe, almost neo-classical narthex. The vaulting is of concrete. The
general effect of the inside is indeed Italian, but a severe and sedate sort of
Italian. The coupled Corinthian pilasters are grand enough, but half a
dozen ways of taking Corinthian orders round corners better than burying
one column in the internal plastering and leaving it to cry 'let me out' had

been in use for two centuries when Gribble built. And the curious Ionic capitals of the side-chapel columns, which resemble nothing so much as jubilee hoseclips, go badly with their Corinthian big brothers. It may be that Gribble was uneasy with his commission, and hankered for sedateness throughout. The black and white altarpiece in the Chapel of the Seven Dolours, in which he himself completed every detail, shows a narrow and severe imagination.

There are many altars and statues imported from Italy and the Low Countries, and many modern pastiches. The twelve Berninesque apostles who line the church are by Giuseppe Mazzuoli; they stood for 200 years in Siena Cathedral. They look rather small in the London Oratory, and must have looked even smaller in Siena; but they give some authentic Italian bravura to the nave.

The Chapel of the English Martyrs is a more satisfying design, perhaps because it is not straining for exuberance but is frankly sedate. It contains a fine triptych by the modern English painter Rex Whistler; it is interesting to see how this sweet vernal painter handles the horrific subject of the English Catholics hanged and burned during the reign of the boy king Edward VI. He has dipped his brush in Bosch.

Across the court is the Little Oratory, the domestic chapel of the Oratorian Fathers; sombre wooden stalls, and good grisaille wall-paintings of 1954 by Adrian Brookholding-Jones and Edgar Ritchard. They look like stylish bookplates. Outside stands Cardinal Newman, the Superior of the English Oratorians and one of the greatest Victorian masters of our language, under a quattrocento-type edicule, every inch the Florentine Renaissance cardinal; which in life he was not.

ACCRETIVE

11. THE CHARTERHOUSE CHAPEL
CHARTERHOUSE SQUARE, EC1

IIE2 U: Barbican

At the time of the Black Death a new graveyard was established for its victims close to the Pardon Chapel and Graveyard, and was called the Spital Croft, or New Church Haw (yard). Twenty-two years later, in 1371, Sir Walter de Manny founded there a Carthusian Monastery. Manny, the son of a noble of Hainault with the splendid name of Le Borgne de Mauny, was a soldier in the service of Edward III. He was buried under the altar. The Carthusian monks lived uneventfully each in his little separate house and garden, wrestling with the Devil and receiving legacies. At the Reformation their prior, the Blessed John Houghton, was hanged, drawn and quartered at Tyburn for refusing the Oath of Supremacy. One of his quarters was hung on the gate of the Charterhouse, but his monks still refused the oath.

After this Charterhouse passed to the Howard family, and presumably the Duke of Norfolk had the mass continued in the old monastic chapel. In

1611 Thomas Sutton, a wealthy colliery-owner who had also married money, bought it and founded a school. In 1872 the Charterhouse School moved to Godalming, and the Merchant Taylors' School acquired part of the old buildings. They in turn moved to the country in the 1930s.

The buildings bear traces of all the changes and are confused and picturesque. Much was destroyed during World War II, but the chapel was unharmed. This was long thought to be on the site of the monastic chapel, and some smart detective work involving what one sees through a certain squint enabled Lord Mottistone to locate the grave of Manny; and there, sure enough, he was, clutching a papal bull. It has always been known that Manny was buried under the high altar of his chapel, and this means that the present chapel was started afresh by Sutton's executor on the site not of the old one, but of the old chapter house. It is very jumbled to look at; Sutton's monument is an enormous compendium of figures by Nicholas Stone, who had worked in Amsterdam (and who was to have done the skyline statues for Inigo Jones's Whitehall), of columns, strapwork, allegorical scenes and scenes illustrating Sutton's benevolence. The effect is grand, and as busy as an antheap. Then there is an arcade of Sutton's time, and a ceiling, pulpit, bench-ends and communion table. The northern aisle and the gallery in it are of 1841.

---

12. CHRIST CHURCH SPITALFIELDS

NICHOLAS
HAWKSMOOR

COMMERCIAL STREET, E2

1714

ID2   U: Liverpool Street

This is one of England's greatest architectural glories: it is one of the six London churches of Nicholas Hawksmoor, an architect whose genius went uncelebrated, even undiscerned, during 250 years of other fashions. A quarter of a century ago this particular church, perhaps Hawksmoor's greatest, narrowly survived threats of demolition.

Until the end of the 17th century the Spital Fields were green. A monastic hospice providing lodging for poor travellers, called St Mary Spittle without Bishopsgate, stood on the site of the present Spital Square from 1197 until the 16th century. The Spital Cross, an outdoor pulpit like Paul's Cross and used in conjunction with it for Easter sermons, survived until the Commonwealth. 'The Mayor and his brethren the Aldermen were accustomed to be present in their violets at Paules on Good Friday and in their scarlets at the Spittle in the holidays.'[1]

A few silk-workers already lived at Spitalfields in the time of James I, who incorporated them as Silk Throwsters in 1629. They worshipped in a chapel of ease at Whitechapel and in Stepney Church until Sir George Wheler built a small wooden chapel for them on his land in 1693. He had lived in France, and when he returned he made himself a champion of the

Christ Church
Spitalfields

---

[1] Stow, *Survey of London*, Everyman edn, London 1945, p. 151.

Huguenots, sending circulars to Members of Parliament about their troubles. Perhaps it was his owning land there as well as there being a small silk industry already which made the Huguenot silk weavers, refugees from the revocation of the Edict of Nantes in 1688, settle in Spitalfields. In a few years they had built themselves eleven chapels, in which they seem to have used the Book of Common Prayer in a French translation. Nearly half the names on the 18th-century gravestones and coffins in and around Christ Church are French. This was the period of Spitalfields' greatest prosperity; the Huguenots arrived as a community, lived in fine houses, and only after three or four generations did the richer ones move away. By 1766 there were four French chapels left. Gradually the parish became poorer. The silk trade stagnated whenever the fashion was for muslin, whole families of poor workers from the City moved into single rooms of houses the rich had left, and the power loom was the end of large-scale hand silk-weaving. In 1832 there were 50,000 weavers unemployed.

A few French names still remain, but in 1881 Ashkenazi Jews began settling in Spitalfields, thousands yearly. Tailoring (a trade particularly subject to sweating), a furriery and cigar-making quite replaced weaving. But as late as 1870, when the Pope wanted a seamless silk garment to symbolise the infallibility he was about to assume, it is said that only in Spitalfields of all Europe could a weaver be found for it, the descendant of Huguenots. After the Jews came people from the Indian sub-continent. The last of the Huguenot chapels, a stone's throw from Christ Church in Fournier Street, after some years as a Wesleyan Chapel became, in 1898, Spitalfields Great Synagogue, and now that the Jews have moved out and away it is a mosque. Gentrification is restoring the Huguenots' houses.

Throughout the 19th century the poverty here seemed bottomless. A soup-kitchen had been started in 1797, and served 3,000 quarts a day at a penny a quart. There was an association for the cheap sale of salt fish, and a public meeting in 1816 was so horrified by what it heard that it subscribed £43,000 for relief on the spot. But little money could be spent on the church, once the Commissioners of the Fifty had paid for it. The spire was renewed after a fire in 1836, but plainer. In 1866 the north and south galleries were taken away, doors and windows were closed or altered, the pulpit was moved and lowered, and the east end made more amenable to a choir, all hurriedly and insensitively by the architect Ewan Christian. The glass in the west window was put in by a Soho firm in 1876. But it continued very much Hawksmoor's church.

In 1960, the building having become technically a 'dangerous structure' and expensive repairs unavoidable, the relevant diocese began in private to think of demolishing the church and selling its site: the law then allowed this without any external consultation or permission. The news leaked out, and those who were successful in aborting the proposal, with a few other enthusiasts, formed themselves into the Hawksmoor Committee, with the aim of promoting appreciation of one of Britain's greatest architects.[1] The diocese later used part of the proceeds of the sale of ST

---

[1] Among the sponsors were T. S. Eliot and Bud Flanagan.

JOHN'S, SMITH SQUARE, to repair the roof, and the Friends of Christ Church Spitalfields embarked on the full and expert restoration of the building.

This is difficult and entirely rewarding architecture: alternative 'readings' of the spaces and the solids coexist and fuse and separate and reassemble.

'Take a block of holy air,' (we can imagine Hawksmoor saying) 'and surround it with decorated stone; make sure you pierce your air with transoms of sufficient size that the stone fall not apart, and corrugate the edges of your air with barrel vaults of sufficient depth that the stone slip not lengthways.' The decoration is all large, complex, static; in the nave, movement is suggested only by the soffit-sweep from the edge of the galleries to the columns which support the organ above the main door. With Hawksmoor one is equally aware of the form of the contained space and of the containing solid. And there are other spaces and solids: the rooms and closets and staircases in the east corners and the west end pierce with a strict warren of complex forms the monumental solidity of the Portland stone. Through them light originally filtered, east and west, into the body of the church.

The portico is colossal; its central barrel-vaulted arch sums up the pattern of the nave within and carries the eye up to the triumphal arch which encloses the belfry. And on one goes, persuaded by strict proportion, up to the tremendous spire which dominates the Tower Hamlets. It is no

Christ Church Spitalfields

longer quite Hawksmoor's spire; when it was rebuilt in 1836, the decoration was left off. The three small openings surmounted by urns on each flat face and the six small bosses up each angle, which were originally there, explained the shape more clearly than the present bare ashlar. As you move round outside the church the triumphal arches of the east and west aspects of the tower separate, show a hemi-cylindrical hollow, then join again. The discovery of this hollow gives a poignant gentleness to the otherwise uncompromising solidity of the whole church. The body of the church supports with static and imposingly regular detail the enormous weight of the spire.

JOHN RAPHAEL
BRANDON
1850–4

13. THE CHURCH OF CHRIST THE KING
GORDON SQUARE, WC1
IIC1   U: Euston Square, Goodge St

Edward Irving, minister of the Scotch Church and friend of Carlyle, drew such crowds to hear him preach in his chapel at Hatton Garden that he had constructed a large brick box in Regent Square with a portentous Bath stone façade modelled on York Minster. This was in 1824–7. Irving's extravagances and lapses into heresy are part of the history of religion in 19th-century England. He laid increasing emphasis in his preaching on the rapid approach of the end of the world and on the sinfulness of Christ's nature. The Presbyterian church was deeply disturbed and when members of his flock commenced gibberish 'utterances' and the prophecies became undoubtedly heretical, Irving was expelled. His followers, the Irvingites, succeeded well enough and, calling themselves the Catholic Apostolic Church, built themselves this veritable cathedral in the style of the 13th century. It was never finished: two bays of the nave and the central tower are missing. Nevertheless, their felt presence is so strong that the west end appears amputated, the church's interior held in place by a strong slice of heavily buttressed and muscular brickwork, and the tower chopped off above a small arcade and flat-capped with grey slate.

The way in from Gordon Square is indirect, and by taking the visitor along one side of a cloister implies acres of monastic buildings up to the north. (They are not there either.) Entry into the church itself is at a right angle from a small baptistery and in under the organ. To the west the nave stretches away below its hammerbeam roof, to the east the huge chancel (stone-vaulted) and, visible through the 'decorated' screen behind the altar, the yet more glorious Lady Chapel.

The architect Brandon had written with his brother an analysis of Gothic architecture in 1847 and the lucidity of this great building displays as few others of the Gothic revival a real sense of Gothic lived.

Since 1963 this has been the University Church of London University and it is evidently put to energetic use – an impression to which its incompleteness somehow contributes.

14. GEFFRYE MUSEUM
The Former Ironmongers' Almshouses Chapel
KINGSLAND ROAD, HACKNEY, E2

ID2   U: Liverpool Street, then buses

1715

In 1910, when the almsmen moved to Mottingham, these almshouses were sold to the London County Council and became a furniture museum. The chapel is central to the design. The little sanctuary apse remains behind its rails, and so does a complicated four-decker pulpit with two box pews

Geffrye Museum, chapel interior

beside it. Why four decks? Sometimes a fourth is a churching pew for mothers newly brought to a bed of a child; but the almsmen were hardly likely to require this service of their chaplain. In an adjacent room is kept one of the little upholstered benches which, at right angles to the apse, filled the rest of the chapel. Neither apse nor rails nor pulpit nor bench can be of 1715; 1770 seems a more likely date.

This is a pretty little apartment; now that the museum is absorbed into a scheme for brighter history lessons it is full of children rushing and jotting.

JAMES ('ATHENIAN')
STUART and WILLIAM
NEWTON
1789

15. GREENWICH ROYAL HOSPITAL CHAPEL

GREENWICH, SE10

IF3

BR: Greenwich

The buildings of the Royal Naval College and the National Maritime Museum make up the grandest organised display of classical and baroque architecture in the country. The architectural history is too complicated to summarise; Jones, Webb, Wren, Hawksmoor, Vanbrugh, Stuart, all added to it, and hundreds of unexecuted drawings survive.[1] It is the nearest thing in England to the royal set-pieces of Versailles or Caserta or Schönbrunn, and more fluent, more lively, than any of these.

Greenwich: the Queen's House (Inigo Jones), behind, and the Hospital (Wren, Webb, Hawksmoor). The Chapel is under the left dome

The Queen Mary Block which contains the chapel was finished by Ripley, largely to Wren's design, only in 1752. The place had started as a royal palace, but was by then a hospital for naval pensioners in their declining years. In 1779 the chapel was burnt out, and by 1789 the veterans of the War of Jenkins' Ear and the colonial wars with France were accommodated afresh in a building which, at least inside, owed very little to Wren. During the rebuilding, 'Athenian' Stuart, who was surveyor, sacked his clerk of the

[1] Including one by Hawksmoor for a gigantic chapel and forecourt, reminiscent of St Peter's, to be put between the south end of the Wren colonnades and the Queen's House. It is described by Laurence Whistler in *The Imagination of Vanbrugh*, London, 1954, pp. 14–15.

*Greenwich Royal
Hospital Chapel*

works, Robert Mylne, because Mylne would alter the drawings he sent him. In his place he took on one William Newton, to whom much of the excellent interior decoration is due. The interior is well preserved and the whole has this great interest, that it is a large and rich church built at a time when thought and money were mostly going into private houses. The first thing to strike the eye is that instead of the usual heavy gallery resting on columns there is a high narrow one supported by swooping cantilevers. Stuart[1] has turned back to the arrangement used by Inigo Jones at Whitehall and in the Queen's House at Greenwich. The treatment of space

---

[1] There is a shadowy possibility, resting on an undated print, that the galleries are a survival of the earlier interior by Ripley.

is plain enough – a box – but the segmental vault is answered by little segmental half-domes in the gallery soffit over each window. These and the console cantilevers give between them a pitching and bucketing traverse to the glance as it runs along the walls. The colours are submarine; fouled anchors, mermen and shells abound in the decoration, and over the gilt Coade stone and marble altar St Paul is shipwrecked in a huge picture by Benjamin West. The round pulpit, high on columns, is in red limewood and the plaques on it are in Coade stone. So are the big statues of Faith, Hope, Charity and Meekness in the octagonal vestibule. These too were designed by Benjamin West. There is a tiny gilt font, rich in seahorses and rather domestic, but the great panelled mahogany doors in their marble jambs and the full-blown Ionic marble porch or loggia they give on to, under the organ, are fit for admirals. In 1955 the whole interior was excellently redecorated. The little caryatid altar was raised an inch or two and slightly added to at the sides, and some coarse plate marble rails were replaced by the original wrought iron ones. These were found lying in bits in the dome, and have been well restored. They are worked in a very clear and chaste symbolism of corn and grapes.

The naval pensioners left in 1879 and the Royal Naval College took over, but every Sunday until 1933 nine hundred boys, the sons of seamen, marched over the road from the school in Inigo Jones's Queen's House to this chapel, led by their band. The buildings now house the Combined Services Staff College, as well as senior officers. In this chapel and the Hall opposite, built by Wren and painted all over by Thornhill, the Royal Navy has two of the most splendid 18th-century interiors in England.

RICHARD JUPP
1780

IIE3

16. GUY'S HOSPITAL CHAPEL
ST THOMAS' STREET, SOUTHWARK, SE1
U: London Bridge

The courtyard of Guy's which opens towards London Bridge Station was laid out in 1738, but the chapel was not built until 1780. The interior is a very charming piece, built at a time when, in church architecture, anything might happen. It is square; an Ionic order supports three galleries. Above the galleries rise orders compound of the Ionic and the Tower-of-the-Winds which support, between themselves and the walls, a stretch of complex groining which gives the impression of a sort of Gothic vault. Inwards a groined cove leads up to a square ceiling with some ordinary chaste plasterwork on it. The effect is at once dainty and surprising.

The big monument in high relief to the founder at the east end, by John Bacon, is a work of capital merit. A water-colour of 1825 shows a central double door where is now the monument, and blind niches where are now the doors on either side.

Guy's Hospital Chapel

---

17. HOLY TRINITY, LATIMER ROAD
SHALFLEET DRIVE, W11

IB3

U: Latimer Road

R. NORMAN SHAW
1887–9

Norman Shaw was one of the architects to move away from Gothic towards 'Queen Anne': 'Arts and Crafts' were not far away. The church has been converted into a boys' club, a hugely tall set of 'Queen Anne' school buildings remaining standing in a desolation of motorways and caravan lots and some new building. The large plain brick building, a faint Dutchness about the one great gable, still has its two vast windows east and west, the one seen through the other, full of delicate and lively convolvulant tracery which leaves *flamboyant* far behind.

SIR JOHN SOANE
1824–8

IIB1

18. HOLY TRINITY, MARYLEBONE
MARYLEBONE ROAD, AT ALBANY ST, CAMDEN, NW1
U: Great Portland Street

The exterior differs from Soane's other two churches (ST PETER'S, WALWORTH, and ST JOHN ON BETHNAL GREEN) principally in having giant Ionic columns half-sunk in the side walls. The main façade, to the south, has a shallow Ionic portico. Soane originally exhibited a design showing only pilasters on the lower stage of the tower, and the people of Marylebone were so impressed by the parsimony of the Waterloo Commission which made this necessary that they subscribed a sum to enable Soane to put on the present free-standing columns with their characteristic urns. Until 1876 the north elevation had a portico sunk flush between wings, like the principal front of ST PETER'S, WALWORTH; then Somers Clarke added the present round apse. The interior, which used to be the same as that at Walworth, is now occupied by the Society for Promoting Christian Knowledge. The nave houses a bookshop, and the rest has been screened off for offices. There is still an altar, and services are occasionally held in the chancel.

The tower's surmounting lantern is one of Soane's serious and entertaining essays: the capitals have sprouted curls, the vases are – perhaps – inverted; the Grecian idioms have adapted and separated out. From the west, the church is now framed by a rectilinear office block, which thereby acquires a role.

J. D. SEDDING
1890–1907

IIA4

19. HOLY TRINITY, SLOANE STREET
BY SLOANE SQUARE, SW1
U: Sloane Square

'The outstanding London example of the Arts and Crafts Movement', according to Pevsner.[1] Anson quotes the historian of the church on its architect's *gentillesses d'oiseau*; . . . he was exactly like a bird hopping from twig to twig and from bough to bough . . .'[2] and the church indeed is a magpie's nest of delightful things, starting with the black and gold fence along Sloane Street. The effect is of a spacious living room, where boyish glee has laid out most pleasant wrack collected from a sunny seashore, the storms of Victorian soul-searching and the energy of Victorian building spent, both the rational calm and the *enthousiasme* of the 18th century gone, the arduous battles of the 17th healed, the great busy landscapes of the Middle Ages all forgotten. Sedding promised: 'We will have designs by

[1] Nikolaus Pevsner, *London except the Cities of London and Westminster*, Harmondsworth 1951, p. 89.
[2] P. Anson, *Fashions in Church Furnishings 1840–1940*, London 1965.

living men for living men – something that expresses fresh realisations.' Basil Clark quotes him picturing a church 'wrought and painted over with everything that has life and beauty – in frank and fearless naturalism covered with men and beasts and flowers'.[1]

He collected his artists and craftsmen well, but did not live to make of their offerings more than a collection of 'dam' nice things'; although the windows, for instance, are very fine, although the lectern, with its three foot high bronze angel and the marble 10th-century pulpit on 16th-century columns with an 18th-century sounding-board individually please, and sometimes delight, and the copper entrance to the organ and the silver fronts to the choir with their imaginary portraits even astonish, yet all does not come together.

It is the afternoon before the earthquake; when less was enough.

Yet John Betjeman found worship here;

> Bronze triptych doors unswing!
> Wait, restive heart, wait, rounded lips, to pray,
> 'Mid beaten copper interset with gems,
> Behold! Behold! your King![2]

20. LINCOLNS INN CHAPEL

BY CHANCERY LANE, WC2

JOHN CLARKE
1620–3

IID2   U: Chancery Lane

Here, as at the Temple (see TEMPLE CHURCH) and at Gray's Inn, the lawyers settled before the Reformation. A medieval chapel, probably mainly of the 13th century, was pulled down in 1618 and the present building put up. It was designed by a mason called John Clarke, though the fact that it had earlier been the intention of the benchers to employ Inigo Jones has misled almost every historian of Lincolns Inn into attributing this odd little hybrid to him. It is in the main a Perpendicular building raised on an open short-legged undercroft. It was restored in 1795, in 1843, and again after a bomb of World War I. The most westerly of the present four bays and the western porch were added only in 1882. The proportions, high and short, were odd until this last addition, but odder still were the flaming urns, a wholly classical device, which anachronistically topped the buttresses until the 18th century, and the Tuscan responds which still lurk in the four-centred arches of the undercroft. Apart from these things the chapel might as well have been built in 1520 as in 1620. Good 17th-century glass was destroyed in the air raid during World War I, but most of the original pewing remains and makes a fine show with its poppyheads and tall doors.

---

[1] Anson, op. cit., p. 251.
[2] John Betjeman, *Collected Poems*, London 1979, p. 59.

John Donne laid the foundation stone and returned as Dean of St Paul's to preach the consecration sermon. Listen: 'And in these walles to them that love Profit and Gaine, manifest thou thyself as a Treasure, and fill them so: To them that love Pleasure, manifest thyself as Marrow and Fatnesse, and fill them so: And to them that love Preferment, manifest thyself as Kingdome, and fill them so, that so thou mayest be unto all.'[1]

incolns Inn Chapel

21. MORDEN COLLEGE CHAPEL
ST GERMAN'S PLACE, GREENWICH, SE3
IF4   BR: Blackheath

Sir John Morden, a Turkey merchant, having himself according to tradition known poverty, founded this almshouse. Decayed merchants were long the only inmates, but with the growth of limited liability merchants found a means of preserving themselves from decay, and officers of the Merchant Marine are now admitted too.

The College is a pleasant piece of ornate domestic architecture. The Wren Society[2] attributes it to Wren, but without adducing documentary evidence. The little chapel leads out of the quadrangle by a splendid carved door. Except for the modern organ, it is almost untouched inside. Box

---

[1] John Donne, *Encaenia. The feast of dedication celebrated at Lincoln's Inn in a sermon there upon Ascension day 1623*, London 1623.
[2] *Wren Society*, vol. xix, p. 151. Edward Strong, who was responsible for the masonry at several of Wren's City churches being built at this time, was in charge of the mason's work.

*Morden College
Chapel*

pews are dominated by a full-sized pulpit and sounding-board; the altar-piece, too, is big enough and fine enough for a City church. The east window, a gift of 1850, is a colourful hodge-podge of 16th- and 17th-century glass from various sources.

22. PALACE OF WESTMINSTER
St Stephen's Chapel
WESTMINSTER, SW1

IIC4 U: Westminster

SIR CHARLES BARRY
and E. BARRY
1837

St Stephen's Chapel and the crypt church under it, sometimes called St Mary Undercroft, were the chapels of the old Royal Palace of Westminster. They were rebuilt in the early 14th century. The brotherhood established there was dissolved at the Reformation; in 1547 the chapel was given to the House of Commons for their debating chamber and became known usually as St Stephen's Hall. For nearly 300 years the Commons met in it, and in it English democracy from the Elizabethan church settlements to the Great Reform Bill was constructed. The building lost much of its medieval outline: Wren put in galleries and wainscots and rounded the great east window. Later a flat ceiling was run across, in the middle of which, above the central chandelier, was a ventilator round which ladies were allowed to sit and squint downwards through a current of foul air, catching sight of Pitt's crutch, perhaps, while just above them the medieval vault stood forgotten. The crypt meanwhile became part coal store and part the Speaker's dining room.

The fire of 1834 which destroyed the Palace of Westminster destroyed St Stephen's Hall with it. Sir Charles Barry built a new Commons Chamber and rebuilt the old Hall on the original medieval lines. It is now a passage and contains historical wall-paintings. The crypt was damaged but not destroyed. Barry's son Edward restored it and painted it all over in what he said was a reconstruction of traces of the medieval decoration he had found under whitewash. It may well be so, and in any case the effect is very magnificent. What one sees there is essentially the lower church of a double church forming part of a medieval royal palace, as at the Sainte Chapelle in Paris. Other examples are found in monasteries like Assisi. In St Stephen's Chapel, with its handsome octagonal baptistery Members of Parliament may marry and give in marriage and have their children baptised. It is non-denominational. The iron screen is a 19th-century copy of the grille round the tomb of Eleanor of Castile in Westminster Abbey, but the two candlesticks on the altar are 15th century.

Palace of Westminster, St Stephen's Chapel

23. ST ALBAN'S HOLBORN

BROOKE STREET, EC1

U: Chancery Lane

IID2

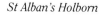

WILLIAM
BUTTERFIELD
1859–62

Here Butterfield carried the tall saddleback tower design further than at ST MATTHIAS, HACKNEY. The angle is not so bitter, but the tower has acquired a new breadth and substance without losing any of its authority. It rears and soars above an appropriately low local authority housing development like a tethered beast. The body of the church, though not the attached school and clergy house, was destroyed in World War II and has been rebuilt differently. The tall space under the tower inside is still as Butterfield built it, and still impressive.

St Alban's Holborn

St Alfege, Greenwich

24. ST ALFEGE, GREENWICH
GREENWICH CHURCH STREET, SE10
IF4   BR: Greenwich

NICHOLAS
HAWKSMOOR
1714–18

Tower
JOHN JAMES
1730

Greenwich was a Roman settlement; in Greenwich Park remain some 20 Saxon barrows. There was a church here by 964 and in 1012 St Alfege, Archbishop of Canterbury, was killed by drunken Danes when he refused to order his people to pay the ransom they demanded for his release. In the 15th and 16th centuries a royal palace was built and enlarged, an industry which made Greenwich into a small town, and by the early 18th century the borough contained buildings by all the great architects of the previous 100 years.

At the Reformation the parish church was richly furnished and, to judge by the number of altars it contained, fairly big. Of this building nothing remains visible, but the present tower includes behind its smooth stone part of the previous one of 1617. It would have been in this church that

Henry VIII was baptised, and his sister Mary married. During a storm of
1710, at midnight, the nave collapsed, probably due to burial excavations
underneath. The inhabitants of Greenwich put their case before
Parliament, pleading that their town was 'depopulated and deserted by the
Richer Sort',[1] that the few gentlemen left were all merely tenants-at-will,
that the parish supported innumerable widows and orphans of sailors, and
moreover that in paying coal tax they had contributed to the building of St
Paul's and many other churches which were now nearly finished. They
suggested that the coal tax be continued and that it should pay for their
new church. Parliament agreed, and thus began the scheme for building
Fifty New Churches.[2]

Hawksmoor, at this time Clerk of the Works at Greenwich Hospital,
started building in 1714 and though the church was gutted in May 1941,
Sir Albert Richardson's restoration is so careful that the church is now,
except for the spire, near Hawksmoor's very intention.

John James, Hawksmoor's assistant and later colleague in building the
Hospital, also assisted him here, at least in 'framing the Roofe'.[3] The tower

St Alfege, Greenwich

[1] *Case of the inhabitants of Greenwich*, 1710.
[2] See p. 12.   [3] *Wren Society*, vol. vi, p. 67.

which James built at the west end in 1730 is a weak early version of the 'pepperpot'. It is sadly irrelevant to the rest of the structure and, riding above the Greenwich roof-tops, misleading about the glories it flags. A design[1] for a tower by Hawksmoor himself survives and shows it attached to the church by a narrow vestibule reaching only as high as the caps of the pilasters. This tower is square and powerful and is crowned with a gushing piston-like lantern.

The church is in the shape of a temple made just cruciform by central projecting vestibules north and south. Enormous Tuscan pilasters support an entablature with large clear detail. Between the pilasters on the north and south sides the aprons of the twice inset gallery windows and the keystones of the aisle windows establish by their weight and complexity the balance of the building. The east end, facing the street, is neither open nor closed: the bottom of the large plain pediment is cut by a deep arch, as in Wren's Great Model Design for St Paul's, and behind it a portico is scooped out of the three middle bays. Small doors facing each other across it lead into the side aisles and in the centre is the wide east window with a curious edicule above it, almost in bas relief. At each corner and at each end of the ridge of the roof is an enormous, magnificent and final quadruple urn.

The interior is more domestic and genial. Its chief beauty is the great, clear, hanging expanse of the ceiling. To show off this ceiling Hawksmoor set his galleries on little posts like turned table-legs instead of the usual pillars. The effect is to make the galleries seem part of the floor space and not a landing half-way to the roof, and the finest view of the interior is from the galleries; where, indeed, is the royal pew. The apse, with its depressed half-dome, is also set low so as not to interfere with the ceiling. The east window, in those proportions to which the external aspect of the windows has accustomed us, is supported, it seems, by the reredos of four Corinthian columns with pilasters behind and a plain entablature. It is simple and impressive. On either side, under a curved triangular entablature level with which springs the arch of the window, are three giant Corinthian columns. They carry nothing; or do they carry the shadow above the window? Or what?

Much of the original woodcarving was by Grinling Gibbons, and a little of his work remains in the posts under the galleries and the Beasts on the Royal Pew. The new woodwork is of a pleasantly light colour. The grisaille painting by Thornhill in the east end has been well restored, and the communion rails and those in the galleries, the work of 18th-century craftsmen with a strong sense of the three-dimensional possibilities of wrought iron, remain.

The organ, destroyed in 1941, had some Tudor pipes in it which came from the organ played in the old church by Thomas Tallis. There is some argument over whether any now remain. Tallis was Gentleman of the Royal Chapel from 1530 to 1585, and was buried in the old church. His

---

[1] Reproduced by Howard Colvin in the *Architectural Review*, March 1950.

memorial brass vanished in 1710 but a reproduction of it, and a commemorative window, are in the south aisle. General Wolfe was buried in the present building.

Luckily for us St Alfege's church was gently treated by its 19th-century vestries and architects. It is refreshing to read a report like that of Basil Champneys to the Renovation Committee in 1883, where he praises the church both for its beauty and for the soundness of its construction, and lists its defects only under the headings heating, lighting and arrangements for the clergy and choir. He painted the interior white, moreover. Before this, in 1870, the pews had been remodelled in a sensible way. As Champneys said, St Alfege 'has been especially fortunate in . . . that . . . no attempt has been made to Gothicise it'.

---

25. ST ANNE'S, LIMEHOUSE
COMMERCIAL ROAD, AT WEST INDIA DOCK ROAD, E14
IE3   U: Aldgate East, then buses

NICHOLAS
HAWKSMOOR
1712–24

All of Hawksmoor's great churches in Stepney are odd: CHRIST CHURCH SPITALFIELDS and ST GEORGE'S IN THE EAST achieve greatness through oddity, St Anne's remains just magnificently odd. White and gigantic, it rears like a startled horse at the appearance of London upstream, and the peculiarity of design which gives it this effect is now enhanced by the tower's in fact leaning backward, and the flagstaff's leaning sharply forward again. The best part of the outside is the west aspect of the tower; the spreading steps which meet the strange cylindrical chamber half in and half out of the tower at one angle, and the fanciful free-standing pillars which meet the lantern above at another, give it a look of wry vivacity. These horizontal triangles are answered in the big pyramidal tomb, possibly of a number of sea captains, which stands near. It seems that at one time Hawksmoor meant to have pyramids on the eastern turrets[1] (though the earliest prints show none) and there is a school of thought that this tomb was made of a pyramid provided but not used for that original purpose.

The church was not consecrated for six years after its completion because of difficulties in raising the money to pay a rector. After the belated ceremony, 'the bishops drank a little hot wine and took a bitt of the sweetmeats, and then the clergy and the laity scrambled for the rest.'[2]

The church was gutted by fire on Good Friday 1850 because, said the *Illustrated London News*,[3] one of the roof timbers entered the flue of a stove. There arose a difficulty about the rebuilding because two Nonconformists had been elected against their wills as churchwardens and

---

[1] Elevations in the King's Maps at the British Library.
[2] Letter quoted by J. G. Birch in *Limehouse Through Five Centuries*, London 1930, p. 67.
[3] 6 April 1850.

St Anne's, Limehouse

they, of course, could not square it with their consciences to pass a church rate. That there was as much as £5,000 insurance money was already to their credit; the church had not been insured at all until their election, and they had seen to the payment of the first premium of £13 4s 8d only just in time. But these two excellent men thought this was not yet enough to discharge the responsibilities they had not sought to an institution they did not approve of, so instead of passing a rate they went from door to door among the churchpeople and collected a sensible proportion of the £8,000 that was still needed.

Philip Hardwick and John Morris carefully restored the interior on Hawksmoor's model and it still has all his serene grandeur, though it is now in poor repair and the church is mostly kept closed. It is to be restored as part of London's dockyard redevelopments. The great circular ceiling, like Hawksmoor's more famous 'hanging ceiling' at Blenheim Palace, answers the brooding chancel arch, and all is held together by the giant Corinthian columns of the tetrastyle Roman atrium which lies, a germinal authority, behind many of his interiors. The organ, prizewinner at the Great Exhibition of 1851, is all that jars: it entirely obscures the apsidal recess which should frame it and at the same time join in the solemn dance of ceiling and chancel arch.

SIR ROBERT SMIRKE
1820–2

IB4

26. ST ANNE'S, WANDSWORTH
ST ANNE'S HILL, SW18
BR: Wandsworth Town

This large and excellently-placed church was built as a chapel of ease for the part of Wandsworth parish which lies east of the River Wandle. The vestry bought the land and the Waterloo Commissioners paid for the church. The district was rapidly being developed and the Wandle now claims to be the most heavily industrialised river for its length in the world, but the church still keeps its long apron of grass hillside in front of it. It is only Smirke's usual church, near twin to St Mary, Bryanston Square, and the others. Here the portico, Ionic, is at the west end; its splendid position and a fine day can flatter it into a certain unwrinkled magnificence. But the steeple is too tall and too phallic, the pediment too small, the stone portico tied, it seems, to the brick body, by a string-course, and the round tower, as one walks round the church, appears unsteady in its saddle over the portico.

Half the vestry wanted the fence round the churchyard to be of iron, the other half wanted it to be of oak. In the end they compromised and decided to have it half oak, half iron. Here the Bishop of Winchester stepped in and forbade them to have a mixed fence. But the vestry, having reached their domestic compromise, defended it tooth and nail and the bishop was so cross that the churchyard was never consecrated. There are still no graves in it.

In 1850 St Anne's became a parish and eventually had chapels of ease built to it. In the 1890s the galleries were cut back, the box pews were replaced by open benches, choir stalls were put in and a new chancel was built, designed in a quiet Wrennish style by E. W. Mountford.

The church was slightly damaged in World War II. It has been repaired and painted, and now, set high on its hill, it is weathered and clean as are few others in London.

J. L. PEARSON
1871–98

IB2

27. ST AUGUSTINE, KILBURN
KILBURN PARK ROAD, NW6
U: Kilburn Park

Is there anywhere a Victorian church which is entirely harmonious, which is pleasing without and within, which lacks neither prettiness nor grandeur, which invites the eye both to dwell and to proceed, which is in short quite beautiful? There is, and this is it.

St Augustine, Kilburn

St Augustine, Kilburn   The building results from a church scission in which the High-Church
faction split away from a Low-Church parish and, being wealthy, built
themselves a great new church of brick without and brick and stone
within. Pearson had a simple motto: 'It is my business to think what will
bring people soonest to their knees.'[1] He did it by kindness, and succeeded
better that way than most of his contemporaries, some of whom used too
much force. His secret perhaps lay in his free use of the central device of
classical, not gothic, proportion: the golden section.[2]

   The red brick exterior with its majestic tower and spire are a heartening
sight from wherever you see them. The west front is very striking. There
are many receding and advancing insets and setbacks and many pinnacles
and turrets, some suggesting structure in a Ruskinian way, others there
for the balance, and one tall buttress folded back across the face of the
tower like a hand shielding it from the wind. The *nicchione* on this front is
admirably bevelled, and even vaulted above. The corner pinnacles at the
base of the spire can only remind this generation of the space shuttle: they
even have fins. At the top of the tower, above the lancets and the Venetian

[1] Quoted in B. F. L. Clarke, *Church Builders of the Nineteenth Century*, London 1938,
reprinted 1969, p. 204.
[2] Nikolaus Pevsner, *The Buildings of England: London 2, South*, Harmondsworth 1983,
p. 210n.

dials, the surprised eye meets that most classical of all motifs: dentils. Over the crossing there is a black flèche to wake you up if you have dozed with delight at all the white and red.

St Augustine, Kilburn

The inside is modelled more or less on that of the cathedral of Albi in south-western France although, unlike Albi, its plan includes a square. The buttresses which take the spread of the vault are enclosed within the church itself and pierced so as to yield vaulted aisles. This is managed because, as at Albi, the spaces between these internalised buttresses are divided laterally half-way up, which provides both a gallery and a strong horizontal emphasis. Here, though not at Albi, there is another strong horizontal above that: a white string-course right round the upper walls which acts like a drawstring, holding together the whole space, including the great vault, which might otherwise seem to spread. Wherever you are there is enough architecture to keep you happy; the columns and vaults stand about in wonderful ordered profusion. Pearson gave himself an awesome task; to make his church speak the same language not only from every point on the ground, but also from every point in the gallery which runs round all four sides and makes a visual equivalent of sanctity itself: the earth is below but the Cross is still above. He succeeds; the language is one felt and understood by worshippers and visitors alike.

WILLIAM
BUTTERFIELD
1870–7

28. ST AUGUSTINE, QUEEN'S GATE
SOUTH KENSINGTON, SW7

IB3

U: South Kensington

Butterfield is the Beethoven of Victorian architecture. He used all the old vocabulary of forms, all the old tunes, but combined them newly to make astonishing and heroic effects.

This is in fact a rather quiet Butterfield church, as they go. The outside is only moderately amazing; it is set slightly at an angle to the street frontage and has absolutely square shoulders with only a small belfry for tower in the middle. But the shoulders are so high that the effect is deeply striking.[1] The inside is dominated by the broad chancel arch and the echoing dual perforation in the high screen above it, which looks through from the nave on to the more complicated chancel roof. All – high and broad nave, small aisles, harmonious decorated arcades, square chancel the same width – was whitewashed in the 1920s[2] and scrubbed clean only in 1975. The scrubbing revealed a lot of light, cheerful polychrome banding and splashing of stone, brick and tile. The columns are painted because not all the whitewash would come off: the original stone shows only in the north-east corner. The boarding of the nave roof is laid so that only the bottom unit of each timber arch shows clearly: diagonals are thus headed straight on to the capitals of the clerestory columns, both original and 'correct', as Butterfield (and Beethoven) so often are.

The corbels under the chancel springers consist of angel heads with wings upraised around like acroteria: eleven feathers a side, all gilt. The pulpit has been moved one bay west. Perhaps it can be replaced, and perhaps the huge flat 'baroque' altarpiece by Martin Travers can some day be removed. It is quite a good piece, but jars in this church just about as much as the Rubens in King's College Chapel at Cambridge.

---

[1] Paul Thompson relates this, obviously correctly, to the even taller west front of the North German Cathedral of Chorin: see Thompson, *William Butterfield*, London 1971, p. 93.
[2] Even the usually appreciative Goodhart-Rendel, in his *English Architecture since the Regency* (London 1953) wrote of this event: 'people perhaps cannot be blamed, if, wincing under some blow between the eyes delivered to them by the master's violence, they feel tempted to protect themselves by counter-attacks with pails of whitewash.' Butterfield's 'zigzags and stripes', he felt, 'are too many, too congested, and often too large in scale; there can be no doubt of that' (p. 129). We disagree.

29. ST BARNABAS, PIMLICO

PIMLICO ROAD, SW1

U: Sloane Square

IC3

THOMAS CUNDY

School 1846

Clergy house 1848

Church 1850

This is one of those developments of church-plus-clergy-house-plus-school which amount almost to a mission-village, of which there were so many in the slums of Victorian London. It was built by the incumbent of St Paul's, Wilton Place, in the slums at the southern end of his parish. It was also built as a model Puseyite church, aimed to satisfy, that is to say, Tractarian not 'Ecclesiologist' principles. The liturgical practices carried on there

St Barnabas, Pimlico

soon caused trouble: matins and evensong sung daily, the daily celebration of Holy Communion, the separation of the sexes. It became famous, and was lampooned as the 'Convent of the Belgravians'. It had become fashionable.

You go into the church between and among buildings, through gates. The texture is rough pale ragstone, but the forms are smooth and correct early English. Its simplicity and correctness and its resemblance to the best medieval rural models were admired at the time of its construction. Gas lighting was installed at once.

As the district smartened up, so the furnishings became ever richer: through the very fine wooden screen surmounted by a majestic Christ crucified, you gaze on to the glories of the chancel and altar beyond – all gold figures and finialed and crocketed niches. (By Bodley in 1893.)

The whole 'village' makes a cheerful effect, Cundy's rather obtuse spire, now brilliant white, laying its silent muezzin call over the roads and railway lines into the Victoria Stations.

1123–60

30. ST BARTHOLOMEW THE GREAT
WEST SMITHFIELD, AT CLOTH FAIR, CITY, EC1

IIE2   U: Barbican

This church is all that remains, the nave and the crossing, of a great Augustinian priory.

Rahere, a frivolous and obsequious courtier of Henry I, experienced a religious crisis and went on pilgrimage to Rome. He fell ill of malaria in the marshes and vowed to found a hospital 'for the restoration of poor men'. It was not enough. On his way home he saw in a vision St Bartholomew (the apostle who had been flayed alive in India) who told him to build a church at Smithfield. He did both. Smithfield (the smooth field) was then the site of a gibbet, and also of a horse fair which continued until the 18th century and was succeeded by the famous meat market. Rahere had the gibbet moved to the other side of the field and in 1123 began to build a priory for regular canons of the Order of St Augustin (Black Canons). He became the first prior, but his nature did not wholly change: it is recorded that he feigned madness to ingratiate himself with the children of the place and to encourage them to collect rubble for the building. He built the choir and ambulatory of the present church, and a Lady Chapel which was replaced in 1335 by the present one. His successor built transepts and crossing, and between 1230 and 1240 a great nave was added, stretching to the edge of Smithfield. The present gate into the churchyard, under the little Elizabethan house, was the door into the south aisle of this nave. The hospital which Rahere founded at the same time was finally separated from the priory in 1420 after continuous quarrels about tithes, about who was to have bigger bells and ring them earlier, and about whether the hospital brethren should spare time to join in the numerous processions of the priory. The present St Bartholomew's Hospital stands on its site, and is its descendant. It has a small church of its own inside its walls: St Bartholomew the Less.

Rahere died and was buried – his present monument and effigy were put up in the 15th century – and the priory continued a history like that of the other great monastic houses outside London's gates. In 1250 the hectic and extortionate Archbishop of Canterbury, Boniface, after

St Bartholomew the Great

excommunicating the Dean of St Paul's, visited the canons at St Bartholomew wearing armour, against their will and outside his rights, and assaulted the sub-prior in the church so that he was bedridden for life. That, at least, was the sub-prior's story. Another story is that it was an unordained cousin of the queen masquerading as the archbishop.

In 1405 the clerestory windows were given their present form and the Norman apse was cut off by a straight wall thrown across from side to side. In 1515 Prior Bolton, a great builder, Clerk of the Works at Westminster Abbey and in charge there of the building of the Henry VII Chapel and Torrigiani's monument, built his window in the south triforium.

At the Dissolution the church became parochial like many others. The nave was destroyed, the priory buildings given to lay use, and the transepts fell into ruin. The history since then has been one of encroachment after encroachment on and into the church. Already in the 14th century a lay physician from the hospital had rented a chamber and latrine in the south triforium arcade, but after the Restoration the encroachment became wholesale. The Lady Chapel was split up into three private houses and at various times there were a Nonconformist meeting house and school in the south triforium arcade; a parish school in the north triforium; also rooms for the servants of the house in the Lady Chapel; a blacksmith's forge in the north transept; a carpenter's shop and a hop store in the sacristy, and a heap of bones called 'Purgatory' behind the 15th-century wall at the east end. Benjamin Franklin is reported to have worked in a print shop in the Lady Chapel in 1724. Thomas Hardwick did some useful repairs in 1790; in 1830 fire destroyed some of the excrescences and in the 1860s funds at last sufficed to sweep away the others. The little houses of Cloth Fair and Duck Street which had grown over the church like ivy were scraped off. At the same time the square 15th-century east wall was removed, the bones cleared away and the first order of the Norman apse learnedly and satisfyingly restored. But there remained the fringemaker. Since 1833 the 14th-century Lady Chapel had been a fringe factory, and its first floor stuck out above 'Purgatory' as far as the 15th-century wall. The fringemaker held out for a still unreachable price, and for 20 years the attic of his factory obtruded over the high altar of the church, supported on cast iron columns. In 1885 the price was reached, and Sir Aston Webb completed the restoration with the admirably harmonised upper two orders of the apse. At the same time he gave the ruined transepts their present horribly jarring ends.

The church as it now stands, a huge fragment suffering by the amputation of the nave, is still among the grandest Norman works in the south of England. The deep and heavy arcades, the vast trajectory of the crossing arches and, a detail, their curt and violent corbels, are all admirable. The church has five pre-Reformation bells and a 15th-century octagonal stone font, the cover of which is decorated with the tonsured heads of monks.

31. ST BENET, PAUL'S WHARF
ST BENET'S HILL, UPPER THAMES STREET, EC4
IIE3   U: Blackfriars

SIR CHRISTOPHER
WREN
1677–83

The medieval church was also called St Benet Wood Wharf or St Benet Hithe.

The church Wren rebuilt after the Great Fire is one of his prettiest and most cheerful, also one of the luckiest since it suffered no damage during World War II and remains essentially as Wren built it. It is of Dutch extraction, almost cubic, and the tower has a lead-covered cupola-cum-spire which it is worth climbing up a neighbouring building

St Benet, Paul's Wharf

to have a proper look at, it is so merry. The exterior is in red brick with stone dressings and delicate stone swags pinned on. These swags complete the effect of vernal gaiety. Inigo Jones was buried in the old church and although only his paternal grandfather was Welsh this was perhaps the beginning of the Welsh connection with St Benet's. Sir Leoline (Llewellyn, really) Jenkins gave the heavy caryatid altar and some other woodwork to the new church. He was the lawyer and diplomat who is commemorated at such length in the porch of Jesus College, Oxford. Since then many London Welsh have been buried at St Benet's, and with them some heralds from the College of Heralds across the way. One of these was crushed to death in 1797 in the excitement of a royal occasion. Here in 1747 Henry Fielding married his second wife. She had been his first wife's maid and when he was widowed Fielding turned to her for sympathy, receiving it in such measure that their first child was born three months after the wedding. The marriage was long and happy.

In 1877 the church was saved from destruction under the Union of Church Benefices Act and became the London church of the Welsh Episcopalians, which it still is. They use the Book of Common Prayer in a Welsh translation, and there is a harmonium opposite the pulpit. The church is locked from one week's end to the next. The interior is one of Wren's routine designs, with Corinthian pilasters and columns, a box-like nave and one aisle. But the font, with four cherubs' heads, is pretty.

NATHANIEL WRIGHT 1790

32. ST BOTOLPH, ALDERSGATE
EC1

GEORGE DANCE THE ELDER 1744

ST BOTOLPH, ALDGATE
EC3

JAMES GOLD 1728

ST BOTOLPH, BISHOPSGATE
EC2

Destroyed 1666

ST BOTOLPH, BILLINGSGATE
IIF2 — EC3

St Botolph (or Botulph) was the son of noble Saxon parents who became a Benedictine monk, and was one of the foremost missionaries in England in the 7th century. More than 70 English churches were dedicated to him, including these four at gates to the City of London.

All three remaining churches show proper burgher-like solidity, St Botolph Without Bishopsgate being particularly substantial and four-square.

33. ST BRIDE'S, FLEET STREET

AT BRIDE LANE, EC4

IID2

U: Blackfriars

SIR CHRISTOPHER
WREN
1671–1703

St Bride or St Bridget – the church was usually called St Bridget's until the beginning of the last century – was an Irish saint of the 5th century, and a very pleasant saint, too. She hung her cloak upon a sunbeam and the sun was then unable to set until she noticed her mistake and took it off again. Her father sold her because she kept giving things away to the poor. At another time she changed well-water into beer, and it was perhaps in the hope she might do it again that a small church was dedicated to her beside a well above the mouth of the Fleet river.

There were seven churches on this site between the 6th century and 1134. There was also the only undoubted Roman building between the City

St Bride's, Fleet Street

and Westminster, which may have been a church; if it was, it would be the oldest known church in London. Roman burials and pavement, and a 1st-century ditch of unknown purpose, were among the discoveries made by Professor W. F. Grimes in his excavations between the destruction of the church in 1940 and its rebuilding in the 1950s. The crypt has now been devoted to an interesting display of Fleet Street bygones.

St Bride's, Fleet Street

In spite of its smallness, the privilege of sanctuary of St Bride's was so undoubted that in 1321 a man taken in the church and imprisoned was returned there on appeal. About 1480 one William Venor, the Warden of the Fleet Prison across the stream, keeping the old church as chancel, built on to it a big nave and aisles and perhaps also the tower which it is later known to have had, and caused the masonry to be, as Stow says, 'wrought about' with grape-vines as a pun on his name. It had a separate curfew tower in the 14th century, one of four London churches which rang bells to tell people to stay home. By the time of the Reformation it was a large Perpendicular church with two pious brotherhoods, six altars, five chantries and a rood loft with an organ in it. Wynkyn de Worde, who was the first man to print music in England, was buried there in 1534, and, 90 years later, Thomas Weelkes, the great composer of madrigals. Pepys was christened there. The last entry in the churchwarden's accounts before the Great Fire was 'paid to the ringers for ringings that the Duch was routed . . . 6s'.

Wren finished the new church in 1678. Having for once a perfectly regular and large site, he built an ambitious great nave, in a rather traditional manner. Coupled Tuscan columns, and they were the most unusual thing about it, bore a barrel vault with bullseye windows groined in; from outside, these windows look like a true clerestory. The church was completely gutted in one of the great incendiary raids of 1940 and there was properly revealed for the first time the vestibule under the tower, an excellent little domed and arched space which seems to reach at once back to the Pazzi chapel in Florence and forward to Hawksmoor.

The interior has now been completely restored – it was rededicated in 1957 – and is in many ways a success. Godfrey Allen, the architect in charge, followed Wren's original plans. The galleries and the organ have not been replaced. The sides and the west end of the church were opened up, revealing the aisle windows and the little vestibule under the tower, and the windowed aperture higher up. The old pews, though, have been replaced by collegiate-style seating, a huge neo-Grinling Gibbons reredos has been introduced, pleasant enough in itself but bearing, among the putti, two lurid decorations by Glyn Jones: a stained glass Christ in Glory and a painting of the Crucifixion. Behind the reredos the flat east wall has been transformed, again by Glyn Jones, following a description of Wren's original plan in Hatton's *New View of London*, 1708, quoted in the church's pamphlet for visitors: 'painted nebulous and above the clouds appears (from within a large crimson festoon painted curtain) a celestial choir or representation of the church triumphant.' It is dated already, to a date quite inappropriate to the rest of the church. The statues of St Bride and St Paul on the western ends of the stalls, by David McFall, suffer similarly.

The interior of Wren's church achieves grace and grandeur by simple repetition in the arcades, and the spire which he put on the tower a quarter of a century later does the same. John Summerson[1] points out that the repeated identical storeys, diminishing as you go up, may be connected with illustrations in early editions of Vitruvius which show the Tower of the Winds with several stages. Also that some of the vivacity and upthrust of Wren's spire comes from the fact that though the pilaster-and-arch part of each stage gets shorter as you go up, the pedestal part actually gets higher. The idea of music is inseparable from this spire. To look at it is to hear bells. It has also been called 'a madrigal in stone'. Those with a taste for parallelisms in the history of the arts may see an analogy between this spire and a Schusterfleck or rosalia which, in musical terms, is what it is. Both provoke an immediate pleasure, followed by a guilty rejection of the facile; which is followed in turn, if they are well done, by a lasting respect. And St Bride's is well done.

In 1803 it lost the urns below the obelisk which answered those on the angles of the tower and gave a regular outline to the whole. They could surely be replaced now.

---

[1] John Summerson, *Architecture in Britain 1530–1830*, London 1953, p. 134.

34. ST CLEMENT DANES

STRAND, WC2

U: Temple, Aldwych

SIR CHRISTOPHER
WREN
1680–2

Steeple
JAMES GIBBS
1719

IID2

Near here, where the Law Courts now stand, was the tilting ground of the Templars. Before that the place was in some way connected with the Danes, perhaps because Danes married to Englishwomen were allowed to settle here between the two cities of London and Westminster. According to one story there was a massacre of Danes at the altar during the reign of Ethelred, and another tale says that when Hardicanute dug up his brother's body and flung it into the Thames, it was the Danes who fished it out again downstream and reburied it. The church was held by the Templars, who lost it before their expropriation, then by the Prior of Warwick. Rebuilt after being bombed during World War II, it is the headquarters church of the Royal Air Force. The Air Council has a special pew and ceremonial services take place there.

St Clement Danes

The old church was not touched by the Great Fire, but it became ruinous except for its tower at about the same time, and in spite of all his other commitments Wren made designs for the rebuilding in 1680. The masons were Edward Pearce and John Shorthose, the former of whom was a talented baroque sculptor.[1] Perhaps to him was partly due the great richness of the interior decoration which has been very well restored. The galleries curl round at the east end, the profusely ornate ceiling bends to a lower chancel arch, and the rather loose plan of the nave is repeated and tightened in the chancel apse.

The woodwork is fine; it suffered in the 1870s and 1890s from a plague of angels and early fathers inflicted on it by worthy people who thought Wren and Pearce and the others would have liked them, but these were not replaced after the war. The Commandments on the reredos were first covered over in red flock paper, later with a Deposition by James Robinson confidently compared to Michelangelo's Pietà in St Peter's, and now with an inappropriate Annunciation by Ruskin Spear. The Creed and Paternoster were replaced by stained-glass windows, but are now back where they belong.

St Clement Danes, Samuel Johnson's pew

Cunning telescopic pews have been put in, which when folded back leave clear the pavement, studded with air force badges. The effect is excellent, of clear darkness below and clear light above the woodwork, with the curly roof well displayed. The church contains a lot of RAF memorabilia – flags, mementoes, the complete roll of the dead – without clutter.

Wren covered the rather squat medieval tower with Portland stone, disguised its buttresses as attached obelisks, and topped the vestibules on either side of it with little domes. The south side of the church is rather more ornate than the north, which used only to give on to a narrow alley.

---

[1] Known particularly for his bust of Wren in the Ashmolean Museum at Oxford.

James Gibbs in 1719 added to the tower and instead of the bellcote put on a nice bobbly steeple. It has, without sharing any of its features, a family resemblance to that of ST MARY-LE-STRAND – a resemblance of expression. A half-domed portico over the south-west door was removed in 1813.

There was a fine scandal in 1725 when a 'ridiculous, superstitious, Piece of Popish foppery'[2] was placed over the altar. This was a painting in which an angel 'supposed to be beating time to the Musick' was recognised as the Princess Sobieski. The Bishop of London had it removed and was acclaimed as another Moses for having 'commanded the Tinctured Abomination to be taken down'. It was returned in 1900, and remained until World War II.

Dr Johnson worshipped regularly here. He may have heard the charity children singing a hymn which included, referring to the Christian, these lines:

Thou Lord his Spirit will sustain
And turn with tend'rest Care his Bed.

This is the church whose name has rhymed for centuries with 'lemons' in the children's song which begins: 'Oranges and lemons / Say the bells of St Clement's.'

HUGH ROUMIEU
GOUGH
1884–7

35. ST CUTHBERT, PHILBEACH GARDENS

EARLS COURT, SW5

IB3   U: Earls Court

A large red-brick church in a dull crescent, interesting, even important, for its furnishings. These are mainly by William Bainbridge Reynolds, one of the stars of the Arts and Crafts Movement, though the powerful reredos was by the Revd Ernest Geldart.

Sunbeams strike down across a dark mysterious space, the walls all over carved with a half-inch-deep pattern of formal leaves in squares. There are niches, saints, royal arms, a huge rood screen, several other screens, pictures, wrought iron, repoussé copper. The blue copper flèche now looks down on karate in the clergy house and there is a rubbish dump in what was once the tree-lined haunt of Anglo-Catholicism: this was the first Anglican church in which the Host was reserved.

---

[2] 'A letter from a parishioner . . . [to the Bishop of London]' 1725, p. 3.

36. ST CYPRIAN'S, CLARENCE GATE
(GLENTWORTH STREET), MARYLEBONE, NW1
IIA1 U: Baker Street, Marylebone

BUCKNALL and COMPER
1903

The church here owes its existence to Father Charles Gutch, who was taken, as a young man, with the Oxford Movement, and was curate at ST MATTHIAS, HACKNEY, St Paul's, Knightsbridge, and ALL SAINTS, MARGARET STREET. Always longing for his own church, he encountered many difficulties and although he was able to set up a ministry in this 'miserable part of Marylebone', his church was never more than a rather sad conversion of two houses and a coal shed. His ministry, though, involved a wide range of organisations for the amelioration of the lot of the poor. There was the St Cyprian's Sisterhood; there were the schools; there was the Society of the Holy Name, with the Associated Guild of St Pancras for men and boys, and the Guild of St Faith's for young women and girls; the Women's Meeting; the Blanket and Coal Clubs; St Cyprian's Club for men and youths over 18, with a reading room and a library as well as a canteen, and cricket and swimming in the summer. There was an orphanage and a 'House of Mercy' for unmarried mothers. There was St Cyprian's Infant Nursery; St Cyprian's Home for the Aged Poor; and finally a 'Home for Incurables'.

During all his 30 years at St Cyprian's, Father Gutch was faced by a persistent refusal on the part of Lord Portman to allow a site on his land on which a larger and permanent church might be built, because he so disliked Father Gutch's churchmanship. Only after his death was the church Father Gutch so much wanted built.

Although it was put up as a memorial to him, little of his missionary purpose is suggested by the elegant interior we see today. The exterior is unexciting but inside it is agleam with gilded fan-vaulted screens, the chancel screen surmounted with a Calvary and angels, the east window beyond glowing with delicate primary colours. The expanse of the smooth parquet floor suggests a Holy Ballroom.

37. ST DOMINIC, SOUTHAMPTON ROAD
Our Lady of the Rosary and St Dominic
HAVERSTOCK HILL, NW5
IC2 U: Belsize Park, BR: Gospel Oak

C. A. BUCKLER
1874–83

A huge towerless church, big and dusty as Dominican churches in the Mediterranean. As the BROMPTON ORATORY is Italian Jesuit Mannerist so this, in feeling if not in detail, is a kind of Italian 'Friars' Gothic'. It is in yellow brick, with black brick and stone dressings emphasising the rather stiff rhythms of its eight identical bays. Within a great airy space each aisle is lined with eight high-gated dark chapels. A single transept serves to cathedralise the sanctuary which is dominated by the elaborate altar: this is framed on three sides by a construction of 15 stepped open niches, all crockets and finials and crestings, the whole surmounted by a small steeple.

38. ST DUNSTAN IN THE EAST
IDOL LANE, OFF GREAT TOWER ST, CITY, EC3
IIF3   U: Monument

SIR CHRISTOPHER
WREN
1670–99

The dedication suggests a pre-Conquest church, but this is solitary evidence. The building was enlarged 'solom la devyse de Mestre Henry Iveleigh'[1] (Yevele) in 1382, when presumably the walls were built which survived the Great Fire. The medieval parish was prosperous, the church rich, the rector well paid (only the incumbent of ST MAGNUS THE MARTYR had a larger stipend) and, at least according to Vissher's rather impressionistic view of 1616, the spire taller than any except St Paul's. There was a college of priests, a choir school and a grammar school attached.

St Dunstan in the East

The walls were throughly repaired with Portland stone in 1632, and after the Great Fire gutted the church only the tower and spire had to be newly built. A vague tradition maintains it was designed by Wren's daughter. It is, whether Wren's idea or his daughter's, a charming piece of unserious Gothic: the 19th-century architect Sir Reginald Blomfield found it insincere. The idea of perching a spire on four flying buttresses was not new: Newcastle Cathedral has a squat medieval version and St Mary le Bow before the fire had something of the kind. But Wren built at St Dunstan's a

---

[1] 48 E. 43: quoted in A. G. B. West, *The Church and Parish of St Dunstan in the East*, London 1923, p. 14.

lantern gay and flexible beyond either of these two. The buttresses are supported on internal corbels 28 feet deep, but to the eye the spire darts weightless upward. The detail was not approved by 19th-century purists, but purity of detail would not have allowed the little cushioning steps at the base of the spire proper, nor the athletic plainness of the buttresses and angle turrets.

Wren put in a Tuscan arcade, and a Corinthian reredos and organ case were provided. About 1810 the walls were seven inches out of line and the body of the church was taken down and replaced in coherent and modest Gothic by David Laing, architect of the nearby Customs House. None of the handsome 17th-century fittings were put back, except later the font which was recovered from a Warwickshire garden. The east window was glazed to symbolise the growth and origins of the Church of England. Figures of Moses and Aaron were of course included. During the rebuilding substantial walls of chalk and rubble were traced, mainly to the north of the church, perhaps marking the site of the priests' college and the schools. The level of the church floor was found to be two feet higher than a medieval one of glazed tile, which is not surprising as an Act of 1680 ordered the levels of the streets here to be raised some six or seven feet.

The body of the church was destroyed in World War II, and only the Wren steeple was repaired. The hollow shell is now a 'Public Open Space' of definite charm. A great magnolia stands at the west end, a small fountain in the middle, japonica and vines creep about the remaining tracery and city workers eat lunch and pursue intrigues under the open sky.

The vestry minutes show, without explanation, that in the 17th century the kennel-raker got two shillings a year, and also that in 1643 a silver basin which had been used for the communion service was to be put inside an iron hoop and used for baptisms.

There is a Montagu and Capulet story: in 1417 the servants of Lord Strange and Sir Tussell, whose wives had quarrelled, fought inside the church; many were wounded and one was killed. Lord Strange's wife was held by the proper court to have been in the wrong, and so for their penance Lord Strange, bareheaded, Lady Strange, barefooted, and all their servants, in clothes of shame, walked before the rector from St Paul's to St Dunstan's.

ACCRETIVE

39. ST DUNSTAN, STEPNEY
Stepney Parish Church
STEPNEY HIGH STREET, E1

IE2   U: Stepney Green

To the Bishops of London in 604 was granted the manor of Stepney (Stephen's Hithe). It stretched from the Portsoken to the Lea, from the Thames to Hackney, and so did the Parish of Stepney when it was formed. Traditionally, a small church on the site of St Dunstan's called All Saints, was rebuilt by Dunstan himself late in the 10th century, probably while he was Bishop of London, and was named for him after his canonisation. Dunstan, brought up at Glastonbury, was an all-round saint combining gifts political, administrative, spiritual (he pulled the Devil by his nose through a grating with red hot pincers) and beatific (he hung his chasuble on a sunbeam). Perhaps the Saxon Rood now over the communion table is a relic of this church.

Stepney developed slowly in the Middle Ages; a little along the river at Ratcliffe, at the new bridge at Stratford Bow, near Aldgate, and round the Parish Church. Otherwise it was open country, where Londoners hunted and fished on the bishop's lands and a few rich men built houses. Until the end of the 13th century St Dunstan's was the only church. It was then partly (at least) rebuilt and two chapels of ease were added: the White Chapel (later St Mary Matfelon)° and a chapel at Stratford Bow (later St Mary Stratford Bow). After 1404 no bishop ever lived in Stepney, but more merchants built country houses. St Dunstan's was rebuilt again late in the 15th century and given much the appearance and shape it now has, a large church, as was needed by a very large parish, of Kentish rag with a fine solid buttressed tower. The 13th-century chancel was retained, which may account for the odd, two-roofed look of the church until 1899 when the nave's small east gable window looking out on to the west pitch of the chancel roof was rationalised away.

Throughout its history the East End has held views opposite to those held in the West End; Lollard, Lancastrian, Puritan, Sectarian, Low Church, Radical and finally Socialist. In the 16th century shipbuilding developed Thames-side Stepney, while the northern part continued to be inhabited by City merchants who took little part in parish affairs. In 1551 Bishop Ridley handed the Manor of Stepney back to the king. In 1585 an afternoon lecturer was appointed, and there being no more use for it, the organ was sold.[1] About 1610 a curious, inappropriate and unneeded 'Tuscan' porch was added to the tower.

The population continued to increase. St Dunstan's was filled with galleries and three new chapels were built on the water front, at Wapping (ST JOHN'S), at Poplar (St Matthias), and at Shadwell (St Paul's). The plague, particularly deadly in 1625 and 1665, when about one in five of Stepney's inhabitants died, expanded the churchyard. The churchyard at Stepney was famous. A correspondent of the *Spectator* wrote in 1712: 'There are more remarkable inscriptions in that place than in any other I have met with ... there is not a gentleman in England better read in tombstones than myself'. Alas most of them now are vanished or indecipherable.[2]

Stepney continued to swell, slowly with shipbuilding and suddenly after the exodus from the City at the Great Fire of 1666. Then in 1669 St Paul's Shadwell became a separate parish, in 1694, ST JOHN, WAPPING, and the

---

[1] At this time too there was a vestryman called Afabell Partrydge. And in 1649 Contrition Sparrow was christened.
[2] Among them, a rather late one recalls Betsey Harris 'who died suddenly while contemplating on the beauties of the moon ... in her 23rd year'.

parishes of ST ANNE'S, LIMEHOUSE, ST GEORGE'S IN THE EAST, CHRIST CHURCH SPITALFIELDS and St Mary Stratford Bow were split off. The newly built churches were paid for with the coal tax and already, with cheap gin and with churchless Irish labour working in the shipyards, Stepney was losing its respectability. In the early 19th century the improved roads, constructed primarily for traffic to and from the new docks, deposited the city's middle-class workers in Stepney, where the streets of houses built for them still stand, and later carried them further east. Stepney became poor, vicious, filled with slums, and after the 1880s absorbed an enormous population of Jewish refugees from Russia and Poland. And now, as the Russians and Poles have moved out, they are followed by Muslims and Sikhs, and mosques and temples arise.

Nevertheless St Dunstan's was much and expensively restored and altered and 'improved'. Its exterior was stuccoed in 1767; the east window was partly blocked outside, and partly draped in. In 1806 the stucco was removed; so were the porches and the brick battlements; the little turret remained on the tower. In 1808 two Gothic stoves were put in. In 1848 the east wall was built up higher in brick, the galleries were reduced and the seating changed. In 1871–2 the whole church was refaced, coloured glass was put in the west window and the old organ (which Renatus Harris had made in 1678) was sold to the Drury Lane Theatre. In 1899–1900 the last galleries were removed, paint from the beams was removed, plaster from the walls, skylights from the roof were removed. In 1901 a serious fire damaged the eastern end of the church, the organ, vestry, chancel and nave roofs, so that still more repairs were needed. Paying for all this was beyond the means of the parish, which had to depend largely on the generosity of the Charringtons, who brewed beer in the Mile End Road and were about the only wealthy Church of England family left in Stepney.

During World War II bombs flattened everything round St Dunstan's. It was shaken and lost its glass, but still stood, and is now surrounded by a lot of rather drab open space enlivened by a small urban farm. Post-war Stepney is the background to the Crucifixion (of an extremely Nordic Christ) in the new east window. St Dunstan's is an airy church; the winds of time blow calmly through it. The battered Saxon rood, the tiny dim 13th-century relief of the Annunciation in the unencumbered chancel, and in the south wall the now useless stairway to the rood-loft and to the little external beacon-tower; all remind us, as a stone brought to the church in 1663 from the walls of Carthage has it: 'Time consumes all; it spareth none'.

JOHN SHAW
1832

40. ST DUNSTANS IN THE WEST
FLEET STREET, EC4
IID2 U: Temple

The church which was pulled down in 1829 presented some very odd features. It was highly accretive, sporting a Georgian clerestory above medieval aisles and a Gothick bellcote on an embattled tower. The inside

St Dunstans in the West

was an eccentric jumble of furniture put piece by piece into the spaces left unoccupied by earlier pieces. There was a kind of broad low cupboard-like chancel sticking out beyond and below the nave with a light in its roof: the altar was to one side of it, and the pulpit and sounding-board were attached to a single column in the middle on the way into it. But the general effect of Old Nuremberg was created most of all by a giant toy of a clock which was built in 1671 and sat on the aisle roof towards Fleet Street. In a substantial Ionic temple two giants or savages struck the hours on a bell with bludgeons. Cowper in his poem *Table Talk* wrote thus of them:

> When Labour and when Dullness, club in hand,
> Like the two figures of St Dunstan's, stand
> Beating alternately in measured time
> The clockwork tintinnabulum of rhyme . . .[1]

---

[1] *The Poems of William Cowper*, ed. R. Bell [c. 1857], vol. i, p. 199.

When the church was pulled down in 1829 the Marquis of Hertford bought temple, savages, and all, for 200 guineas and erected them in Regent's Park. In 1935 Lord Rothermere bought them back and set them up on the new church where they now beat again. Also preserved from the old church are figures of Queen Elizabeth and King Lud and his two sons from the old Ludgate, which was built in 1586 and demolished in the 1760s.

In 1751–2 George Dance made plans for rebuilding, which were not accepted. The church John Shaw built in 1832, set back a little to widen the street, is a very civilised octagonal Gothic job and has on Fleet Street a fine openwork tower after the Boston Stump or, more exactly, after the tower of All Saints on the Pavement in York. It was damaged in 1944 and has been restored.

John Donne was incumbent here, and at the same time Izaak Walton held the parish offices of scavenger, questman and sidesman. Here presumably Walton heard the preaching of Donne, 'a Preacher in earnest, weeping sometime for his Auditory, sometime with them: always preaching to himself, like an Angel from a cloud, but in none . . .'[1]

St Dunstan's was made a Guild Church in 1952, concerned with the work of the Church of England Council on Foreign Relations. It also now serves as headquarters for the Romanian Orthodox Church in London; there is a Romanian screen, a chapel for Old Catholics, and an altar for the Armenian, Coptic, Syrian and Ethiopian churches.

NICHOLAS
HAWKSMOOR
1720–30

41. ST GEORGE'S, BLOOMSBURY
BLOOMSBURY WAY, WC1

IIC2   U: Holborn

This church was put up at the expense of the Commissioners of the Fifty. First designs had included one by Gibbs, one (which was approved by the Commissioners) by Vanbrugh, and two, one of them for an oval church, by Hawksmoor.

Like all Hawksmoor's six London churches, the one finally built is thoroughly unusual and very grand. The interior, box within box as at ST MARY WOOLNOTH but without the groups of columns, presents a problem, in that it can be 'read' as 'working' along either an east/west or a north/south axis. At present the altar is at the north end, but behind two powerful depressed chancel arches, and at the east side is an apparently insignificant groined apse. The altar was originally in the eastern apse and there was a gallery on the north side. This orientation proved inconvenient to the parishioners, and the church was reorientated in 1781 and the north gallery removed. (The south gallery remains.) When Bedford House was pulled down in 1801 the present inlaid altarpiece, which was formerly in the chapel there, was given to the church. The two majestic arches in the former north aisle were probably necessary to support the roof.

---

[1] Isaac Walton, *Lives* . . . , 1670, p. 38.

St George's, Bloomsbury

Externally, the northern projection, its northern face an elegant essay in fenestration, is surprisingly light and gay for Hawksmoor; it is in strong contrast to the very fine, deep, Corinthian portico, modelled on the Pantheon, to the south. On the west side is a tower standing on the ground, with stairs running up to doors north and south. It is surmounted by a beautiful piece of fantasy: starting upwards with Hawksmoor's usual broad and dour arches, his Brobdignagian keystones, and a pediment echoing the one on the portico, there comes a stepped pyramid, his idea of the Mausoleum at Halicarnassus; and on top of all a statue of George I as St George. Down two of the angles of the pyramid crawled, until Street removed them in 1871, two ten-foot lions; up the other two, two ten-foot unicorns: the Royal arms, in short, in action. (Hawksmoor had ordered them from the sculptor Edward Strong, without the Commission's direction or knowledge.[1]) A traditional rhyme goes:

When Henry the Eighth left the Pope in the lurch
The Protestants made him the Head of the Church;
But George's good subjects, the Bloomsbury people,
Instead of the Church made him Head of the Steeple.

---

[1] See K. Downes, *Hawksmoor*, London 1959, p. 186.

*St George's,
Bloomsbury*

42. ST GEORGE'S, HANOVER SQUARE

JOHN JAMES
1712–24

OFF HANOVER SQUARE, MAYFAIR, W1

IIB2   U: Oxford Circus

This is a disappointing work from the Golden Age. The building was financed by the Commissioners of the Fifty and John James's design was as unstinted as the others called forth by that munificent enterprise. But plan, elevation, handling of volume and detail all reveal a narrow and viscous imagination fumbling after the grandeur of Hawksmoor's and Vanbrugh's language. The Corinthian portico has been with reason praised, but all else, whether bold like the north windows or timid like the tower or abrupt like the jagged entablatures within, is second rate.

Above the altar is a blackened Last Supper by Thornhill and above that is the chief glory of the church, the glass in the east window. It is 16th-century Flemish glass, brought from a convent at Malines in the 1840s and altered to fit James's window.[1] The hectic, impure architecture and decoration of the Flemish Renaissance has its apotheosis in brilliant glass like this: when all is a dazzle the florid babu idiom comes into its own. The window was damaged in 1914 by a suffragette bomb. Originally the font was kept under the altar and rolled out on castors.

---

[1] '. . . a seated figure of the First Person of the Trinity being omitted.' T. F. Bumpus, *London Churches*, London 1908, vol. ii, p. 41.

Throughout its history St George's has been a great place for weddings. If all the best people are married at ST MARGARET'S, WESTMINSTER, all the next best people are married at St George's. Most of the heroes and heroines of Victorian novels were married there; so was Theodore Roosevelt; so were we.

NICHOLAS
HAWKSMOOR
1715–23
Gutted in World
War II

43. ST GEORGE'S IN THE EAST
CANNON STREET ROAD, AT THE HIGHWAY, E1
IE3   BR: Shadwell

Hawksmoor built here for the Commissioners of the Fifty one of his gigantic white-gleaming churches, as big as some cathedrals. It had a complex ground plan; the interior was a Greek cross with giant Tuscan columns, depressed elliptical vaults, and a strange and impressive diagonal emphasis. It was burned out in World War II, and stood for years thereafter as a ruin with a tiny makeshift tabernacle in it. In winter the river winds yelled through the deep, funereal arches of the mighty tower and past the ruthless keystones, each as big as a child's coffin, while charred woodwork hung creaking and flapping.

In 1963 a new church was opened inside this great ruin. It is of a friendly but quite undistinguished design, and has the great merit of not being visible from outside. The ruin and its immediate surroundings have been cleared up and tidied; the gleaming, monumental tower and the hunched, close body of the church now ride high and white over one of the least successfully rebuilt bits of blitzed London.

To this most majestic church came as rector in 1842 the Revd Bryan King (see also ST JOHN ON BETHNAL GREEN) and there began an extraordinary battle between good and evil, or between two pig-headed clerics. Bishop Blomfield of London, the first to abandon the episcopal wig, issued a charge that sermons should be preached in a surplice. King, already a ritualist and a Puseyite, willingly obeyed. Now began the trouble, for Bishop Blomfield was succeeded by A. C. Tait who was born a Presbyterian. King, disillusioned at Bethnal Green in the virtue of mere church-building, concentrated at St George's on missions in the docks, and in charge of his missions he put one Charles Lowder, a High-Church prima donna who excited hostility by preaching at the sites of street accidents. King also attacked the organised fleecing of sailors by brothel-keepers and pub-keepers in the Ratcliffe Highway, the street outside his church. But it was from these very people that his vestry was drawn, and the vestry, to keep things boiling, elected to be lecturer a Low-Church prima donna called Hugh Allen. Bishop Tait had already refused to license Allen as lecturer at Stepney Church because of Allen's support for Nonconformist revivalism, but the opportunity of baiting a ritualist rector was too much and, in spite of King's appeals, Tait licensed Allen at St George's. Allen occupied the church with his party while King was preparing a service, waved his licence, and preached against popery.

St George's in the East (1971)

There followed the St George's riots. Every Sunday Allen's party sat in the choir stalls to keep the choir out, and interrupted the services with shouts and even violence. King sought police protection and for a time officiated from among a guard of 60 constables. But the police were withdrawn, and for some months King struggled against threatening letters, a hostile bishop, an indifferent Home Secretary and some dubious proceedings in the magistrates' courts. Allen's party had formed a 'Tower Hamlet Protestant Association' ('Be roused as a lion to resist this foul and false system', said their broadsheets; and 'The man of Sin stalks exultingly abroad . . . Up and be doing against this Popery'), and King in answer formed from among other East End parsons a 'St George's Defence Association'. He announced a commination service. Things went from bad to worse, bedevilled by the bishop's legal secretary (for Tait and King would not meet), one John B. Lee, whose correspondence in this as in other matters suggests he was a hectoring boor. The bishop would not suspend Allen, King would not desist from wearing a surplice, and at last in September 1859 King sought and obtained Tait's permission to close the church.

St George's in the East

There was a truce of six weeks, during which King failed to come to terms with Tait and the vestry failed to get an undertaking from King to abandon his High-Church practices. When the church was reopened the disorders lost all connection with real issues and became nightmare. From all over London the mindless and the crazed were attracted by the weekly uproar. They blew trombones during the service, they pelted the altar with garbage, they let loose in the church dogs which had been given a drug to make them howl.

The credit for bringing an end goes to the Revd Thomas Hughes, the author of *Tom Brown's Schooldays*. He, acquainted with all the parties and respected in the East End, arranged for King to hand over to a locum. King's health had given way, and he went abroad. Within a few weeks Bishop Tait broke the locum and put in his own chaplain. Perhaps the whole story is best set in proportion by the fact that King, vegetating 30 years in the prehistoric Wiltshire village of Avebury, lived to hear that the vestry of St George's had insisted against his successor's will on putting up a life-size mosaic Crucifixion over the altar. It is still there, inside the new, dull church of 1963.

44. ST GEORGE THE MARTYR, SOUTHWARK

JOHN PRICE
1734–6

BOROUGH HIGH STREET, AT LONG LANE, SE1

IIE3   U: Borough

There have been at least three churches on this site. The earliest known was given in 1122 to the Abbey of Bermondsey; the next, described in 1708 as being 'modern Gothic', was nearly square and had a tower half as tall again as the church was long; the third, John Price's, now stands splendidly islanded at the junction of the old Dover Road, Long Lane and the Borough High Street. It partly qualified as one of the Fifty Churches and received £6,000 from the Commissioners. It is a very good sort of brick building embellished, particularly at the west front, with white stone. Here the main door is enclosed in and surmounted by two tall, nearly wall-high, attached columns with a segmental pediment. Above this, and rising from it, is the sensible white spire.

The interior, restored in 1951, has an odd ceiling by Basil Champneys. It was damaged in World War II, but recast from the originals. His cherubs still break through cloud, tinged now with pink and blue and gold. The galleries, which William Hedger put in in 1808, on table-leg posts, would be better without the little boxes from which the ceiling is lit but the pulpit, standing on four Ionic columns, is unspoiled and charming.

There were seven prisons in Southwark; Bishop Bonner, who died in the Marshalsea, is buried in the churchyard, and Dickens's Little Dorrit, born in the Marshalsea, found shelter in St George's and was married there.

GILBERT SCOTT and
MOFFAT
1844

ID4

45. ST GILES, CAMBERWELL
Camberwell Parish Church
CAMBERWELL CHURCH ST, SOUTHWARK, SE5
BR: Denmark Hill

St Giles, Camberwell

Camberwell Parish Church is one of the few in London which really do appear in Domesday Book. From 1152 until the Dissolution of the Monasteries, Bermondsey Abbey appointed the priest. The church was almost entirely rebuilt about 1500, was added to at various times, and a Gothicisation of 1799 culminated in an absurd wooden structure on top of the tower like a child's copy of Wren's open-work lantern at ST DUNSTAN IN THE EAST. A print of the inside in about 1830 shows a pulpit standing on a Gothic arch over the central aisle. Communicants would thus pass thorugh it on their way to the altar-rail, a bold symbol.

All was burned out in 1841. 'The untimely devastation', wrote a local historian, 'of this venerated building, occasioned, as might be expected, a great sensation in the neighbourhood, and for some days after the catastrophe, carriages were seen in unusual numbers rolling towards the ruins, amongst which a few of the more sentimental visitors were allowed under proper restrictions to remain.'[1] Camberwell was beginning then to be built over and the young Gilbert Scott, using a machine to cut the tracery, built the present large, lucid Gothic church. He rescued sedilia, porch and piscina from the old church, and made a summer house of them in the vicarage garden. The sedilia and the piscina have been taken back. There are various pieces of continental medieval glass in the windows. The so-called political gargoyles in the south-west turret were put up at the end of the last century. Salisbury, bearded, and Gladstone went up in spite of the view of the conservative vicar at the time, the father of Sir Gerald Kelly, PRA, that the latter was not fit to appear on a sacred edifice.

---

46. ST GILES, CRIPPLEGATE

ACCRETIVE

BARBICAN, LONDON WALL, EC2

IIE2 　　　　　　　　　　　U: Barbican

St Giles now sits alone on a broad pavement in the new, high, shiny Barbican development, like a respected but not well understood older person at a party.

The postern known as Cripplegate existed before the church, and it may have got its name from the Anglo-Saxon for a covered way, or from a hospital for cripples which may have stood nearby, or from the cripples who begged at it. The church was first built just outside the City wall about 1090 by Alfune, who some years later helped Rahere build both the Priory and the Hospital of ST BARTHOLOMEW: he dedicated it to St Giles, the patron saint of cripples and blacksmiths. At this time the whole parish was bog, pond and drain, and the church was presumably small. It was first enlarged and then rebuilt in the 14th century, as Moorfields became by drainage more capable of supporting a population. In 1545 the church was almost destroyed by fire, and was rebuilt much as before. The parish became drier; gentlemen built country houses in it and others opened pleasure gardens. Galleries were put in the church. The town ditch passed through the churchyard, and in the 17th century proposals to cover it over were made and partly carried out: the bastion still visible in the churchyard has a large drain going beneath it which probably dates from the mid-17th century. This did not prevent the death of half the parishioners in the Great Plague (1665). The Fire the following year just missed the church, and replenished the population with refugees from the city. From this time on the church was frequently repaired, restored and

---

[1] Douglas Allport, *Collections . . . of Camberwell*, London 1841, p. 173.

St Giles, Cripplegate

altered. The top of the tower was rebuilt in brick in 1682, and the present little cupola replaced four tall pinnacles and a centre turret, all five adorned with crosses and weathervanes.

The 1711 Commission intended three of the Fifty Churches to be built in the parish, but in fact only one was: St Luke's, Old Street. Small improvements continued: a crimson velvet cushion with fringe and tassels for the pulpit, new pews, new reredos; 'palisadoes' were removed from round the christening pew, the roof was covered in copper, the side walls were lowered, the chancel was given a new clerestory, the oval east window was glazed in yellow, gas was installed in 1818. By then the richer inhabitants had moved to Hackney and Bow. But still in the late 1860s Gothicisation began: galleries out, pews down, chancel up, ceiling open, pointed windows found and guessed at, battlements up, ragstone facings on. Oddly the reredos remained – indeed another of the same period[1] was later put into the north aisle – and so did the east window in spite of being so alien to the current taste as to be described in 1863 as a 'pale, faded nondescript yellow vitreous transparency'.[2]

---

[1] Originally in St Bartholomew by the Exchange, by way of St Bartholomew, Moor Lane.
[2] W. Harvey, *London Scenes and London People*, by 'Aleph', London 1863, p. 302.

Foxe, of the Martyrology, was buried in the church; so was Milton. In 1790 a search was made for Milton's coffin so that a bust by Bacon might be placed somewhere near it. A corpse in a coffin was found. Hair and teeth were pulled out and sold the next day, when shame had had time to work, for next to nothing. Perhaps it was Milton. Perhaps it was not.

The church was gutted in 1940 by the incendiary bombs which laid waste much of the land surrounding it. After the bombing and in the aftermath of the war St Giles (or what was left of it) became victim of desecration, vandalism and arson. In the war period virtually all the church furnishings and contents disappeared save the registers dating back to 1561, the church plate, vestments and the Victorian eagle lectern commemorating Bishop Lancelot Andrewes, one of the very few Church of England saints, who was vicar of St Giles from 1588 to 1604.

The sanctuary roof is now panelled and bossed. The west gallery and organ (from St Luke's, Old Street) was installed after the war. So was the light braced roof, pews and panelling. The marble font and cover also came from St Lukes.

In the south-west corner of the churchyard is a large bastion of the old City wall and to the south two more bastions revealed by the bombing. To the north-east is the City of London School for Girls, completed in 1969. Directly facing the north is the Barbican Arts Centre.

---

47. ST GILES-IN-THE-FIELDS
ST GILES HIGH STREET, WC2

IIC2   U: Tottenham Court Road

HENRY FLITCROFT
1731–3

A lazar house was founded here by Matilda, Henry I's queen, and its chapel may have served as a church for the parish of St Giles which existed by the 13th century. The hospital was suppressed at the Dissolution of the Monasteries and the old chapel or church was pulled down in 1621. Laud consecrated a new one in 1630 which, according to old views, had triple lancet windows below and oval windows above, a very Transitional arrangement. In this church Andrew Marvell was buried, lying nearly a century in his fine and private place before an inscription was put up. So too was Chapman, the translator of Homer. His monument, much weathered, has been brought into the church from the graveyard and an inscription on it of 1827 says it was put up by Inigo Jones at his own expense.

The 17th-century church became ruinous and was pulled down in the 1720s. The 1711 Commissioners agreed to bear the cost of a new church if the parishioners would find the stipend for the incumbent of the new church of ST GEORGE'S, BLOOMSBURY, which they proposed to build in the northern part of the parish. Gibbs and Hawksmoor were among the unsuccessful in the competition for the design. Hawksmoor's design had a steeple with a peristyle bearing a dome bearing in turn an obelisk. Henry Flitcroft won the competition and built the present St Giles. It is fairly

Giles-in-the-Fields

much after the model of Gibbs's new ST MARTIN-IN-THE-FIELDS and, though it lacks such grandeur as that church has, it lacks also its main blemish: Flitcroft's tower does not ride on a portico. The interior is remarkable for three strong details: the junction of galleries with columns is well done, showing the bases of the upper orders in a pleasantly rhythmical way: the corbels on which the aisle vaults rest are rather grand; and the square apse with Decalogue, Moses and Aaron and so on, in separate small panels, is pleasant.

A little Grecian font of 1810 has been found and replaced. In it in 1818, probably at the same ceremony, were christened Allegra, the daughter of Byron and Clare Clairmont, and the two children of Shelley and Mary Wollstonecraft.

EARLY 13TH
CENTURY

IIF2

48. ST HELEN'S, BISHOPSGATE
GREAT ST HELEN'S, OFF BISHOPSGATE, EC3
U: Liverpool Street

Some of London's parish churches were originally built by religious orders and only became parish churches after the Dissolution of the Monasteries. But St Helen's was first built as a parish church: even when a Benedictine convent was attached to its north side, the south remained parochial and merely absorbed at the Dissolution what had never been, physically, detached from it.

Naturally it was long supposed that the Emperor Constantine erected the original church to the memory of his mother St Helena, presumably in the 4th century; and the body of St Edmund the King, martyred in 870, is supposed to have lain here. But the first certain record is that of an agreement in 1181 between the Dean and the Canons of St Paul's and one Ranulf and his son that these two should hold the church for their lifetime on payment of twelve pence yearly. Later, at the beginning of the 13th century, William, the son of a goldsmith, had permission from the dean and canons, to whom it had reverted, to hold the church and to found there a priory of Benedictine nuns, and it is to this time that the present rather garbled buildings go back.

The earlier church probably stood where are now the chancel and the eastern part of the nave. Starting with the nuns' choir (with lancet windows) and the second nave, the whole church was built more grandly than before. Outside, the western aspect of the two naves, conventual and parochial, suggests an exact equality. An elegantly waving string-course provides a long eyebrow over the two west windows and the small 17th-century bell-turret is centrally perched above. The convent buildings were to the north, reached through several doors in the north wall. There remains an odd little staircase in the north wall, which originally led to the nun's dormitory and gave easy access to the church for night services. A high screen separated the two naves, and the parish was served by a parochial chaplain in the southern one. In 1285 Edward I presented a piece of the True Cross which he had found in Wales, and the church had an alternative dedication to the Holy Cross.

The priory appears not to have been rich before the 14th century, but then papal indulgences and many small benefactions, particularly the endowment of chantries, paid for repairs and for the building of the two chapels in the south transept dedicated to the Holy Ghost and to St Mary. In 1385 the nuns were reproved by the Dean and Canons of St Paul's for, among other things, the number of little dogs kept by the prioress, for kissing secular persons and wearing ostentatious veils. But frivolity died hard and 50 years later they were told that 'alle daunsyng and revelying be utterly forborne among you except Christmasse and othe honest tymys of recreacyong among your owne selfe usyd, in absence of seculers in alle wyse'.[1] There was also conviviality in the cloister and kitchen, waving over the screen which separated the parish nave from the convent nave, and too many children running about. The result was debts; Sir John Crosby (see below) left £40 to help diminish them.

The Dissolution passed quietly; the nuns and officers of the priory were pensioned off, the convent buildings were bought by the Leathersellers' Company, the partition between the two naves was removed and in 1576 the parishioners made various Low-Church alterations to the altar and rood screen. In the 1630s the church was repaired and redecorated at the

---

[1] J. P. Malcolm, *Londinium Redivivum*, 1807, vol. iii, p. 548.

expense of various of the Livery Companies. On the handsome door-cases and pulpit, quite classical pilasters and broken pediments are mixed with purely strapwork elements. (The sounding-board is a little later, and its support is partly 18th century.) The south door is on the contrary a particularly clumsy mixture of the architectural idioms of 1633.[1] The pretty, plain marble font and its wooden cover are also of this date. The rich and unusual wooden sword-rest, now on the south side of the chancel, has the arms of Sir John Lawrence, the Lord Mayor of 1665, and is the only one in the City to date from before the Great Fire, which did not touch the church. Perhaps this was heaven's reward to Sir John for staying so nobly at his place during the plague. In the 19th century the chancel was redecorated 'after the best West Anglian models'[2] (that is, to accommodate surpliced choirboys), and the 15th-century nuns' stalls were moved into it from the north nave.

St Helen's, Bishopsgate

In 1966 the Victorian vestries were removed and new vestries, offices and a rectory were built south of the church. There is a small and no doubt useful neon-lit bookstall in the north-west corner, and near it a desk with filing cabinets, bookshelves and so forth. More of a shame is the virtual inaccessibility of the two little chapels, which are now not only blocked off by the enormous 19th-century organ, but occupied by

---

[1] John Summerson, *Architecture in Britain 1530–1830*, London 1953, p. 101, suggests the name of Anthony Lynnett as the designer. This style in general he calls 'artisan mannerism'.
[2] T. F. Bumpus, *London Churches*, London 1908, vol. i, p. 139.

partitioned-off rooms (labelled 'tape room' and 'This door to be kept locked at all times'). Thus the Lady Chapel cannot be seen at all, and the Chapel of the Holy Ghost is (1985) full of unused furniture, piles of ancient sheet music, bits of railing and even a bicycle.

But this is not really our church, nor even the church of the medieval nuns. It belongs to the many and splendid monuments to the substantial dead. In the 19th century Francis Bancroft's nine-foot-square tomb was removed from the north nave. As it was his 'express intention and desire to have the same kept up . . . whether the church be standing or not', it was put in the crypt which is now sealed off. He had also required that his coffin should open and shut like an ordinary trunk, possibly from a fear of being buried before he was dead, possibly so that he should not be left behind at the Resurrection.

Sir John Spencer and his wife, brightly coloured, lie between two black obelisks beneath a fine display of strapwork, heraldry and Florentine arches. He was 'Rich Spencer', Lord Mayor, who died in 1609 and left nothing to charity. His daughter forfeited her dowry when she was abducted in a baker's basket by Lord Northampton; she can be seen kneeling repentantly at a prayer desk by her parents' feet. Between the two chapels lie John de Oteswich and his wife in their smooth flowing robes, who died in the late 14th century and were moved here in 1874 when St Martin Outwich, the church he had helped to build, was demolished. Sir John and Lady Crosby (1476) the builders of the Crosby Hall which was moved to Chelsea in this century, are near them; he, grocer, alderman, MP, Yorkist, in armour; she in a headdress reminding one of Nefertiti. Sir William Pickering (1574), under his fine free-standing arcade, was in youth imprisoned in the Tower for breaking windows at night with bolts from his crossbow. Later he was ambassador in Paris, and was considered as a husband for Queen Elizabeth. Martin Bond (1643) captain of the Trained Bands when they marched to Tilbury in 1588, rests, a little tired, in his tent, no longer invigorated by the queen's great words. Other Bonds, Robinsons, Judds, all piously kneel, their pious families ranged behind them. Hugh and Katherine Pemberton, their daughters and two of their sons, have disappeared from their tombs, but ten brass sons remain. Sir Julius Caesar Adelmare (1636) agrees in the deed which forms the inscription on his tomb to pay the debt of nature as soon as God requires; and Sir Thomas Gresham lies plain but substantial, as befits the financier behind the splendours of Elizabethan government.

---

49. ST JAMES, BERMONDSEY
ST JAMES'S ROAD, OFF JAMAICA ROAD, SE16
U: London Bridge, then buses

JAMES SAVAGE
1829

IE3

This is one of the finest churches built by the Waterloo Commission. It is a large church in a wide churchyard beside a great main road, dominating a shabby district with its own by now shabby grandeur. The cost of £21,000 was shared between the Commissioners and the parishioners of Bermondsey, and Savage, the architect also of ST LUKE'S, CHELSEA, put up a great stock-brick box. But the tower, surmounted by a seven-foot dragon, is an intelligent adaptation of the free-standing groups of columns used in the baroque to the rectilinear fashion of the Grecian, and the east end is very fine and original. The surprise is that it has a strong echo of Vanbrugh. A severe pediment rides a deep and solemn blind arch between two advanced wings; the cliff of anachronistic brickwork suggests a poor man's Seaton Delaval.

The interior also shows a powerful intelligence working on the old problems. Galleries ride on piers from which rise Ionic orders, but the gallery fronts are curved concavely away and up, revealing part and concealing part of the base mouldings of these orders which support not a ceiling, not a vault, but a continuous entablature from which rises a clerestory. The model is thus as much the Roman basilica as the Greek temple. The excellent articulation of the three stages, piers, Ionic orders, clerestory, makes this church of the highest interest. When the eye finally does reach the flat ceiling it is again surprised and convinced by coffering so deep as to be a pattern of negative pyramids. Unfortunately, the area beneath the galleries has been screened off on both sides, and one-third of the way up the nave is a metal beam from gallery to gallery, from which in 1985 hangs a beige nylon curtain. The lighting also leaves something to be desired – but the church is in use, and the excrescences are not immovable.

The olde worlde slide in the churchyard was built in 1921 to save the granite edges of the west steps of the church from final wearing away under children's bottoms. Suggestions for more popular services here in 1919 included a smoker's gallery and lessons from Ruskin and Carlyle.

JAMES CARR
1780–92

50. ST JAMES, CLERKENWELL
Clerkenwell Parish Church
BY CLERKENWELL GREEN, ISLINGTON, EC1

IID1   U: Farringdon

When St John's Priory (see ST JOHN'S, CLERKENWELL) was founded, that is to say about 1110, there was also founded the Benedictine Nunnery of St Mary's and it is on the site of the nunnery that the present Clerkenwell Church stands. The nunnery was rather rich, and continued mostly on good terms with the nearby house of St John's. In 1269 the prior of the Hospitallers gave to the nuns 'one of the six pots in which Jesus turned the water into wine', a gift noted in the Convent's books along with others in cash and less startling kind. The nunnery possessed a chapel on Muswell Hill called Our Lady of Muswell. It was a place of pilgrimage and that not always of the most becoming. 'Our Lady was a Virgin, and yet at her pilgrimages . . .' The church at the Convent of St Mary's was used by lay people, and acquired about 1500 a second dedication to St James. Or it may be that a parish chapel in the church had this dedication.

After the Dissolution of the Monasteries the church and conventual buildings passed through various private hands until in 1656 the parishioners bought the church, or rather the chancel and tower, for the rest had been allowed to fall down. With it they bought also the advowson and, like the people of other parishes during the Commonwealth, they began to elect their vicars. But somehow this practice was never stopped at the Restoration, and Clerkenwell continued a sort of Congregationalist enclave in the Church of England. Vicarial elections went on until the beginning of the present century with all the inconveniences one would expect; frantic canvassing, competitive claims to Almighty backing, litigation about the franchise. The upshot was a strong evangelical tradition. Robert Maguire, vicar in the 1850s, lectured the working classes on *The Pilgrim's Progress*, wrote a pamphlet called: 'The Irish Church Independent of Rome till AD 1172', and another: 'One Hundred Defects of the Mass', and yet more trenchant: 'Perversion and Conversion, or Cause and Effect'. The vicar is now elected by the Parochial Church Council, no longer by the parishioners at large.

By the end of the 18th century the old church was patched and tattered like most: the tower had twice fallen in the 1620s and the part of the nave it destroyed had been rebuilt with the ridge of the roof running north and south, like transepts at the wrong end. The three aisles were a jumble of Norman and Perpendicular work with some 18th-century oval bullseye windows, and the tower was embattled and bellcoted. The church was declared ruinous and demolished in 1788: the people worshipped for the time being in the nuns' cloister, which was pulled down when the new church was finished. James Carr (not to be confused with John Carr of York) built this, setting it high on an undercroft. The unusual thing about the design is the stone facing of the west front under the tower only, leaving the wings plain brick.[1] This gives an impression of the tower's having been slid into place in a prepared slot. On this stone centrepiece certain Palladian exercises go on, but the spire above is rather dull, rather old-fashioned, like Flitcroft's work of 40 years before. It was rebuilt to the original design in 1849. But the ceiling inside has mouldings which make one remember Carr was the contemporary of Holland and Chambers, and the curved west end is an altogether pleasing arrangement, deriving perhaps from the curved east end at ST CLEMENT DANES. The iron children's galleries are an addition of 1822, but they go well with the deep recesses behind Soanesque arches which they cut. Blomfield, unobtrusively for him, modernised in 1882. The central pulpit and the high pews went, the pavements and present dark windows came. In 1910 the brick piers in the undercroft which supported the church were cut away and iron columns substituted, which gave more floor-space to what is

---

[1] The Younger Dance had done something like it 25 years earlier at ALL HALLOWS ON THE WALL.

now the church hall. Basement areas were dug at the same time, which increased the apparent height of the church.

Bishop Burnet lies here; his monument, preserved from the old church, is on the left in the entrance vestibule.

SIR CHRISTOPHER
WREN
1676–83
IIE3

51. ST JAMES GARLICKHYTHE
GARLICK HILL, BY UPPER THAMES STREET, EC4
U: Mansion House

The old church was repaired in the 1620s and 1630s with money raised at 6 per cent, but when the parson was deprived in 1647 for continuing to use the Book of Common Prayer the parishioners were rich enough and loyal enough to club together and make him a pension in his successor's

*St James
Garlickhythe*

despite. After the Great Plague, perhaps to enable its future incidence to be observed, the cause of death appears in the burial registers: 'gripe of the guts' some died of, 'lethargy' others; 'convulsions', 'rising of the lights', 'worms', 'stoppage of the stomach', and, terse, but after these catastrophes, somehow domesticated: 'tooth'.

The church Wren rebuilt after the Great Fire has on its tower one of those complex and graceful turrets, all pillars and vases, which to Sacheverell Sitwell suggested the grinding out of bell music by turning, as in hurdy-gurdies.[1] ST MICHAEL PATERNOSTER ROYAL and ST STEPHEN WALBROOK have others, and there is good reason to suppose they were put on, long after the churches were built, at the time when Wren was thinking about the west turrets of St Paul's. The interior of the church has crossed vaults, as at ST MARTIN LUDGATE. Three and fourpence was spent on sherry and pipes at the opening of the church, and the party evidently lasted until nightfall, since the vestry had also to bear the cost of links 'to enlighten my Lord Mayor home'.

In 1815 the curate presented a painting of a biblical scene by Andrew Geddes, ARA. The altar-piece was chopped in half and the east window removed to make room for it. It is still there. Later the remains of the altar-piece were painted over in a sub-Pre-Raphaelite manner. Some windows on the north side were blocked and some on the west opened in 1838; at the same time the tall windows in the transepts, which had eared architraves, were closed up into the present toy wheels. A 500-lb unexploded bomb and extensive fire damage to the tower during World War II led to the church being closed from 1954 to 1963. The work carried out in this period by architects Lockhart Smith and Alexander Gale was in Betjeman's opinion the best restoration in the City.[2] Indeed, the many-windowed interior that gained St James's the appellation 'Wren's Lantern' is once again resplendent.

The pulpit is fine, and so is the organ gallery and the stairs up to it. Best of all is the profusion of wrought iron, some of it from St Michael Queenhythe, sword-rests, hat-stands, columns under the gallery, and just ornaments. A mummified person with a pleasant smile is kept in a cupboard.

52. ST JAMES, PICCADILLY

PICCADILLY, WESTMINSTER, SW1

IIB3   U: Piccadilly Circus

SIR CHRISTOPHER WREN
1682–4
Restored 1953

Among the loyalist diplomats and courtiers whom Charles II rewarded at his Restoration was William Jermyn, Earl of St Albans, to whom he gave crown land in Westminster. The houses St Albans built soon filled up with the new governing class who had different ideas about how to live from those of the Parliamentarians they replaced, and it was chiefly in Jermyn Street and St James's that what we think of as Restoration *moeurs* went on. The district still called St James's, and still full of a more stolid kind of masculine good living, took its name from St James Church, finished by

[1] S. Sitwell, *British Architects and Craftsmen*, London 1945, p. 54.
[2] John Betjeman (ed.), *Collins Guide to Parish Churches*, London 1980.

Wren in 1684 as a chapel of ease to ST MARTIN-IN-THE-FIELDS and made parochial the same year. The church in turn took its name from the nearby royal palace.

> 'Pray which church', says Berinthia in Vanbrugh's *The Relapse*, 'does your lordship most oblige with your presence?'
> LORD FOPPINGTON: 'Oh! St James', madam: there's much the best company.'
> AMANDA: 'Is there good preaching too?'
> LORD FOPPINGTON: 'Why, faith, madam, I can't tell. A man must have very little to do there that can give an account of the sermon.'

The tradition continued; Gillray was buried there, and d'Urfey, whose *Pills to Purge Melancholy* was for long the standard collection of bawdy songs, and there in 1810 the fourth Duke of Queensberry was buried under the altar, Wordsworth's 'degenerate Douglas', or to another circle 'Old Q'. He it was, the father, more or less, of the Turf, who gave Charles James Fox his taste for gaming; he also held for a time the unlikely office of the First Lord of the Police.

St James, Piccadilly

But the church is of a more serious interest because it was the only one in London which Wren built on a new site, without having to take account of an earlier church. He himself told a correspondent that it best embodied his idea of what a parish church should be. The proportions are 2:3:4. An arcade rises from the galleries and bears a barrel vault; an entablature runs out from each column of this arcade to a corbel on the side wall and the space is thus richly framed overhead. The church was badly knocked about in World War II and Sir Albert Richardson in restoring it took the opportunity of doing away with Victorian solecisms while adding some of his own. The marble font, a civilised and graceful piece by Grinling Gibbons, has been saved: Adam and Eve still transact their crucial business round the stem, but its cover, on which an angel precariously rested and which was lowered from a sheave framed in cherubs' heads 'all gilt with gold',[1] was lost early in the 19th century. It is said, improbably, to have been stolen and used as a sign over the door of a nearby liquor shop. The reredos, which has Gibbons's characteristic easy profusion of falling vegetation under a single wide segmental pediment, was saved and now has a cedarwood sunburst of Richardson's design as centrepiece. The organ-case, which came to this church from the Roman Catholic Chapel Royal at Whitehall, also survived. When the organ was being repaired in 1897 a tiny coffin was found in it containing the skeleton of a bird. Dust to dust and music to music. Richardson hoped to put on the tower the little domed steeple which Wren designed, but in the end the nondescript bellcote which was put up by one of Wren's own carpenters and which was knocked off in the war was replaced.

St James, Piccadilly

An Ionic doorway on the Jermyn Street side was removed in the middle of the last century, and the outdoor pulpit on the Piccadilly side was set up at the beginning of this century. It is not used now.

The present incumbent, Donald Reeves, is full of bright ideas: an annual festival, a coffee house, famous guest preachers and lecturers, a clown service, concerts, modern art (sometimes misplaced) and a strong sense of what he prefers to call 'community' to parish.

---

[1] *Parentalia*; quoted in *Wren Society*, vol. x, p. 27.

INIGO JONES
1623–7

53. ST JAMES'S PALACE
The Queen's Chapel, also called the Marlborough Chapel[1]
MARLBOROUGH ROAD, OFF PALL MALL, SW1

IIB3 U: Piccadilly, St James's Park

The chapel was begun for the Infanta who never married Charles I and was finished for Henrietta Maria, the French princess who did. She worshipped in it with a very young bishop and 29 other French priests; the ostentatious focus of Catholicism which she kept up here was one of the many causes of scandal and friction during her husband's unhappy reign, although at one time he sent home no less than 440 of her 'French Court'. The chapel was reinstated in 1660 for Charles II's queen, Catherine of Braganza, and Portuguese priests took the place of the French ones. Since the 17th century it has always been the chapel of queens: Dutch Reformed and French Huguenot services were said there in the reign of William and Mary, German Lutheran services under the Hanoverians, and Danish services for Queen Alexandra. In 1809 the passage connecting the chapel with St James's Palace was burned down and it now stands separate across a public road, in the same compound as Marlborough House.

The outside is not of much interest, but the inside is. During the Commonwealth the chapel was sacked; it was restored in 1660 and in the 18th and 19th centuries the east end was often remodelled to carry an organ, and so on. There is an enormous royal pew, a room really, fitting loggia-like into the top half of the west end, which was gradually filled up with living accommodation two-deep. As late as 1950 the Ministry of Works cleared away three servants' bedrooms from against the top halves of the three windows which look from the royal pew into the chapel; they also cleared away the organist's bathroom which had its floor level with the cornice of the great fireplace and enclosed the arms of Braganza in the pediment. Only 30 years ago the way into the royal pew lay through the sub-dean's bedroom.

The last restoration in 1950 brought the interior very nearly back to the condition of 1660; before that there is no record. The lovely reredos is curved and recessed, suggesting the Teatro Olimpico of Palladio and Scamozzi at Vicenza, and is probably in the main a reconstruction of 1660 on the lines of Jones's original. The wood carving along the top is of the time of Grinling Gibbons, soon after 1660. The altar-piece itself, under its chaste pediment, is a modern guess; restrained but satisfactory. It contains an early painting by Annibale Caracci. The two reading-desks level with the altar-rails were almost certainly composed, some time back, from the two halves of a pulpit shown on the north wall in a print of the 1680s. The little late 18th-century organ has been put back where it belongs in the

[1] Divine service is held in either this chapel or the Chapel Royal on most Sundays in the year; the public is admitted at these times only.

recessed gallery on the south side. The windows into the great royal pew are open again, and all the woodwork and the coffered elliptical ceiling vault are learnedly restored and pleasingly painted.

Proportion, exactitude, control, balance and calm show here as they do in everything Jones built.

54. ST JOHN ON BETHNAL GREEN
CAMBRIDGE HEATH ROAD, AT ROMAN ROAD, E2

IE2

U: Bethnal Green

SIR JOHN SOANE
1824–8

St John's was erected by the Waterloo Commission as a district church within the parish of St Matthew, Bethnal Green. It became a parish church in 1879. Soane placed it facing squarely down the Bethnal Green Road and the west front, now obscured by a railway bridge, is the most interesting aspect. The eye happily follows the triangles its features indicate and is arrested by the two deep recesses for the side door: 'obstinately original', Pevsner[1] calls them. An earlier design in the Soane Museum shows that Soane thought of a much higher turret, like the pencils at HOLY TRINITY, MARYLEBONE, and at ST PETER'S, WALWORTH, but abandoned it for the present button, which better shows the triangular dispositions. Along the parapets north and south, and on the freestanding pillars of the tower, are those

St John on Bethnal Green

[1] Nikolaus Pevsner, *The Buildings of England: London, excluding the cities of London and Westminster*, Harmondsworth 1952, p. 68.

curious urns Soane was so fond of and under one of which he lies buried in OLD ST PANCRAS churchyard. Summerson[1] has pointed out that they are as it were negative casts of a dome on pendentives, or rather of a dome and lantern. The negative lanterns were higher here; various designs show objects suggesting pawns, or asparagus, or pineapples on chimneys, and so does Schnebbelie's early view. But they were taken down some time before 1849, leaving only the negative domes.

In 1870 the church was gutted by fire; the windows were then given their present inappropriate tracery and the ornamental roof-timbers were put in. Later the chancel was extended. The appearance of Soane's interior can be recalled by the two bays which survive from it immediately east of the new chancel arch. Those in the nave were rather narrower, and lacked the two intermediate columns under the gallery. The best things of Soane's to survive inside are the soffits of the galleries (their upward swoop counterpointed by the very shallow segmental arches), and the high, solemn, somehow extreme, vestibule under the tower. The original altar-rails were like the balcony railings on the Soane Museum in Lincolns Inn Fields.

To this church in 1837, immediately after his ordination, came Bryan King, one of the most controversial and tragic figures of Victorian church history (see ST GEORGE'S IN THE EAST). His answer to the dreadful slums which were growing up in Bethnal Green was churches and always more churches. He got Gladstone and the Barings and Buxtons of the day on to an appeal committee, and in eleven years no less than ten new churches were built, named after the apostles. Few went.

St John's is now (1985) High Church. You get incense with the service, and tea and toast after.

ACCRETIVE

55. ST JOHN'S, CLERKENWELL
ST JOHN'S SQUARE, EC1
IID1   U: Farringdon

Shortly before the First Crusade some Amalfi merchants in Palestine either founded a new Christian hospital, or rebuilt an old one originally dedicated to St John Almoner but dedicated by them to St John the Baptist. So when the Crusaders arrived the hospital was in full swing. The brothers who served it formed themselves into an order of soldier-monks and built both forts and hospitals along the pilgrims' routes. They wore a black habit over their armour, with a white eight-pointed cross on the breast. Their rule required them to be knighted and of noble blood. Priests and serving brothers were inferior members of the Order, and a few women were enrolled as sisters. Together with the Knights Templar (see TEMPLE CHURCH) and some other military orders they defended Palestine against the attempts of the Arabs to retake the land they had lived in for 600 years.

---

[1] John Summerson, *Sir John Soane*, London 1952, p. 32.

Beaten back, they defended the Christian foothold in the Levant, first from Acre, then from Cyprus. In 1312 the Templars were dissolved and their property in the east passed to the Hospitallers, who carried on defending from Rhodes, whence they were expelled in 1523. In 1530 they settled in Malta. After withstanding a particularly horrible siege by the Turks in 1565, the Knights Hospitaller led a quiet life there until they surrendered to Napoleon in 1798. A few knights fled to Russia, taking with them their most prized relic, the Baptist's right hand, which in 1919 was taken from the Cathedral of Gatchina by the retreating White Guards of General Yudenich.[1] When the Tsarina Maria Feodorovna was dying in Denmark, she gave it to the Orthodox Patriarch of Serbia, but it is now believed to be in Sofia.

About the year 1145, ten acres of land were granted to the Hospitallers near Clerkenwell, and here they built the chief priory of the English Langue, as the national divisions were called. They acquired much other land, and had some 1,900 manors when the Langue was dissolved in 1540. The Grand Prior, or Lord Prior, of the English Knights often filled great offices of state and had precedence of all barons; the Clerkenwell Priory was one of the chief houses of royal entertainment and hospitality.

The Priory was built as soon as the Knights settled in Clerkenwell; nothing now remains of it but the much restored St John's Gate, once its main entrance, and certain parts of the church. Like the TEMPLE CHURCH, St John's had a round 'nave' to the west and a rectangular 'chancel' to the east, a combination favoured in the 11th and 12th centuries when the thought of the Church of the Holy Sepulchre at Jerusalem was much in men's minds. The Round has gone; part of its circumference is marked in cobbles in St John's Square outside.

At some time the round nave of the church was replaced by a rectangular one with a large tower at the north-west corner. Stow says this was 'a most curious piece of workmanship, graven, gilt, and enamelled . . . and passing all other I have seen'.[2] Was it some kind of minaret, incongruous and fascinating in medieval London? Wat Tyler's comrades murdered the prior on Tower Hill and set fire to the church; it was rebuilt. The tower and all the church except the chancel were blown up in Edward VI's reign after the order was dissolved; the stone was used to build Lord Protector Somerset's new house. The porch went to All Hallows, Lombard Street, and later disappeared.

The square chancel was for a time the office of the Master of the Revels, and many of Shakespeare's plays received their licences there. Later it became the property of Lord Burleigh, who made a chapel of it, and in the early 18th century it was a Presbyterian meeting house. In 1721 one Simon Michel bought it, repaired it thoroughly, and sold it for £2,500 to the Commissioners of the Fifty, who made it into the Parish Church of St John. A century later a carved panel was put up over the door and, since

---

[1] Information courteously supplied by the Acting Deputy Directory (Scientific) of the State Hermitage, Leningrad.
[2] Stow, *Survey of London*, Everyman edn, London 1945, p. 387.

the vicar did not know to which St John the church was dedicated, the Baptist, the Evangelist and the Almoner were all three shown on it.

The box-like nave was gutted in World War II, and restored by the architects Seeley and Paget in the 1950s. It has an 18th-century west wall, and in the other three walls are fine priory windows from the early 16th century, in a style then a century out of date. Other openings and closings in the wall are now clearly whitewashed into anonymity. The fine 12th-century crypt has been carefully cleaned and restored from being a mere repository of coffins in the late 19th century. Its first three bays are round-arched, the two easternmost and the two little side chapels are pointed; a difference of some 40 years. (In a crypt, that flight which the later builders could give to an arch is hardly felt; it is only embryonic.) It contains a magnificent 16th-century Spanish alabaster effigy of a knight of the order, Juan Ruyz de Vergara, recumbent, with the eight-pointed cross on his breastplate and a boy asleep against his legs.

The church was deprived of its parish in 1931 and it belongs now to the new Order of St John of Jerusalem, a Church of England charitable and medical organisation founded in the reign of Queen Victoria.

JAMES SPILLER
1797
Porch and steeple
1813

IE2

56. ST JOHN AT HACKNEY
Hackney Parish Church
MARE STREET, E8
BR: Hackney Downs

This yellow brick church stands, huge, ponderous and wide-eaved, at the edge of a forest of blackish-yellowish-trunked London planes. White tombstones are densely serried among the trees and the white, curious steeple floats high above all.

Spiller's church is the successor to the church whose tower still stands down the hill at the other end of the churchyard. In the late 13th century there was a rectory of St Augustine at Hackney. Gradually the church changed its name, perhaps because the Knights Hospitaller of St John of Jerusalem had property here, and certainly since 1660 it has always been known as St John's. It was rebuilt in the early 16th century (the fine tower is from this rebuilding), again in the early 17th century and yet again (the east end) about 1730. The fabric appears nevertheless to have been fairly uniform, in neatly worked ragstone, and the interior, according to the *Gentleman's Magazine*,[1] was a 'respectable . . . remnant of antiquity' with nave, two aisles, pointed arcades and a number of galleries rather irrationally placed; one appeared to hang from the ceiling by iron hooks.

Hackney, some three miles from the City, was convenient during the 17th and 18th centuries for rich merchants to live in and for small boys and young ladies to go to school in. By the 1790s the old church was too small, as well as out of repair, and the parishioners promoted an Act of

---

[1] *Topography of London. Collected from the Gentleman's Magazine*, London 1905, p. 193.

St John at Hackney

Parliament allowing them to raise money for building a new one and to repay it by means of a church rate. James Spiller, their architect, built them an enormous church in the shape of a Greek cross, elongated a little to the north and south, so big that it could hold 4,000 people. When the new church was consecrated the old one was pulled down and only the tower remained, deprived of a stook-shaped topknot. An old south chapel containing monuments of the Rowe family remained by it until 1894.

By 1831 there were in Hackney 34 private schools. The young ladies, to judge from prints, filled the three galleries of the new church. These galleries spread back into the arms of the Greek cross and made a great horseshoe facing the east end. By skill or by chance Spiller managed to keep straight, for the eye as well as for the ruler, the fronts of his north and south galleries: a feat not achieved by Wren in the Sheldonian Theatre at Oxford or by David Stephenson at All Saints, Newcastle upon Tyne. A neat, strong-looking railing surmounts the gallery entablature. The size and the enormous sweeping curves of the ceiling, unsupported by columns or pillars, diminish the beholder; perhaps to counteract this effect, the frame of the east window, designed by Spiller as a single huge composition with the reredos, has been painted to match the walls. The ends of the north and south arms of the Greek cross contain vestibules and stairs to the galleries. These are not very carefully designed and appear dank and oppressive. The east window, the steeple and the porches were added after the building had been completed. For the north façade, Spiller considered a recessed Soanesque porch flanked by two enormous Tuscan columns standing inside it. The wall was to be rusticated to half-way up. Above this, set back on the roof, was to rise a rather ordinary steeple, a little like the lower half of ST MARY LE BOW. Another steeple he considered was square-topped, with a spiky weathervane, and eagles on all four sides under the clock-face.[1] The existing steeple is extremely individual with its great long inverted consoles, sad as a bloodhound's ears, looping out at each corner.

The church was gutted on Ascension Eve 1955 when a builder working in the roof left his blow-torch on: the resulting fire took three days and forty fire engines to put out and the roof collapsed into the interior. Rebuilding commenced almost immediately and the interior has been restored. The church was reconsecrated by the Bishop of London on St John's Day 1958. The great ceiling now hangs from steel roof supports, in place of timber, and the columns supporting the galleries are also steel-cored.

The central feature of the rebuilt church is the high altar, standing in a small circular sanctuary, with elaborate metalwork communion rails and surmounted by a corona of light. (The original table is in the Urswick Chapel, by the north entrance porch.) The reredos, scorched by the fire, has been restored and gilded and on the altar are 17th-century Italian carved and gilded cross and candlesticks. The wooden pulpit somehow survived the fire and is in its old position. The 18th-century font has been moved to the north door. The original east window (1811) depicting the first day of the Creation was damaged in World War I and destroyed in World War II; a new window by Christopher Webb, depicting the ascended Christ supported by the Virgin Mary and St John the Baptist, was installed in 1958.

The vast space has proved difficult to use and a war memorial chapel under one part of the south gallery and a new clergy vestry under another part of it leave acres of unfilled parquet floor. Of the baby blue and beige decor, it can only be said that the magnificent exterior promises – or deserves – better.

There are some fine monuments from the old church rather ill-arranged in the north vestibule, Lady Latymer, 16th century, in recumbent effigy on a large box-tomb, and several others. Inside the church are few: two

---

[1] Drawings in the Hackney Public Library.

balancing monuments on the east wall to serving officers, by Regnart, remind one this church was building throughout the French War. Most citizens of Hackney – and how many and wealthy they were – were buried in the churchyard.

---

57. ST JOHN'S, HAMPSTEAD
Hampstead Parish Church
CHURCH ROW, HAMPSTEAD, NW3

IB2   U: Hampstead

JOHN SANDERSON
1745–7

The early status of the church here, which is mentioned since the beginning of the 14th century, is obscure. Probably it was a separate parish church but Westminster Abbey, to which the church belonged, used from time to time to spare expense by having only one parson for the two parishes of Hampstead and Hendon. It remained the property of Westminster Abbey until the Reformation and Thomas Thirlby, first and only Bishop of Westminster, was rector of both Hampstead and Hendon from 1540 to 1550. Prints show the old church small, dormered, accretive, with weather-boarding on the top stage of a short square tower.

In the 1740s the vestry of the by now rich village, without going to Parliament for funds, decided to have a new church. They refused Flitcroft's offer of his services because he would not submit to a competition, and employed instead a minor Burlingtonian called John Sanderson. Both architects were parishioners. Sanderson did his work badly; within five years much of the woodwork had to be renewed because of damp, and within twelve the tower had to be largely rebuilt. It was at this time that it acquired its little battlements. The piffling copper-covered spirelet was added in 1784.

Sanderson's church, set among yews at the end of a contemporary street on the hilltop, has every advantage of situation, but its sloping shoulders and mean brick tower seize none of them. The interior is better, and strongly shows the influence of the rejected Flitcroft; very probably Sanderson talked over the designs with him. It has the chunks of entablature and the swoopy vaulting which Flitcroft adapted from Gibbs and used at St Olave's, Tooley Street,° and it is marred by a characteristic fault of Flitcroft's: too narrow columns, the same fault which mars his great country house Wentworth Wodehouse. The galleries are high and unobtrusive, the original pulpit remains (cut down) as does the stem of the original font, which has been built into that most typical Victorian addition, a piscina in the north-west chapel.

In 1843–4 the church was lengthened and given transepts. In the 1870s a chancel, of course, had to be added, but the east tower stood in the way. It is greatly to the credit of the people of this enlightened suburb that they did not pull the old church down but simply reseated it so that it faced the other way. A very large chancel was added at the west and all the nave was

St John's, Hampstead

redecorated. The architect was F. P. Cockerell, the wood carver Sir T. G. Jackson and the painter Alfred Bell. By and large it was one of the more sensitive and pleasing Victorian enlargements.

The wrought iron gates to the churchyard were bought, when the church was built, at the sale of Canons Park, the Duke of Chandos' enormous house at Stanmore.[1]

---

[1] Other ironwork from Canons is at New College Oxford. The grand staircase fetched up at the Odeon Cinema, Broadstairs, where it was destroyed in World War II.

58. ST JOHN'S, SMITH SQUARE
WESTMINSTER, SW1
IIC4
U: Westminster

THOMAS ARCHER
1714–28

St John's, at £40,000, was the most expensive of the Fifty. It is a great turbulence of architecture, playing for astonishment, and thus fully baroque. Broken pediments face in all directions; four tall pierced towers, each a cluster and disgregate wobble of familiar elements, amaze. But there was a hex on the church. For a not-yet-explained reason the towers were finished with lead cupolas and pineapples instead of the pinnacles Archer intended. In 1739 Westminster boys (Palladians perhaps) broke the windows. In 1742 the church was gutted by fire and the twelve great columns inside, which formed an atrium like Hawksmoor's at ST MARY WOOLNOTH, were sold for ten shillings each. It was rebuilt by James Horne, the architect of St Katherine Coleman,° with a grant from Parliament, as a simple room with a tiled roof.

St John's, Smith Square

St John's, Smith Square

In 1812 it had to be propped up by huge untrimmed balks of timber. Inwood got rid of these in 1824, refurnished the church in the Grecian style, and opened some new windows and doors. It had long been believed that the church had begun to sink while it was still building and that Archer only put on the four great towers 'that the whole might sink equally'.[1] Lord Chesterfield said it was like an elephant lying on its back; Dickens, in *Our Mutual Friend*, that it was like a petrified monster. The story current now is that Archer, or more often Vanbrugh, asked Queen Anne what it should be like. She kicked over her footstool and said: 'Like that'.

In 1941 St John's was bombed and burnt out. For 20 years it stood gutted while some people proposed schemes of varying degrees of sense for its salvation and others hoped that it might conveniently fall down of its own accord. It was to be a home for the diocesan archive or a centre for liturgical experiments, it was to house excess statuary from Westminster Abbey, it was to have four levels, an art gallery, a TV studio, a cinema, a roof garden, underground parking . . . Fire, nature, mischievous childhood, gossip, the profit motive, bureaucracy and the king's enemies had all conspired to keep out the foreign architecture, but a happy ending finally came in 1968 when St John's opened as a concert hall and as like

[1] H. Chamberlain, *A New and Compleat History and Survey of the Cities of London and Westminster . . .* , London 1770, vol. ii, p. 590.

as possible to Archer's original design, including galleries. Plans for the interior had turned up: the twelve Corinthian columns were replaced; the ceiling was invisibly adapted with felt, muslin, paint and pinholes to give good acoustics; simplicity and a good colour scheme were agreed upon. The architect was Marshall Sisson. The first-rate acoustics, the great beauty of the white interior, even the salads and wine in the crypt, all combine to make it the finest middle-size concert hall in London.

59. ST JOHN, WAPPING
SCANDRETT STREET, E1
U: Wapping

IE3

JOEL JOHNSON
1756
Gutted in World
War II

In the 16th century Wapping-on-the-Woze (on the Marsh) was drained, and Wapping wall built. The Rector of St Mary Matfelon° built a chapel of ease there in 1617 in an attempt to subdue and civilise the tough waterfront inhabitants. In 1694 Wapping became a parish and was later

St John, Wapping, in the 19th century

declared by the Commissioners of the Fifty to deserve a new church (see ST GEORGE'S IN THE EAST). The old chapel was a house-like little building. Its tower was low and weather-boarded, and had a tiled roof and a chimney-like spike on top. The new church which succeeded it in 1756 was badly damaged in World War II; only its tower and some dangerous-looking walls, awash with nettles and plane saplings, remained. The tower is pleasant, of dark brick with stone dressings to make it identifiable through the river mists, and has a lead lantern rising square from the clock-stage by concavities to a squared cupola. Beside it is a little 18th-century school; the two charity children, he and she, in niches on the façade, may still be there, boarded up like the windows.

The body of the church is to be converted for use as a house. Opposite is still the old cemetery. The rest of Wapping is all wharves and warehouses, derelict or awaiting gentrification; high, dark; enormous doors at all levels; cobbles, right angles, dying docks and the invisible Thames.

ST JOHN IN THE WHITE TOWER
see TOWER OF LONDON

SIR EDWIN LUTYENS
1910

60. ST JUDE ON THE HILL
and the FREE CHURCH
HAMPSTEAD GARDEN SUBURB, NW11
IB1

U: Golders Green

The Central Square of Hampstead Garden Suburb, with its two magnificent churches and its Institute all designed by Lutyens, is without doubt the grandest surburban layout in London, and perhaps in England. The grass between the huge and splendid buildings has remained unworn and an almost country wind blows across the great space. It is true that, as Pevsner elegantly puts it, 'Institute education and divine worship have not proved to be as much of a permanent and non-intermittent attraction as the social reformers behind the Suburb had hoped',[1] but it is a fine place for all that.

St Jude's has a monumental tower of great height with a characteristically Lutyensian mixture of Byzantine and Perpendicular proportions. The huge nave roof comes almost to the ground, and is reminiscent of a certain 17th- and 18th-century style of farm building in the Franche Comté. Seen from Southway, the overall massing has an almost Japanese look to it. The major windows have a Dutchish sort of pediment, the minor dormer windows have a gusty baroque ambiguity in

---

[1] Nikolaus Pevsner, *The Buildings of England: Middlesex*, Harmondsworth 1951, p. 62.

the alignment of the bricks; all of which adds up to one of Lutyens' best   *St Jude on the Hill*
bouillabaisses.

This splendid outside seems to offer promises about the inside, but they
are belied. It is barrel vaulted, with round arches. The quite ingenious
capitals are spoiled by the loudspeakers inserted into them. If you were to
see this inside first, you would expect it to have a neo-classical outside.

What grandeur there is gets further compromised by the messy, slightly
mad timbering in the aisle ceilings, which shows through and among the
smaller round arches. Perhaps it looked fun at the design stage.

The not very good murals are by Walter Starmer (1877–1961).

The Free Church at the other end of the square uses many of the same design elements, including the low-reaching roof, on a smaller scale and in a more restrained way. It has the same classical-looking interior and the aisle ceilings are equally awkward, though a bit less frank about it.

1628

61. ST KATHERINE CREE
LEADENHALL STREET, CITY, EC3
IIF2   U: Aldgate

A parish of St Katherine is immemorial here. In 1108 it and three other parishes were merged and the new Augustinian Priory of Holy Trinity, Aldgate, was built over them. The civil and ecclesiastical connection was so intimate here that the prior became ex-officio the alderman of Portsoken Ward and the parishioners of the new single parish of Christ Church used part of the priory church. This latter arrangement was not satisfactory and

St Katherine Cree

eventually a new parish church was built in the parishioners' part of the priory cemetery, and called St Katherine Cree. Cree, although Laud called the church St Katherine Creed, is supposed to be an abbreviation of Christ Church, the name of the parish. It was served by a canon appointed by the prior, but even this did not work and from 1414 the parishioners maintained their own parson.

The priory was surrendered by the prior and convent to King Henry VIII in 1532, first of the big houses in England, and first of any in London. This aroused little regret, for the prior, as alderman, was unpopular in the City, and the priory was seriously in debt because of good living and because it had allowed its property to deteriorate. Parliament confirmed the gift to the king 'because the Prior and convent had departed from the monastery leaving it profaned and desolate'.[1] Lord Audley was granted the priory, and he offered its church to the parishioners of St Katherine, who refused it, 'having doubts in their heads about the afterclaps'.[2] It was then pulled down; the stone sold cheaply, as Londoners still preferred brick and wood for building their houses.

The parishioners decided to rebuild their church in 1628 and pulled down everything but the tower of 1504. They broadened the nave, except for the two westernmost bays of the north aisle. The tradition that Inigo Jones designed the new church is only a survival of the days when he was thought to have designed everything built in England during his lifetime. The colonnade, rounded arches resting without chunks of entablature on Corinthian columns, though definitely in the Italian style, is not what a follower of Palladio would allow himself. The medieval ground-plan is simply accepted, with no attempt made logically to incorporate either the tower or the bite out of the north aisle which remained from the old church. The detail, except on the columns and the pilasters of the clerestory, is of the appliqué kind common in northern Europe at this date – particularly the aprons of the windows, the west door and the odd inverted bobble-and-fringe castellation along the parapet, shown in an early print, of which a tiny fragment remains between the tower and the west front. The gate, now in the churchyard against the parish room, which used to make an entrance into the churchyard from Leadenhall Street, is very like the south door at ST HELEN'S, BISHOPSGATE, which is also traditionally and impossibly attributed to Jones. The perfectly nice but perfectly usual groined ceiling has nothing to do with the Renaissance. The church was consecrated in 1631 by Bishop Laud of London, as he then was, and his vestments and the form of service he used were later held against him at his trial. That the church itself was designed for Arminian worship is hard to see. There was no screen, but then screens were approved neither by High nor Low Churchmen, only by Middle Churchmen who saw them as a convenient protection for the communion table. The communion table could indeed be seen immediately one entered the church; but though to some this might provide an opportunity for worshipping the altar, to others it would seem a way of ensuring that all equally could take part in the service. In fact the layout is disappointing to anyone hoping to find a church specifically designed by Laudians for their worship.

The church escaped the Great Fire and was indeed 'resorted to by the Corporation' when the others were destroyed.[3]

The Catherine wheel in the top of the east window is contemporary with

[1] *Victoria County History: London*, vol. i, 1909, p. 472.
[2] Stow, *Survey of London*, Everyman edn, London 1945, p. 129.
[3] Pepys, *Diary*, 18 August 1667.

the building; so are the rather touchingly knobbly font, the plate and the painted bosses in the ceiling. The vestry is shown on a plan of 1677. The pulpit and the carving on the lectern are from the end of the century. The sounding-board has been used as a table in the vestry, but is now restored to its original use. The reredos comes from St James's, Duke's Place,° replacing an earlier one with a perspective of columns, cherubim, seraphim and Moses and Aaron. The best monument is one saved from the previous church, that of Sir Nicholas Throckmorton, a reclining figure between columns supporting an entablature. He was ambassador in Paris, and later Chief Butler. Throgmorton Street is called after him.

There is also a modern plaque just before the communion table to Sir John Gayor, who gave the font and also endowed the 'Lion Sermon' in thanks for the gentleness of a lion he met in a desert in the Near East. This sermon is still preached.

The generations since the church was built have added a sundial, removed the battlements and the segmental pediments which had stood over some of the windows, altered the broken pediment over the door in the tower, rather spoiling its balance, put pillars round the turret on the tower, cut down the pews to make benches, raised the chancel by one step, put in more stained glass and built more and more closely up to the sides of the church.

Against the east wall of the tower in the south aisle there is the top part of an octagonal respond. The capital is about two feet from the floor. The present tower was built in 1504, the church in 1628. Stow, in 1598, said one went seven steps down into the old church. Strype, in 1720, described this respond and said there was 15 feet more of it underground. The Royal Commission on Historical Monuments says it is a 15th-century respond.

This church is altogether inconclusive: it is the only complete Jacobean church to survive in London but it answers no questions about its time, informing us only that it was a time of change and indecision. It is now one of the Guild Churches and is devoted to the Christian life in finance, commerce and industry. It is the headquarters of the Industrial Christian Fellowship. The side aisles have had to be blocked off to provide offices and a library for these purposes. All in all, it tells us more about our time than about its own.

SIR CHRISTOPHER
WREN
1671–7

IIE2

62. ST LAWRENCE JEWRY
GRESHAM STREET, BY THE GUILDHALL, CITY, EC2
U: Bank, St Paul's

In the late 12th century this church belonged to the convent of St Sauve and St Guingalaens[1] of Montreuil in the diocese of Amiens, and a century later to Balliol College. The name Jewry came from the neighbourhood where, before their expulsion by Edward I, the Jews of London had lived.

[1] Perhaps the Cornish Winwalloe.

The church that was destroyed in the Great Fire was a rich and fine one, thoroughly repaired in 1618 and with much stained glass.

Wren's church is no architectural *tour de force* but, like its predecessor, it is handsome and richly decorated though not, alas, as richly as it was. At street level it is substantial and plain, except for the eastern façade, which gives on to the approach to Guildhall; this is substantial and ornate, sporting pediments, attached Corinthian columns, niches, festoons and heavy swags. It is based on one of the designs Wren made for St Paul's: the Model Design.

By thickening the east wall at its south end and by adjusting the vestibule, tower and vestry into the west end, Wren managed a nave of regular proportions. There is a north aisle but, placed behind the entablature and clerestory, it does not interfere much with the regularity.

Dreadful things almost happened to St Lawrence in the 1860s, when the vestry asked Digby Wyatt for estimates for restoring the church. (See

Introduction, p. 25.) But they were too high; and Blomfield restored in a comparatively harmless manner.

At the same time St Lawrence's was in the throes of ritualist experiment. The churchwardens disapproved – particularly of a festival in which 50 colonial bishops and the Bishop of New York took part – but the Bishop of London did not. Between September 1867 and December 1869, there were 47 sermons preached by bishops, and all the bishops different.

St Lawrence's was gutted in the same raid as ST BRIDE'S, FLEET STREET, in 1940. Between 1954 and 1957 the church was admirably restored by Cecil Brown, who was responsible for both the fabric and the decoration. The stone tower with obelisks at each corner supporting a tall lead lantern in turn surmounted by a slender obelisk – all this straight and tapering in contrast to the curving delicacy of ST MARY LE BOW a few stone's throws away – has been rebuilt. The steeple is a glass fibre copy of the original. The weathervane in the shape of a gridiron, the symbol of St Lawrence's martyrdom, was preserved, and has now been incorporated with the shape of an incendiary bomb to top the steeple.

The interior, despite having lost its original ornaments, remains fine. An appropriate dark oak reredos, a carved oak screen separating the north aisle (the Commonwealth Chapel) from the nave, the organ (built to

St Lawrence Jewry

Harris's original design) and gallery in no way detract from the building itself, save that the organ is a little cramped against the ceiling. The latter is a replica of the original. Some tactful stained glass has been put in to defend the church against the encroaching 20th century. The pews come from HOLY TRINITY, MARYLEBONE; the Lord Mayor's pew (this being the corporation church, since the demolition of the Guildhall Chapel in 1368) incorporates his sword-rest, and there is a stall for the Master of Balliol in the front row. The font is dated 1620 and comes from Holy Trinity, Minories.° Its cover incorporates wood from the old roof of the Guildhall. At the base of the tower is the tiny chapel in which the church survived between destruction and rebuilding.

On 12 February 1664 Pepys came to St Lawrence. He was not impressed by the sermon but thought the church 'a very fine church'. Fortunately it once more is.

---

63. ST LEONARD'S, SHOREDITCH
Shoreditch Parish Church
SHOREDITCH HIGH STREET AND HACKNEY RD, E1
ID2   U: Old Street

GEORGE DANCE THE ELDER
1736–40

Shoreditch Church is documented from the middle of the 12th century. Exterior views of the 17th and early 18th centuries show a building with four aisles, of which the north one had probably been a chantry, and with a tower having a weather-boarded top stage and a small bellcote.

In this church were buried Richard Burbage, the first actor to play Hamlet, and others of his family. The 16th-century registers are full of the births, marriages and deaths of actors from the two theatres in Shoreditch, the Theatre and the Curtain, including Gabriel Spencer, who was killed by Ben Jonson in a duel at Hoxton Fields. A sentimental connection between the church and the stage continues to this day. The bells of this church were famous, pleased Queen Elizabeth, had quaint inscriptions. But we extract the following lines from verses written after a team of ringers visited the old church during the last years of its existence:

> The peal of bells are not extra ornary
> For some are very ornary
> They'd be much better if they had
> A good second and third, for those are bad.[1]

The Commissioners of the Fifty marked Shoreditch for two new churches, but they were never built and even a move by the parish to get Commission money for the rebuilding of St Leonard's itself was unsuccessful. In 1734 a survey by Flitcroft, Dance, James and one Cordwell pronounced the medieval building to be not only unsafe, which everybody

---

[1] Quoted in A. S. Bradley, *The History of Shoreditch Church*, London 1914.

knew because bits used to fall off during services, but also insanitary, because the floor was by then many feet below ground level. An Act of Parliament was obtained empowering trustees to raise £8,000 at 8½ per cent secured on the burial and other rates. The old church was pulled down and George Dance began to build the present one. His builder provoked a riot by employing Irish labour at cut wages, and the soldiery had to come out from the Tower.

St Leonard's, Shoreditch

Dance's design was ambitious. The steeple is a great landmark in that part of London, very high, very slender, very complicated. Dance must consciously have invited comparison with Wren's steeple at ST MARY LE BOW; he must consciously have been trying to go one better, to accept the general pattern and to make it even slenderer, even more graceful. The result is a grandiose failure, neither substantial nor airy, neither original nor traditional, and all perched anxiously on top of a portico in the manner unhappily devised by Gibbs at ST MARTIN-IN-THE-FIELDS. It is hard to judge the rest of the exterior since six of the ten steps Dance set his façade upon were put underground in 1766, a great square recreation room was slapped on to the south side in 1902, and the high-pitched east end was made perky at some time or other by the addition of two chimney pots.

The interior, though not structurally altered, is distorted by the usual removal (in 1857) of north and south galleries, by the insertion in 1923 of a large rood-beam complete with figures and by each pillar's sprouting from the top a pair of pendant neon tubes. There is also a row of gas heaters at window level, but these things do not disguise the interior's being as ambitious as the exterior, and more successful. Tuscan arcades with interrupted entablature carry a low clerestory above a string-course, and the nave, spectacularly lofty, skips gaily thus to near the altar where the movement is calmed by the heavy horizontal lines of the apse. If you peer beneath the rood-beam you can see that this is one of the best of all Georgian apses: its complex gravity is matched by vestibules at the west end between which the rich and substantial organ of 1757 sits on the only remaining gallery. The rococo clock-case on the front of this gallery, said to be Chippendale, is one of the finest pieces of woodcarving in London; 18th-century benefaction boards in the chancel and peal boards in the entrance vestibule record feats of charity and of bell-ringing in frames of discreet jubilation; and the monument in the south aisle to Elizabeth Benson, of 1710, is a fully developed essay in the sophisticated making pretty of the ghoulish. On it skeletons hitch their shrouds over oak trees and symmetrically drag down their branches. The pulpit, once high and solemn, has been cut off at the knees in Victorian mutilation and now looks like Porgy on his trolley. The church was lit by gaslight as early as 1817. It was damaged by a flying bomb in 1944, has been repaired and redecorated, but is still kept locked most of the time.

---

64. ST LUKE'S, CHELSEA
Chelsea Parish Church
SYDNEY STREET, SW3

IC3   U: South Kensington

JAMES SAVAGE
1820–4

When the riverside village of Chelsea began to spread inland a new church was needed and the parishioners fortunately decided to leave ALL SAINTS, the Old Church, as a chapel of ease and to build afresh among the new streets. The rector, deputising for his brother the Duke of Wellington, laid the foundation stone and James Savage raised the great church which was perhaps the first in England consciously to emulate, not merely to recall, the churches of the Middle Ages. It is indeed a brave affair. It cost £40,000, all raised by subscription, and attracted the most serious interest when it

St Luke's, Chelsea

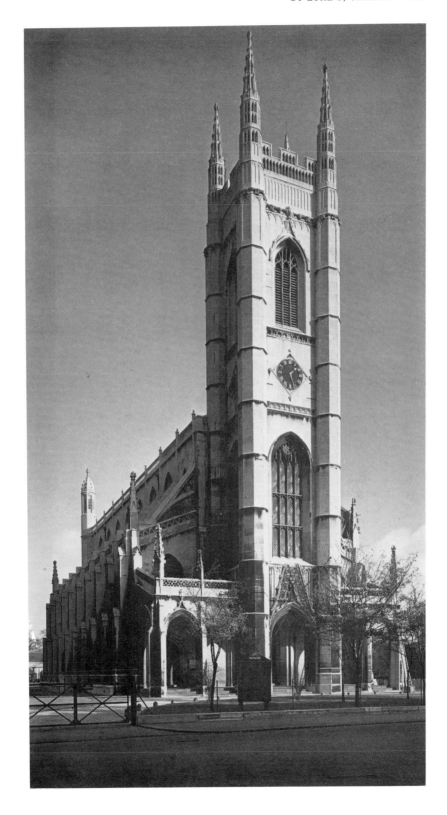

was new.[1] It has a stone vault throughout a tremendous tower,[2] flying buttresses, a broad lateral porch, and even a triforium below the clerestory. It is easy to find the faults: the ornamental top of the tower is laboured, the flying buttresses look all wrong without any pinnacles to pin them down and, worst of all, the exterior articulation between tower and nave is utterly clumsy and unthought-out. But the grandeur is all the same undeniable, even if it did not satisfy the Ecclesiologists' requirement for 'correct' Gothic. There is a wide playground, and to the east Savage built parochial schools to match the church, with two great arches open to the sky, oddly set askew on the axis. These have been converted, but the setting still allows the church to look fine and bold. The galleries remain, but the furniture is Victorian. A Deposition over the altar, by the Academician Northcote, contemporary with the church, is a dramatic and exciting piece.

65. ST MAGNUS THE MARTYR

LOWER THAMES STREET, CITY, EC3

IIF3

U: Monument

SIR CHRISTOPHER WREN

1671–1705

Of the eleven martyrs called Magnus the one favoured as the patron saint of this church is the governor of the Orkneys who was murdered in 1116 for political reasons and canonised in 1135. Nevertheless, there exists a reference to a stone church of St Magnus during the reign of William I.[3] The chapel of St Thomas on London Bridge paid an annual sum to the rector of St Magnus to compensate for any diminution of alms.

Henry Yevele, who built the nave of Canterbury Cathedral, founded a chantry and was buried here in 1400 among many other 'men of good worship'.[4] Miles Coverdale, jointly responsible for the 1532 English translation of the Bible, has now joined them, brought from St Bartholomew by the Exchange. By the end of the 15th century, however, 'priestis and clarkes, in tyme of dyuyne service, be at tauerns and alehowsis, at fyshing and other trifils, whereby dyuyne seruice is let.'[5] The church was particularly convenient for fishing, for it was then, and remained until the 19th century, on the waterfront, immediately to the east of London Bridge. In the late 16th century an ingenious Dutchman passed pipes from the river over the steeple through which to pump water to the houses in Lower Thames Street. The church avoided a fire on London Bridge in 1600, but was burnt in the Great Fire. As it now stands it differs from the one Wren built after the Fire in many ways. The widening and improving of London Bridge in 1756–8 brought the

---

[1] E.g. Britton and Pugin, *The Public Buildings of London*, London 1825, vol. ii, p. 205 *et seq.*
[2] Savage had desired a stone spire like that of ST DUNSTAN IN THE EAST, but this was not allowed.
[3] *Victoria County Histories: London*, vol. i, 1909, p. 180.
[4] Stow, *Survey of London*, Everyman edn, London 1945, p. 290.
[5] *Arnold's Chronicle*, London, edn 1811, p. 278.

pavement right up to the south-west corner of the church. Soon after this there was a fire in an oil shop next door and not only was the church re-roofed but the two aisles were cut back so that the pavement might pass under the tower. Part of the deal governing the widening of the bridge was that a room would be built attached to the vestry, 'for the reception and preservation of the fire engine of the said united parishes'. A wise move, after such a history. There had previously been a doorway set forward with a window on either side in the middle of the north wall; this was now blocked up and the rich decoration of this whole aspect of the church was thrown out of balance. In 1827 the north windows were blocked up into small circles. Internally, abolishing the door made nonsense of the wide spacing of the columns level with it; extra columns were placed here in 1924 to restore regularity. Because the ceilings were rebuilt at the same time, one cannot know if originally there was some reflection of this cruciform arrangement in the ceiling.

St Magnus the Martyr in the early 20th century. It is now even more hemmed in.

Until old London Bridge was pulled down and the new bridge built in 1832 St Magnus had a fine position, its west front and steeple sentinel at the City end. The space left between the church and the new bridge sprouted a horribly fertile crop of buildings, one of which, Adelaide House, sprang up in 1921 cutting off St Magnus from the river, the bridge, and the skyline. The Midland Bank's St Magnus House, to the east and south-east, the dual carriageway, the concrete spiral stairs, the two bridges and the seemingly constant roadworks, do little to encourage the still small voice of calm. The steeple, pushing and muscular, is one of the very best, establishing itself at each stage: square tower, tower with chamfered corners, eight-sided peristyle, eight-sided dome and plump eight-sided pinnacle.

Inside is 'inexplicable splendour of Ionian white and gold',[4] now again made beautiful by affectionate care. The reredos, once cut in two, has been put together again, the north doorway is a diagonal side altar and a pair to it in the other aisle has been built up. Light glass has been put in the windows. Most of these improvements were the work of Martin Travers, in 1924 and 1925.

The organ, basically that of 1712 with what is said to be the first ever swell organ, still stands on its original little wrought iron posts (compare those under the west gallery at ST MARY'S, ROTHERHITHE). The font and its house-like cover, the reredos and the altar-rails, the table of benefactions, the churchwardens' pews, the pulpit; all are fine. There is also a ghost for those who have eyes to see it.

Until 1883, there was a clock on the tower embellished with figures of St Magnus, St Margaret, Hercules, Atlas, two eagles and several cherubs. The clock, dated 1709, has now been replaced, but alas without the figures. It was originally given by George Duncombe, the Lord Mayor, who when an apprentice was once thrashed for being late and who had promised to provide a clock so that the next generation might avoid a similar experience.

For many years in the middle of this century the church had some claim to be the highest *in partibus*. But it now seems to have been outdone.

---

66. ST MARGARET, LOTHBURY

CITY, EC2

IIE2

U: Bank

SIR CHRISTOPHER WREN

1686–90

This church is now congested with woodwork from other Wren churches demolished since 1780.

The pre-Fire church was rebuilt in 1440, part of it carried on a vault over the Wall Brook. Wren rebuilt a very plain middle-sized church on the medieval plan (the foundation arch of the old east wall is still there, below ground) and probably on more or less the medieval elevation, since there

---

[4] T. S. Eliot, *The Waste Land*, 3. 'The Fire Sermon'.

is a low side aisle to the south, now arcaded off by a low screen with alternate wood and iron uprights, designed by Bodley in 1891 and incorporating woodwork from St Olave's, Old Jewry.°

The most prominent piece of woodwork is the fantastic chancel screen brought from All Hallows the Great° when it was demolished. It is an exercise in the top-heavy, related in pattern to the only other screen in a Wren church, that at St Peter, Cornhill, but cocking a snook at our ingrown feeling about the weight-bearing capacities of wood in a way that the other does not. Vast central pediment, double spread-eagle, two subsidiary pediments, swooping entablature and the royal arms of William and Mary, all stagger on fairy-light twisted skeins and open-work carving. It is hard to see anything else in the church, but the effort is worth making, for the sounding-board of the pulpit is a lovely work. This also came from All Hallows the Great,° though the pulpit beneath is indigenous. (The sounding-board's original pulpit, being too large for St Margaret's, went to St Paul's Hammersmith, while the reredos and the entire Portland stone tower went to Twickenham.) The sounding-board suggests a coronet, with its rim of standing cherubs, thin swags and long-winged bird. The font, originally under the organ gallery, is, though undocumented, often attributed to Gibbons himself, probably from its similarity to the undoubted Gibbons font at ST JAMES, PICCADILLY. It is a very gay and urbane piece of carving featuring Adam and Eve, the Dove returning to the Ark, Christ's baptism and Philip and the Eunuch. The reredos in the aisle is from St Olave's, Old Jewry.° The paintings of Moses and Aaron beside the modern plaque above the reredos in the chancel are from St Christopher le Stocks,° and so is the blank-visaged bust of Sir Peter le Maire. Two pilasters beside the chancel reredos, painted in Wren's day to resemble lapis lazuli, have disappeared. The central south window shows the arms of the Worshipful Company of Scientific Instrument Makers.

Some little shops on Lothbury, against the south side of the church, were removed in 1771. The slender lead spire, rather absurd, is best seen from the north.

Various other pieces of wood carving from the churches mentioned and from St Bartholomew by the Exchange° are incorporated about the church.

1504 and later

67. ST MARGARET'S, WESTMINSTER
PARLIAMENT SQUARE, SW1

IIC4 U: Westminster

The parish was originally the whole of what is now the City of Westminster except a little bit in the Strand. There is some reason to think that until the reign of Edward the Confessor the parishioners worshipped in Westminster Abbey, and that they were then put out by the abbot who built them their own church right beside the Abbey, where the present one

stands. Later the Abbey certainly claimed that St Margaret's was within its jurisdiction and not that of the English hierarchy. The two are now administratively merged.

St Margaret's, Westminster

The present building follows the pattern of an early 16th-century church, but all that survives of the old work are the regular, graceful and spacious arcades inside and an unusual and pleasing 16th-century arch leading from the tower into the church proper: instead of coming down to corbels or capitals the ribs just turn sharply away into the wall like so many hot water pipes. The tower was rebuilt in the 18th century by John James and the rest of the exterior dates from various times between then and 1905, when the famous east window was reset in a new east wall. The east end had been several times rebuilt.

St Margaret's is one of several churches in London on which one could hang a history of England. In 1540 the parishioners put up armed resistance when the Lord Protector Somerset decided that the fabric of the church would be useful for building his new palace.[1] In 1614 the House of Commons, probably on account of the increase of Puritanism among the members, ceased going as they commonly had to worship with the Lords in Westminster Abbey and took Communion by themselves in St Margaret's. This they have done ever since, and the revolutions of 17th-century England were played out in little through the quarrels and emotions about the form of worship here. It was in St Margaret's in 1642 that the members raised their right hands and took the Solemn League and Covenant against Popery which was the first crude, senseless cry of

---

[1] Cf. ST MARY-LE-STRAND.

that infant juggernaut, the democratic nation-state. In 1667, on the other hand, Pepys took his 'perspective glass' to St Margaret's, and 'had the pleasure of seeing and gazing at a great many fine women, and with that and sleeping I passed the time away till sermon was done.'

St Margaret's, Westminster, with monument to John Churchill (right)

Later furniture for the comfort of legislators – a Corinthian edicule for the Speaker to sit in; a splendid high central pulpit, octagonal, composed of cartwheels and flamboyant ogees and supported by flying buttresses – has been swept away, and the church is now dully and demurely furnished. The east window is a bright piece of Flemish painted glass of the early 16th century. The story goes that it was made to celebrate the betrothal of Catherine of Aragon to Henry VII's eldest son Arthur, and was perhaps the gift of her parents, King Ferdinand and Queen Isabella. Either side of a crucifixion stand, if this is true, Prince Arthur, all visor and nose, and the lady, apprehensive in blue (though her head is a later substitution). The window arrived after Prince Arthur's death, after his brother Henry VIII had married Catherine, perhaps even after he had divorced her. Naturally he packed it off out of sight and it passed through several hands until it was acquired in 1758 by the vestry of St Margaret's for 400 guineas. The Dean and Chapter of Westminster prosecuted the vestry for setting up a superstitious image but, defended by a lecturer at St Margaret's called Thomas Wilson who wrote the most exemplarily learned and handsome book about it,[1] they were acquitted.

Raleigh's body was buried here after his execution (though his head is in West Horsley, Surrey) and Milton was once married. Both are commemorated in handsome windows, the gifts of Americans in the last century. The south aisle windows were blown out in 1941 and now contain some rather meaningless coloured glass by John Piper, called 'Spring in London'. The poet Skelton, who is, or ought to be, held in especial affection by all who care for creative dottiness, was also buried here, but lacks grand commemoration. All the best people are married in St Margaret's; all, that is, except those who are of such exalted bestness as to be married in the Abbey itself.

68. ST MARK, DALSTON
SANDRINGHAM ROAD, E8
ID2
BR: Hackney Downs

CHESTER CHESTON
1866
Tower
E. L. BLACKBURNE
1877

A fine, cheerful stock-brick church with stone quoins. It is very large indeed, and was designed as the centrepiece for the growing estates of Hackney built with their two, three and four stories, for all conditions of persons. Some of the housing nearest the church goes admirably with it and vice versa.

All that is known of the architect, Chester Cheston Junior, is that he was the son of the agent of a wealthy parishioner called Amherst who had a lot to do with the commissioning of the church. Other work by him has not yet been traced, except for a few houses and a pub. His own proposal for a tower was rejected in favour of the present one by F. L. Blackburne. The church forms part of what we call elsewhere a 'holy village'; this one includes also a spirited hexagonal vestry and a clergy house, attached to the south-east corner of the church.

The interior of the church is at once dark and graceful. This is a grand display of the wide open spaces conferred upon Victorian church builders by the technology of cast iron. The six clusters of columns forming the nave arcade have four iron units cast as one in a very good approximation to the Early English style. The four crossing piers have the same unitary cluster as a core and five free-standing cast iron columns arranged round it. The large and small capitals required by this programme are excellently devised. The ceiling is of boards laid on vaguely Jacobethan members. In

---

[1] Anon, *The Ornaments of Churches considered* . . . etc., London 1761.

St Mark, Dalston

the spandrels of the transept windows there are stained glass panels let in, of pale blue sky and golden angels. The effect is strikingly decorative, and contrasts very well with the rest of what John Betjeman rightly called the 'scalding glass' (by Lavers and Barraud). The original gasoliers were simply turned upside-down when electricity came, and they serve the purpose very well. There is much excellent furnishing throughout, though the pews are plain.

On Blackburne's powerful tower one of the clock face sites is occupied by a barometer, an idea said to have been borrowed by the then vicar from two churches he saw in Paris. The machinery for multiplying the tiny movement in the mercury column to the almost cathedral-size arm on the 'stormy–set fair' face is thoroughly ingenious.

A forthright sort of Christianity is practised here. The parish magazine for Spring 1985 carried a full-page imprecation as follows:

> In 1945, A. Hitler was DEMOLISHED.
> In 1985, A. Scargill is being ROUTED!
> SO MAY ALL THINE ENEMIES PERISH, O YAHWEH!

The church is defiantly open despite severe and visible thefts in the past, but parishioners walk through it as often as they can.

69. ST MARTIN, GOSPEL OAK
VICARS ROAD, NW5
IC2
BR: Gospel Oak

EDWARD BUCTON
LAMB
1866

To include this church is not an expression of the authors' liking or approval: rather an expression of faith in the oddness of the human, and therefore of the divine, imagination. Thus must Adam have felt on first seeing the duckbilled platypus.

The building's main characteristic is unlikelihood: the stretched look of the tower, porridgy in texture and now lacking some of its turrets: was it to be viewed looking down from Parliament Hill? On plan there is a basic square, but it scarcely reads like one. Pevsner describes it thus: 'Hammer beam roof running right through, with the fanciest, busiest details, and resting on shafts which do not go down to the ground but start from Cistercian-looking brackets. The square piers between nave and aisles have four such bracketed shafts attached to their four sides (a sight never before seen).'[1] The overall effect is that all these curious structures are holding one piece of the organism apart from another.

The building is important in the surrounding desolation of two-storey flat-top terrace houses and bloodless tower blocks.

70. ST MARTIN-IN-THE-FIELDS
TRAFALGAR SQUARE, WC2
IIC3
U: Charing Cross

JAMES GIBBS
1722–6

When Nash opened up Trafalgar Square in 1829 St Martin's suddenly became one of the most splendidly situated churches in London. Gibbs had built it closely confined in St Martin's Lane, and had perhaps thought of the temple portico as seen only from close to and its spire as riding not the portico but the surrounding rooftops. Certainly he had regretted not having his earlier design for a circular church accepted. But whatever allowances we make, the way the spire rides the temple is absurd, the interrupted string-course and rusticated window surrounds neither graceful nor appropriate; and the east front, the flattest aspect of the church, is by far the most satisfactory. The model kept in the crypt is slightly different and rather better.

St Martin-in-the-Fields

By the 12th century there was a small chapel here in the fields owned by Westminster Abbey. In the 16th century it was given a parish cut from the northern part of ST MARGARET'S, WESTMINSTER. In 1543–4 the church was rebuilt, still very small; only 45 feet by 25. In the next 200 years it grew piecemeal and in 1721 measured 84 feet by 62; the tower had a cupola by

---

[1] Nikolaus Pevsner, *The Buildings of England: London excluding the Cities of London and Westminster*, Harmondsworth 1952, p. 361.

Wren. It is said that Henry VIII parochialised the church so that plaguy bodies should not be carried past his new Palace of St James's for burial at St Margaret's. The royal family certainly accepted St Martin's as the church of the royal parish; several royal babies, including Charles II, were christened in it (now only Pearly princes and princesses are christened there); Queen Mary I worshipped there and gave hangings; and George I contributed a handsome organ to Gibbs's new church. The foundation stone of this was laid 'with full religious and masonic rites'[1] by the Bishop of Salisbury deputising for the king, and a royal pew was provided, complete with a fireplace. In the church and graveyard a variety of notables was buried: Francis Bacon, John Hampden, Nell Gwyn, Nicholas Stone, Jack Sheppard, Sir Edmundbury Godfrey.

Gibbs studied in Rome and was by upbringing a Roman Catholic, though he later joined the Church of England, and St Martin's shows how difficult he found it to solve the problem of combining Roman architecture and Anglican liturgy. At ST MARY-LE-STRAND the interior is a mere echo of its distinctive and charmingly Roman exterior. At St Martin's, as it was originally built, the nave moves slowly east, turns handsomely into the chancel arch and then has nowhere to go: no splendid baldaquin, no flamboyantly emotional altar. The royal arms symbolically cut off that part of the church most important to a Catholic. 'The ceiling', writes Gibbs, 'is ellyptical, which, I find by experience, to be much better for the voice than the semi-circular, tho' not so beautiful.'[2] This is like Gibbs; he could never quite make a virtue of necessity, make the imaginative leap which turns the theoretically inadequate or outrageous into an individual, a unique beauty. Parts, one might say, excellent; synthesis weak. Yet his published drawings, particularly of St Martin's, had in the 18th century a great influence both in England and in the United States.[3]

Three incumbents of St Martin's in the present century have been remarkable men who have made their parish pump into a fountain of metropolitan importance. Dick Sheppard, Pat McCormick and Eric Loveday, with their broadcast services, ever-open door and parish magazine (the *St Martin's Review*) with a circulation of 10,000, have done by way of the mass media what Wesley and Whitefield did by travel and the Methodist system of circuit preaching. The Revd Austen Williams continued the tradition with exhibitions, peace vigils, anti-apartheid activities (the South African Embassy is a stone's throw away), a soup kitchen and a public relations officer. The central position and high profile are such that a letter addressed in 1983 to 'God, somewhere in London' was delivered to St Martin's. The church is now spruce and much cared for, though the charitable activities always need money and there is probably not a church in London that does not need some form of restoration.

---

[1] J. McMaster, *Short History of St Martin's in the Fields*, London 1916, p. 75.
[2] James Gibbs, *A Book of Architecture*, London 1728, p. 82.
[3] See, for instance, St Michael's, Charleston, S. Carolina; Christ Church, Philadelphia; St Paul's Chapel, New York City; illustrated in Dorsey, *Early English Churches in America*, New York 1952. Also the excellent interior of the King's Chapel in Boston.

SIR CHRISTOPHER
WREN
1677–84

71. ST MARTIN LUDGATE
CITY, EC4

IIE2

U: Blackfriars, St Paul's

The Welsh hero Cadwallader, says Geoffrey of Monmouth, founded the church (and was buried in it) in 677. Perhaps he did. The Romans certainly had had a cemetery here, for their sepulchral stones have been found. The church is dedicated to St Martin of Tours, the Roman soldier who cut his cloak in half to share with a beggar.

In 1561 the steeple was struck by the same lightning that brought down the spire of old St Paul's. The Great Fire consumed the church, and Wren rebuilt it a few feet further north. By filling the south side with a vestibule and gallery under and beside the tower he made his building almost a cube. The site slopes, but the slope is absorbed externally in the inconspicuous range of doors at street level and internally in the vestibules. Four Corinthian columns set up on plinths as high as the wainscotting carry the Greek cross of the ceiling and form a Vitruvian tetrastyle atrium. Everything is very tall, but proportion is kept and only the cut-down pews look submerged. The raising of choir and sanctuary in the 1890s, and the pleasant coloured glass, rather enhance the submarine effect.

The reredos has been altered a little, but it is still a good piece. The inner door-cases in the south wall are satisfyingly complex in design. An open pod of peas among the carving on the south-east door suggests that Gibbons might have been involved. On the east wall is a yellowing Ascension by R. Browne, from St Mary Magdalen, Knightrider Street.° The chandelier comes from the Cathedral of St Vincent in the West Indies.

The steeples of St Martin's and of St Augustine, Watling Street, each of them black and sharp and each on a main approach to St Paul's, have the function of making the great dome of the cathedral appear more hazy, more distant, more impressive. But quite apart from the steeple's function in Wren's skyline, St Martin's whole south front is particularly good. The great angle scrolls are the key to the façade: they help to establish the importance of the horizontal mouldings above the three windows and the relation of the windows to the height of the whole façade. The smaller scrolls are sequential and so is the shape of the cupola and spire; they hold and sharpen the tension. The little balcony, on the other hand, is worn loosely and casually.

St Martin's is now one of the Guild Churches; it serves the Metropolitan Police.

72. ST MARY ABBOTS
Kensington Parish Church
KENSINGTON CHURCH STREET, W8

IB3 U: High Street Kensington

SIR GEORGE GILBERT
SCOTT
1869–79

Kensington Parish Church has the surname Abbots because in the Middle Ages it belonged to the Abbey of Abingdon. A church, probably of the 12th century, was rebuilt in 1370 and this church in turn was demolished in the 1690s. King William III, who lived near by in Kensington Palace, contributed to the building of the next church and gave a pulpit and reading-desk: the pulpit, plain and simple, survives in the present building. There was a royal pew in the church until 1834, when a room in Kensington Palace was fitted as a chapel. Perhaps it was as a compliment to the Dutch king that the parishioners had a Dutch gable on the east end of their new church. Below it a small apse projected. At the west end they kept the tower of 1370, but in 1772 it had to be replaced by a new one, with battlements and bellcote. Photographs of the mid-19th century show the interior with a shallow segmental vault resting on columns with hybrid capitals dating from a restoration of 1797. High pews and galleries filled all the church.

The 17th-century church was found to be ruinous in the 1860s and was replaced by Sir George Gilbert Scott's present near-cathedral. The design is solemn and straight. The huge and well-proportioned tower and spire, the latter derived from St Mary Redcliffe in Bristol, is the largest and finest of the dozen Victorian spires which used to stand round Kensington Gardens and Hyde Park, punctuating the huge treescapes. Those that remain are now jostled by the lumpish hotels and so on permitted in the building free-for-all of the 1950s and early 1960s.

The correct, but uninspired and over-simplified, Early English interior of the church is probably too regular, but it is good enough to make one wish that more Victorian church architects had been given enough money to build stone vaults over their naves and aisles.

The bent and sloping cloister walk, to keep people dry on the way to their carriages, was added about 1890 and is pleasing. The architects were Micklethwaite and Somers Clarke.

Overlooking the churchyard are two painted figures of charity children which survive from a parish school built by Hawksmoor in 1713. This fine building, which had a central tower bursting up through a pediment cleft as it were by its passage, was demolished in the 19th century.

SIR CHRISTOPHER
WREN
1681   IIE2

73. ST MARY ABCHURCH
ABCHURCH LANE, BY CANNON STREET, EC4
U: Monument

The name is usually taken to have come from Up Church, since it does stand on a bit of a hill, but a 12th-century deed has 'Habechirce' which makes the matter obscure.

The church Wren built after the Great Fire is comfortably domestic without, in red brick, with a slender leaden spire. Within it has a fine dome, painted by Thornhill, having pendentives, and all resting on several corbels, a respond and, rather joltingly, one pillar. The church is nearly square and there is none of the intellectual excitement about it that there is about Wren's other domed church, ST STEPHEN WALBROOK. It was six times damaged during World War II, but all the woodwork was saved and restored. This woodwork is the chief glory. The church has kept its original pulpit steps, which is rare, and there are still dog-kennels under the churchwarden's pews, which is even rarer. There was no organ till 1822, but the fine door-cases are original. The font cover is also a good piece; figures stand in niches round a little pavilion. But best of all is the

St Mary Abchurch

altar-piece, very large, very wide and easy and loose in design, with a flop and a lightness of flowers which is quite different from the heavy splendour of most of those in City churches. And indeed it really is by Grinling Gibbons. The following letter was found in a chest in 1946:

May the 12. [1686]

Mr Chamberling
Sr.
I wold beg the favr from you to send me the 30^{li} of the olter pecs but if the gentellmen consarned does not beleave it to be not follen Anof of work then obliage me to send 20^{li} by this baerer and as soon as I kane come in towne Agane I will wait on You and satisfy You youer desire.

Sir I am youer s'ant
Grinling Gibbons.[1]

St Mary Abchurch is now one of the Guild Churches.

---

74. ST MARY ALDERMARY
QUEEN VICTORIA STREET, AT WATLING STREET, EC4
U: Mansion House

IIE2

1510
SIR CHRISTOPHER
WREN
1681–1704

Although no mention of it earlier than the 13th century has been found, this church is generally supposed from its name Aldermary to be extremely ancient; more ancient particularly, claim its partisans, than ST MARY LE BOW, which was known as New Church in the 11th century. Partisans of Bow suggest that Aldermary may mean not Eldermary, but Altera Maria, or 'the other Mary'.

Sir Henry Kebyl or Keeble provided money for rebuilding the church. Maitland quotes a long poem in which he is praised, his fame is pointed out and others are urged to acquire the same fame in the same way. From this passage the date of his generosity may be calculated:

When he this Aldermary Church
   'gan build with great Expence,
Twice Thirty Years Agon, no Doubt,
   Counting the Time from hence
Which Work began the Yeer of Christ,
   Well known of Christen Men,
One thousand and Five hundred just
   If ye will add but ten.[2]

The Keeble church looked roughly like the present one; his work was completed by two other benefactors in the early 17th century, who finished the tower as he had started it. Most of the church was destroyed in the

---

[1] R. M. Laporte Payne, *St Mary Abchurch, E.C.4.*, London 1946.
[2] Maitland, *History and Survey of London*, London 1756, vol. ii, p. 1136.

St Mary Aldermary

Great Fire. The story goes that another benefactor, Henry Rogers, offered £5,000 provided the church was rebuilt in Keeble's style. This condition Wren and his staff accepted. The result has a curious fantasy quite different from the character of building when Gothic is in season. Eastlake, the contemporary historian of the 19th-century Gothic Revival, after pointing out that Wren had been 'utterly incapable of recognising or imitating the most essential elements of [the] grace' of 'Mediaeval buildings' (sic) went on: 'yet it was better that such churches as St Mary Aldermary and St Dunstan-in-the-East should be erected than that the use of the Pointed arch should be clean forgotten in our metropolis.'[1] It is like the difference

---

[1] C. L. Eastlake, *A History of the Gothic Revival*, London 1872, p. 35.

between fairies and angels. Externally this fantasy is not much apparent: the ladder-pattern on the tower continues up unbroken from Keeble at the bottom through the 1630 builders to Wren's, or perhaps William Dickinson's, pinnacled top which was, in any case, renewed in the 19th century. Wren's pinnacles were more onion-like, and frilly at the top. The frills became dangerous and were taken down in the 1920s and used in a rock-garden at the west end. The tracery in the windows, some of which was found in the 19th century to be of pre-Fire Caen stone, matches the tower decorations. But the regularity of the internal arcades has that uniformity which no Gothic architect achieved or perhaps desired. In the spandrels are plaster decorations, charming, appropriate even to this Gothick interior, but very much of their age. And the plaster vaulting, which may be a 'free imitation of former fan vaulting'[1] is a close relation to the ceilings of churches to be built some 50 years later outside London, Hartwell, for instance; plaster Gothick, not stone Gothic. It is beautiful, but with the sweetness of confectionery.

St Mary Aldermary

Most of the fittings were cleared out in 19th-century restorations. There had been a token screen between nave and chancel, simply an extra panel at the top of the front pew, bearing a lion and a unicorn. There is now towards the west end the remains of a taller modern screen which used to

---

[1] Philip Norman, in *Transactions of St Paul's Ecclesiological Society*, vol. viii, London 1917–20, p. 148.

stretch right across the church. The old reredos was removed, and so were the panelling, the sounding-board and a gallery that had been built in 1781 to carry an organ. Stained glass was put in. There is now clear glass, which much improves the light. At some time a pierced parapet was put round church and tower; this was removed in 1911 from the church, but remains on the tower. Of the 17th-century woodwork the fine west door remains; also a handsome wooden sword-rest of 1682 and some railings, probably made up from the old altar-rails, round the font. The font is a routine piece of a good period.

This is the earliest true Gothic Revival church in London and it is significant that it should, quite literally, have its feet in the real thing. It is now one of the Guild Churches and is used for the promotion of retreats and the devotional life.

SIR CHRISTOPHER
WREN
1670–6
JAMES SAVAGE
1848–9

IIF3

75. ST MARY AT HILL
ST MARY AT HILL STREET, CITY, EC3
U: Monument

The church which was burned in the Great Fire was built at the end of the 15th century, and we know from its unusually full records that in 1491 fourpence was spent on 'a peyre of henges for the pewe dore'. The records make it clear the pews were quite substantial.

It was rebuilt to Wren's design and incorporated the former tower and some of the north and south walls, which were still standing. The last Gothic windows in these walls were not superseded till the second decade of the 19th century. Into a space as irregular as most of those he had to work in Wren put a Greek cross and above it a shallow dome on pendentives. This form cunningly relegated the irregularity to the limbs of the cross, and kept the central atrium symmetrical. The author of the contemporary account of Wren's churches in *Parentalia*, never uncritical, says the order of the four supporting columns was 'the Workman's own invention', and the two pilasters at the east end were 'of no order at all, but a specie, partly composed of the *Dorick* and *Corinthian*'. Savage's present capitals are freely copied from the Tower of the Winds at Athens, but Wren's were perhaps of the roughly similar order, probably invented by himself, which he used on the peristyle of Bow steeple. The eastern exterior aspect, which is all that now survives exactly as it was, has a cleft pediment, clumsily used.

But the real interest here lies in the woodwork. In 1827 James Savage, the rather good architect of ST LUKE'S, CHELSEA, and ST JAMES, BERMONDSEY, restored, and in 1848 he restored again, changing the decoration and fretwork to the present not very apt scheme. At this latter time the rector was J. C. Crosthwaite, musician, theologian and archaeologist. Under him, at the height of the Gothic Revival and the Tractarian Movement, Savage employed the woodcarver William Gibbs

Rogers to make some most remarkable additions to the 17th-century woodwork. The pundits say they cannot tell Rogers' work from that of Gibbons' contemporaries, but the pulpit, reading-desk and rector's pew are all dated 1849, and the lion and unicorn have 'VR' on their breasts. Regular, slow, solid, dark, circumstantial, these pieces, and particularly the stairs to pulpit and reading-desk, give a new meaning to the words 'Victorian pastiche'. You come out of the city alleys into a landscape of dark, rich oak, where the work of those to whom the style was living and of those to whom it was dead blend in a paradoxical display of Restoration furniture at its very best.

Of the six sword-rests, two came from St George, Botolph Lane.° One of these and one of the original ones commemorate Lord Mayor Beckford, d. 1770, father of William Beckford, who built Fonthill and wrote *Vathek*.

Edward Young of *Night Thoughts* was married here in 1731. Prebendary Wilson Carlile was rector here from 1892 to 1926: 'the Archbishop of the Gutter' was born a Congregationalist in 1817, took part as a layman in Moody and Sankey's 'Efforts' and, as a curate of the Church of England, founded the Church Army on the pavements of Kensington High Street in the eighties. In St Mary at Hill he preached on the Test Match and on night clubs, and instituted a Doll Sunday and a Bun Sunday, when gifts of these were made. Not often has a City Church been as full and as lively during the last century-and-a-half. His trombone, to whose notes the church used to echo, is preserved.

---

76. ST MARY, BATTERSEA
Battersea Parish Church
BATTERSEA CHURCH ROAD, SW11

IB4   BR: Clapham Junction, then buses

JOSEPH DIXON
1775

It is fairly certain that Battersea Church was granted by the Conqueror to the Abbot and Convent of Westminster. The Infirmarer of the abbey was responsible for the upkeep of the chancel and his accounts survive. Probably he ran a herb garden here. The whole convent would come to Battersea for its yearly outing, and the workmen employed at the abbey were also employed here. These included the Master Mason Henry Yevele, who worked here while he was working on the present nave of Westminster Abbey. In 1379 he built a new eastern gable to the chancel of Battersea Church. The shape of his window survives in the present east window. The medieval church appears to have had a chancel, nave and tower; about 1400 a south aisle was added, and a south chapel in 1489. In 1613 a north aisle was added, and in 1639 the tower was rebuilt.

Until the 16th century Battersea was a small village hemmed in on the south by marshes and on the north by the Thames; its inhabitants were mainly watermen. Then London developed a taste for fresh vegetables. Flemings grew them successfully in Wandsworth; the trade spread to

St Mary, Battersea

Battersea and remained its staple until the late 18th century. In 1771 the first Battersea Bridge was built and from then on mills and manufactories grew up faster and faster.[1] By the 1770s the church was rather too small, its condition rather ruinous and its churchyard rather crowded; moreover its churchwarden Joseph Dixon was very ambitious to build a new one. There was a competition, which he naturally won. (William Newton, who worked for 'Athenian' Stuart at Greenwich, entered a design for a little towerless temple with deep eaves and niches for statues, quite Mediterranean in feeling.) Dixon's church now stands very much as it was built; a riverside village church with the usual white stone dressing on its brick tower, appropriate to its position and its date, its merits useful rather than architectural. The only unusual things are the brackets which support the front of the galleries and the way in which the whole church is lifted up by the crypt. The trustees of the building decided after the outer walls were built that they wished the tower to be differently set at the west end and differently shaped. This put out the plans for the crypt which is in

---

[1] In old prints of the church a thing like a gasometer often appears behind it. This was a 'Horizontal Air Mill' which was first built to grind linseed in the 1780s. Later it ground malt, but it was never a great success. Wind, admitted through a system of venetian blinds 140 feet high, pushed round 96 double planks, which acted as sails, or rather as turbine blades.

consequence badly lit by its round windows. The east window, stonework as well as glass, was kept from the old church and replaced, 14th-century shape and 17th-century glass and stone. The old monuments, font, tables of benefactions and a few oddments were also replaced in the new church. Drawings were made, trying the pulpit centrally in the nave and at the west end, under the gallery. It was finally put at the north-east corner of the nave with the reading-desk and clerk's desk opposite it in the south-east corner. By 1826 they were amalgamated into a central three-decker which lasted until 1879. In 1842 more than £50 was spent on gold lace and trimmings for pulpit and communion table. Sir Arthur Blomfield advised on the condition of the church in 1876; he did not support a parish proposal for a new chancel. On his advice choir stalls were put in and the pews were cut down. He also designed a new basin for the font, which was put on top of the small original basin.

The monuments from the old church, several of them large and fine, are mostly in the galleries. Oliver St John, Lord Grandison, and his wife (she was disliked, and there is no commemorative comment below for her) peer out, mildly surprised so to terminate at the bust, from a neatly classical frame. Grandison had ordered his monument from Nicholas Stone, by whom it may well be. Roubiliac's large urn and bas-relief portraits of another St John, the first Lord Bolingbroke, and his second wife is not really good; and though Bolingbroke was brought up in the manor house at Battersea he seldom returned there. He composed the two epitaphs for the monument. That to his wife is appropriate, but his own implies a self-confidence he never seems to have known in the flesh. In the south gallery is a monument to Sir Edward Wynter, modifying his rather disreputable career and concentrating on his encounter with a tiger; and one in Coade stone, to John Lumden, and his daughter, with a tall nymph.[1] Also a kind of monument is the yellow and gold east window, with its innumerable coats of arms and its portraits of the royal connections of Sir John St John, Lord Grandison: Margaret Beauchamp, Henry VII, Elizabeth I.

In this church William Blake married the daughter of a local market gardener; she, being unable to sign, made her mark. From the vestry window Turner watched the sun set, and the chair he is supposed to have sat in is kept.

Behind the church the new 'Battersea Village' is thriving; in front houseboats are moored, and small boats.

---

[1] In St James, Hampstead Road, is an almost identical monument.

THOMAS HARDWICK
THE YOUNGER
1817

IIA1

77. ST MARYLEBONE[1]
Marylebone Parish Church
MARYLEBONE ROAD, OPP. YORK GATE, W1
U: Baker St

The present Marylebone Church is the fourth. In the early Middle Ages there were inhabitants enough along the Tye Bourne for there to be a little church of St John Tyburn. The famous Tyburn gallows was much further down the stream, where Marble Arch is now. St John's was demolished in 1400; a new church was built and called St Mary le Bourne, and the village began to be called by the new name. This church, small and undistinguished, is said to be that illustrated by Hogarth in the print which shows the Rake progressing into marriage. (You can also see the spider's web over the poor box.) It was demolished in 1740 and the third church was built, a very plain, small, brick one, with a high-pitched roof. The parish grew from 577 houses in 1739 to 6,200 in 1795, most of them belonging to the richer sort, but it was not until 1818 that the fourth church was built. Hardwick, a pupil of Sir William Chambers who himself had made some drawings in 1771, began it as a chapel of ease, a little to the north of the old church. It was to have had a simple Ionic portico. When the façade was already partly built there was a change of plan and the vestry decided to make the new church the parish church, giving it a more magnificent Corinthian portico, and to demote the old one to be a chapel of ease. The old one, the Parish Chapel as it came to be called, was closed in 1926, damaged in World War II, and demolished in 1949. Byron was christened there. There is now a little public garden on the site, towards the top of Marylebone High Street, and some tombstones.

The new church, a few yards to the north, was unusual in several respects. It cost about £75,000, very nearly as much as NEW ST PANCRAS. It lies north and south, facing up the fine vista of York Gate which Nash arranged to face the church while he was laying out Regent's Park. The tower is finished with a beehive stage and caryatids round, which, like the human voice with an orchestra, having once attracted attention never let go. There are two wings sticking out diagonally at the south end, presumably to provide an effective approach from the High Street, where the main entrance originally was. The interior was an extreme example of the arrangements which so shocked the Liturgical Movement 30 years later. There were two tiers of galleries all round the church resting on iron columns. The organ was in the gallery over the altar and was split into two parts, between which was a large transparency painted by Benjamin West, PRA. The light which came through this canvas was the only light at the altar end. On either side, across the diagonal wings, were family pews, one above the other, looking with their curtains very like stage boxes. Each

---

[1] See p. 161, footnote.

had a fireplace in it. This arrangement did not last long. In 1826 the stage boxes were taken out and the galleries carried round in a curve. The organ was closed up and the transparency, which had cost £800, went for ten guineas at auction.

In 1884 the church was Victorianised by Thomas Harris. He took out the top galleries at the sides and entirely remodelled the unusual south end, adding an apse. He took off the old coved ceiling and added the present rather harsh flat one. He put in orange pews, which have now faded, and the symbolic decoration, put the Ionic wood covers over the iron columns under the galleries and even provided designs from which the ladies of the parish knitted cushion covers. The interior now has very little character. A new organ, due in 1987, will halve the upper gallery at the east end. The old organ will remain.

The Brownings were married in this church, and there is a memorial room to them. The crypt of the church has been excavated and many bodies removed and reburied so that the labyrinthine vaults can be converted into a centre for healing, as a link between medicine and the Church.

SIR CHRISTOPHER
WREN
1679–80

IIE2

78. ST MARY LE BOW[1]
CHEAPSIDE, CITY, EC4
U: Mansion House

The great bell of Bow has brought the fame of this church to every English child. 'Turn again, Whittington,' it tolled (there were not until Wren's day enough bells for the full tune to have recalled him), and 'I do not know' just before the dangerous part of 'Oranges and Lemons'. To be born within its sound is, traditionally, to be a Cockney. Wren made room for twelve bells but only eight were put in then; there were ten in 1762, and twelve only in 1907. The great bell is called Cuthbert.

Wren used as foundation for his spire a Roman causeway which he found 18 feet below ground. Under the burnt-out medieval church he found a crypt, with round arches built up partly of Roman bricks, and this

St Mary le Bow in about 1930

---

[1] To avoid confusion of names, here is a list of four churches:

1. St Mary le Bow, or Bow Church, in the City.
2. St Marylebone, or St Mary le Bourne, in Marylebone, Westminster.
3. St Mary Bromley by Bow, or Bow Church, or St Mary Bromley St Leonard or, erroneously, St Leonard Bromley by Bow, in Poplar, Tower Hamlets.
4. St Mary Stratford Bow, or Stratford at Bow, or Stratford le Bow, in Poplar, Tower Hamlets.

But it is No. 3 which is on the site of the medieval convent of St Leonard Stratford Bow, not No. 4. Nos. 3 and 4 are only a few hundred yards apart. The Bow in No. 1 comes from the arches under the church; the Bow in Nos. 3 and 4 from the arches of the nearby bridge over the River Lea – 'My Lady Lea' that gets danced over in another rhyme.

too he took to be Roman. In fact it was, and still is, a fine 11th-century construction. When it was built it was above ground and had large windows. Recent excavations have revealed a bog and running water deep beneath this crypt, and this may partly account for its enormous solidity. It is thought that the name le Bow, or de Arcubus, derives from these bows, these arches in the crypt; the Court of Arches, an ecclesiastical Court of the Province of Canterbury which long sat here, also owes its name to them.

St Mary le Bow

There is an argument, unlikely ever to be settled, about which is the older church, ST MARY ALDERMARY or St Mary le Bow. Bow certainly has the showier history of the two. In 1091 a tempest blew off its roof and flung the rafters 20 feet into the 'marish ground';[1] in 1196 William FitzOsbert barricaded himself in the steeple and had to be smoked out; in 1271 the steeple fell down into the market opposite, partly as a result of the fires lit to eject him; in 1284 a goldsmith called Laurence Ducker was murdered in what was left of the steeple, and the doors and windows of the church had to be blocked up with thorns to purge the sin. After this a new steeple was slowly built up, new bells were mounted in it, and the curfew continued to be tolled. In 1512 the new steeple was completed with a flying finial, like the one Wren built later at ST DUNSTAN IN THE EAST, designed to hold five lanthorns 'whereby travellers to the city might have

---

[1] Stow, *Survey of London*, Everyman edn, London 1945, p. 227.

the better sight thereof'.[1] In the 1630s the churchwardens were excommunicated for not having seen to repairing one of these lanthorns.

The plan of Wren's church is based on that of the Basilica of Constantine in Rome but it is less than a third as big, the aisles are narrower, and there is no apse. The tripartite division of the nave and of each aisle is like the exemplar, so is the way the Corinthian columns stand against the heavy piers which carry the arches and wide vaulted ceiling, so is the lighting of the nave through clerestory windows. The reredos put up in 1706, which was surmounted by seven sham candles, was cut down in the 19th century, and so were the galleries and much of the woodwork. In 1820 George Gwilt the younger unfortunately substituted Aberdeen granite for Portland stone in the top peristyle of the spire and shortened the obelisk. He also discovered the Norman foundations.

The medieval church was set back from Cheapside. Wren, wishing his steeple to abut on the street front, set a lobby, on to which the vestry opened, between the body of the church and the tower. He wanted to build a loggia along the street as far as Bow Lane, but the plan was never fulfilled. The church was gutted in World War II, and was rebuilt between 1956 and 1964 by Laurence King, according to Wren's original design but still without the loggia. Inside, the corbel heads at the tops of the arches in the nave represent the bishop, the architect and others involved in the rebuilding. Other interior changes are some rather fetching glass and a huge hanging rood, both by John Hayward.

The steeple of Wren's Bow Church, his most separate and campanile-like, is also his loveliest. It survived the bombing, though with a noticeable slant. Its detail is more or less classical; all four orders are represented in it. The Roman Doric doorways are held to the tower in a splash of rustication and secured there by lolling cherubs and heavy fruit. Above these, windows with little balconies recall the previous gallery where Edward III watched jousts in Cheapside. Ionic pilasters enrich the bell-stage and above this rises and falls the lantern, a fountain of stone as lively and bright as water. The surmounting obelisk is a quiet gushing over of the central jet of masonry and the scroll brackets at each corner of the tower jump as high as would water dropping from the balcony of flying buttresses. And on the ping-pong ball which the jet holds suspended is a flying dragon.

JAMES GIBBS
1714–17

IID2

79. ST MARY-LE-STRAND
STRAND, WC2
U: Aldwych, Temple

The present church had a medieval predecessor known as the Church of the Nativity of Our Lady and the Innocents. The Lord Protector Somerset, wishing to build his palace between the river and the road to Westminster,

---

[1] Stow, op. cit., p. 230.

pushed the road further north and, promising to rebuild, pulled down the parish church and several other buildings. He did not rebuild, and for nearly 200 years the parishioners used the Savoy Chapel, taking their bell with them. Only when the 1711 Commission began to build did they get a church of their own again.

The exterior of a church is not as denominational as its interior. Gibbs, himself a Catholic, had just returned from Italy when he was commissioned to build this, the first church of Queen Anne's Fifty. He made it engagingly Roman outside and then when it came to the interior he found himself unable to do more than repeat quietly the exterior proportions and idioms, and cover them with a rather busy and dispiriting ceiling. The church is logical and well adapted, with its cheerfully corsetted air, to the rowdy site; the exterior even suggests a contemporary Roman palazzo. There were changes in his commission: at first the church was to be towerless and to have a 250-foot column with a statue of Queen Anne on it 80 feet away. The death of Queen Anne put this plan out of date and a steeple was called for. The church was already half-built; but Gibbs did his best, and on the walls he had standing, he managed to put up a good if rather thin tower. The statue of Queen Anne he proposed to put on top of the little domed portico. He also proposed statues in the niches in the bays of the lower order. They were never made, and Queen Anne went to Queen Anne's Gate, where she still is. But the church, now all clean and spruce, is a success, and swans charmingly down the Strand with ST CLEMENT DANES in its wake.

---

80. ST MARY, PADDINGTON
PADDINGTON GREEN, W2
IB3   U: Edgware Road

JOHN PLAW
1788–91

Until the 19th century Paddington was an obscure village with an obscure village church. The living was so small that when a 16th-century Bishop of London was charged with appointing his retiring porter to it he justified himself by saying its very smallness was proof of the porter's honest intentions. A church of uncertain age, in which John Donne had preached his first sermon, was pulled down in 1678 and replaced by another, which prints show very small and rustic. This in turn became ruinous and in 1788 John Plaw, who later emigrated to Canada, began the present one. The design is quite unusual for its symmetry and rationality. It begins with a simple brick cube from each side of which grows a substantial square apse. Two of these apses have porticoes of different sorts. Above is a stylish cupola with coupled columns diagonally set. The interior is small and complex and lively. Within the central cube is a tetrastyle atrium, the columns bearing a shallow dome on pendentives. Each of the four apses has a shallow segmental vault and the gallery wobbles round nine sides of a dodecagon. Perhaps there is rather too much going on for the eye to be delighted, but it is certainly interesting.

St Mary, Paddington

There are good monuments of around 1800. The church was restored by Raymond Erith in 1972; the floor and the box pews were repaired, a new chandelier and organ provided and the whole tidied up and embellished. Alas no-one can clear away the motorway that sails past the church some yards away; but it was tied money from the land the motorway took up that allowed a modest parish to restore its church to such a high standard.

1714
Tower c. 1739

81. ST MARY'S, ROTHERHITHE
Rotherhithe Parish Church
ST MARYCHURCH ST, SE16

IE3 U: Rotherhithe

Of the Thames-side churches rebuilt in the 18th century, Wapping, Woolwich, the Poplar Chapel,° this is the most metropolitan. It is built of yellow brick with stone dressings and has a neatly defined cornice and parapet. Strongly marked doorways and well related gallery and aisle windows restrainedly decorate the exterior. Tower and spire are less well related. The brick tower seems built for the parish, the stone spire as a landmark for the river.

Rotherhithe is a name of Saxon derivation, and a church has stood here certainly since the 13th century, when the Abbot of Bermondsey held the advowson. In the west wall above the organ gallery are a few uncovered stones, all that remain, together with the foundations of the tower, of the old church. It was lower than the present one and, before the Thames was embanked, in constant danger of flooding. The Reformation passed placidly, with one rector surviving from Henry VIII to Elizabeth; in the following century, too, the rector lasted from 1611 to 1654. He was a moderate Puritan and probably did not acquire the symbolical portrait of Charles I which the church now owns. Although over £1,000 was spent on repairs in 1687 the church's foundations had been nibbled away by the tides, and in 1714 it had to be rebuilt. The parishioners failed to induce the Commissioners of the Fifty to pay anything towards their new church, and the tower, and probably the apse, were finished 20 or 30 years later.

The barrel ceiling, slightly lopsided, is supported by four large columns. These, which hide oak trees within, are of a private order, a combination of Tuscan and Ionic. The sanctuary apse is a curious composition of curved surfaces. The reredos, although deprived of its segmental pediment, is handsome, and the mid-Victorian desire for chancels was here satisfied with a merely symbolic quantity of ironwork in the two eastern bays. The chancel furniture is mainly made up of wood from the north and south galleries which were taken down in 1867. The pulpit was cut down from an early 19th-century three-decker: the original bulging and be-cherubbed pulpit has vanished.

The glass in the chancel windows is a mixture of 16th-century German, early 19th-century English and modern English. The west gallery is supported on wrought iron stanchions with frilly tops, as were also the north and south galleries until their demolition.[1]

Lemuel Gulliver, embarking at Rotherhithe, travelled far from home. Prince Lee Boo, son of Abba Thule, Rupack or King of the Island of Coorooraa, one of the Pelew or Palos Islands, came on nearly as strange a journey and, in 1784, died in Rotherhithe in his 20th year and is buried in the churchyard. His father, reputed a cannibal, treated the shipwrecked crew of the East Indiaman *Antelope* with such gentleness that in gratitude her captain brought Lee Boo to England to show him the sights.[2] In 1892 the Secretary of State for India caused a plaque to be put up in the church to celebrate the kindness of the barbarous people.

The church and its environs preserve the air of a Victorian riverside village. But as with old Battersea village the area is undergoing a certain gentrification. The once active warehouses, long fallen into disuse, are being snapped up, now serving as desirable residences and studios; a southern counterpart to the upwardly mobile world of Limehouse and Wapping, where only the churches – ST ANNE'S, great, and ST JOHN, a mere tower, carry on unchanged.

---

[1] Cf. ST MAGNUS THE MARTYR.

[2] See 'A Letter to Madam Blanchard' in E. M. Forster, *Two Cheers for Democracy*, London 1951; and George Keate, *An Account of the Pellew Islands*, London 1789.

82. ST MARY WOOLNOTH

NICHOLAS
HAWKSMOOR
1719–27

CORNER OF LOMBARD STREET AND KING WILLIAM STREET, CITY, EC3

IIF2

U: Bank

The medieval church, rebuilt in 1442 and 1486, was important enough to have a little cloister for the parson to pace in, playing at monks. It was not entirely destroyed in the Great Fire and was patched up before 1677 by Wren or somebody from his office in a manner roughly matching the old architecture. Within 40 years it was ruinous again, and Hawksmoor put up an entirely new church, which the 1711 Commissioners paid for after the parishioners petitioned them.

St Mary Woolnoth

John Newton was incumbent here from 1780 until his death in 1807. He was an early Evangelical who had served in slave ships in his youth, and was converted in a storm during a trick at the wheel. He inspired Wilberforce in his campaign against slavery, and wrote the hymns 'Amazing Grace' and 'Glorious things of Thee are Spoken'. 'The old African blasphemer' he called himself until his death. He came to St Mary Woolnoth from Olney, where he and the poet Cowper had together reached an extreme of self-accusation.

St Mary Woolnoth

Like all Hawksmoor's buildings St Mary Woolnoth is a work of the very highest refinement of intelligence. Nothing is there simply to hold something else up, or to keep the rain out. The interior consists of one square standing on four groups of three columns enclosed in a wider, lower square. A sort of clerestory is thus formed which has a large semicircular window in each side. The handling of volume within volume suggests the Argument from Design: if the church is built like that, there is necessarily a place appropriate for the altar; if the world is like this, there is necessarily a place for God. The altar space – one could not call it chancel – is held into the design. But the fully baroque black baldaquin, derived from Bernini's in St Peter's, with its crowned and twisted columns and gold putti, is in passionate contrast to the rationally interpenetrating volumes of the church. The same function, that is, contradictions within rationality, is fulfilled by the famous recesses in the north elevation on Lombard Street, each with its inset pediment curved forward and borne by columns set on skewed and concave pedestals. All is as if seen through water, through a groundswell, yet blindly, and it is perhaps only in this one little wall that the hypnotic splendour of the continental baroque reached London.

Altogether, the little church has fared badly. In 1876 Butterfield took out the side galleries but, since the fronts of them were too richly carved to throw away, he stuck them high up on to the walls with their pillars, which are rather like those at ST ALFEGE, GREENWICH, dangling from them. This is a meaningless arrangement, although it is nice to have them somewhere. The pulpit he lowered but left its sounding-board high. The relation between the two objects is now terrible, though either alone is magnificent. He took out the high pews, put the organ down in a corner, and raised the floor of the chancel, covering it with polychrome tiles. The walls he patterned square in polychrome, and the ceiling he spattered with stars.[1] The painting on the walls has gone, but the great black baldaquin over the altar is still bumping its head against the soffit of the chancel arch where it was left by Butterfield. The little old organ has been put back where it belongs, but a large new one has been introduced on the floor of the church and spoils its proportions.

The façade has also fared badly. Hawksmoor's design was, like everything of his, an utterly original, nearly cranky, composition made up of elements new and familiar. From a west front rusticated into monolithic pugnacity from which the doorway and the window above it have been ground out,[2] rises a tower composed of first a podium, then a Corinthian colonnade, correctly cheerful, and finally of two small square turrets which, by virtue of a kind of offhand plainness, seem to be beyond the habitat of custom or the arc of reason. The whole is beautiful. People have always wanted to do away with the whole church but it was saved five times between the 1840s and the 1920s, not because of its beauty, but

---

[1] A letter to *The Times* in 1952 commended this ceiling, which is still there, as an authentic pattern to those who were restoring Wren's churches.
[2] This part of the façade is markedly similar to the north front of Seaton Delaval which Vanbrugh was building in Northumberland at much the same time.

because of its prestige as the Lord Mayor's Church. In 1897–1900 the old City and South London Tube built the Bank station under the church, removing the dead from the vaults, completely undermining the whole church, supporting it on steel girders, and sinking lift shafts directly below it. No harm, and good engineering. But then they made two entrances to the station and threw up round them some screens and poster boards which are still there, and are now the property of London Transport. They blatantly and unncessarily cut off the windows at either side of the façade and unbalance the proportions of this major work of a great architect, situated at the very centre and vortex of the City of London.

St Mary Woolnoth is one of the Guild Churches and is particularly concerned with the relief of stress in the City; meaning psychological stress.

83. ST MARY MAGDALENE, BERMONDSEY
Bermondsey Parish Church
BERMONDSEY STREET, SE16

IIF4   U: London Bridge

Mainly 1680

This little church, which owes its charm to a confusion of styles, is best seen from the churchyard-cum-public garden beside it; the faery Gothick turret rides in a gently scatty manner above the rather large and naïve window in the round gable of the 17th-century porch. The whole is held together by the unity of beige plaster.

At the end of the 13th century references appear to a church of St Mary Magdalene for the 'servants and tenants' of the great Cluniac Abbey of Bermondsey, which was founded two centuries earlier. Under abbots called 'Lords of Barmsey' the abbey grew rich and powerful and the little lay church stood in its shadow as ST MARGARET'S still stands under Westminster Abbey. In time it became a parish church. At the Dissolution of the Monasteries the revenues of the abbey were settled on Sir Thomas Pope, a Roman Catholic, who used them in part to found Trinity College at Oxford. The abbey fell into ruins while the parish church continued. The churchwardens' accounts for 1679 show that for 16s 8d one could still be buried 'in the Cloysters' – presumably of the abbey. The utter expunging of the abbey is striking. Cars and lorries now drive up the nave, which lay along Abbey Street, and every Friday the New Caledonian Market is held in the main courtyard, which was Bermondsey Square until it was bombed. All that now survives is one stone cross bearing the consecration mark of the abbey, which was found in 1922 during the building of the petrol station in Tower Bridge Road and may still be seen there, and a pair of hinge pins at 7 Grange Walk.

In the early 17th century the medieval parish church became ruinous. The present church was built in 1680 and incorporates at the west end two 13th-century arches from the original church. The architect is unknown,

St Mary Magdalene,
Bermondsey

but his style was derived from Wren's. His tower, resting on the medieval arches inside, had a little dome and lantern rising on a square plan, like the Frenchified pattern used by Wren at ST BENET, PAUL'S WHARF. This has been replaced. His interior, which survives, rests on giant Tuscan orders with entablatures which break for one bay on each side; the shallow groined vault of the ceiling is thus made cruciform, the general effect being rather like Wren's ST MAGNUS THE MARTYR before it was altered. But the cross is Latin, with its foot unexpectedly in the chancel. The south aisle of the medieval church had been widened in 1610 and the architect of 1680 followed the earlier plan. His handling of the asymmetry has been stultified by the putting up in 1793 of aisle galleries which rest on tiny columns not related to the main columns. One gallery fetches up right against the main columns, the other one comes only half-way across the south aisle which is now closed off and used as a social club and for services when attendance is particularly low. What remains of the 1680 woodwork is a pleasant reredos which keeps the painted panels of Moses and Aaron as well as the Paternoster, Decalogue and Creed, a square churchwardens' pew at the west end and the gallery above it. There are two graceful candelabra of 1699 and 1703.

In 1829 the old rectory was pulled down; the north wall of the church was thus exposed and threatened to collapse. Repairs were entrusted to one George Porter and led from one thing to another so that by the next year the 17th-century dome and lantern on the tower were destroyed, a schoolroom which rested on columns over the pavement at the west end was removed to expose a medieval traceried window and the present Gothick west front and turret were substituted. In 1883 the chancel was extended to take choir-stalls.

The famous Bermondsey Dish housed in the Victoria and Albert Museum belongs to this church. In the middle of it is a charming engraving, keyed to hold enamel, of a lady putting an enormous helm on the head of a kneeling knight. It was probably made about 1325 and may have belonged to Edward II.

Some of the tombstones along the south wall of the church, outside, are entertainingly macabre in a statistical way. In 1611 a Puritan rector, Edward Elton, himself cut down and chopped into pieces the Bermondsey maypole.

84. ST MARY MAGDALEN, PADDINGTON
WOODCHESTER STREET, W2
IB3   U: Warwick Avenue

G. E. STREET
1868–78
Crypt Chapel:
NINIAN COMPER
1895

St Mary Magdalen was one of the several successful churches built by and for a particular priest in a poor area during the Tractarian Movement. As building progressed but slowly, architect and priest were able to give it all the thought they wanted, and the effect is strong and serious. The church is now the visual gathering point of the Warwick Estate, council-built development of three-floor terrace houses with the occasional tower block, pleasantly leafed and lawned and, on the north side, edged by the Grand Junction Canal.

The raison d'être of the church's asymmetry has vanished with the previous street plan; its high spire, turret and chancel apse now dominate their surroundings with almost military solidarity.

Street it was who introduced Italian Gothic to England, but there is little of it here. His detail often tends to scratchiness: his big Westminster church, St James the Less, is all over spikey railings and sharp corners and jagged brickwork, inside and out; the tower even has slit windows implying fortification and firing across into the Vauxhall Bridge Road.

St Mary Magdalen is tall, decorated all over inside, including the ceiled wagon-roof; saints lean from their niches in the spaces between the windows and the arcade (they were carved by Thomas Earp). The chancel is high up steps, and seems far away as the lowered vault and dim light plays games with the perspective.

Beneath the church in the crypt is a small chapel by Ninian Comper – a seeming three-dimensional enlargement of a blue and gold miniature. The effect is endearing.

C. F. PORDEN
1822–4

85. ST MATTHEW'S, BRIXTON

BRIXTON HILL, SW2

ID4 U: Brixton

This is the most important of the four churches built in Lambeth with the help of the Waterloo Commission and, alone with ST JAMES, BERMONDSEY, of all the Commission Churches in London, is worthy of comparison with that magnificent private venture of the same time NEW ST PANCRAS, on which, under the Inwoods, Porden had worked. The Commission found one-half of the cost of St Matthew's, and the people of the new villas in rural Brixton found the other.

Porden's church is Doric throughout, and of a Doricness like pugs to poodles. The west portico is for once big enough; the powerful entasis of the columns is answered by the equally powerful batter (the inward inclination of the verticals) on the door-jambs behind. The windows are battered in the same way and there is a great battered crypt-doorway half sunk in the ground.

The inside is unfortunately no longer visible: it has been completely cleared and refilled with the trappings of a community centre. It was formerly very fine. Even the organ case was battered Doric; and the altar-rails were a Doric colonnade of iron. The interior was forthrightly built round receding rectilinear spaces, nothing softened, no persuasion; even the setting of the windows under the galleries was inflexibly rectilinear. All tended to the last recession of all; two more Doric columns flanked the east window through which came not immediate daylight but what was left after daylight had crossed a room in the east tower. This window was originally plain, then held a tropical sunrise with a very green palm. Originally, too, the rectilinearity was broken by the straight, banistered staircases which starting one under each gallery climbed diagonally, one to the towering reading-desk, one to the yet more towering pulpit. These, cyclostyle with Doric pilasters, bore crimson cloths. Those two diagonals, one suspects, because they alone contradicted it, drew together and enlivened the horizontal mass.

The western vestibules were admirable; here also Porden contradicted the receding rectangles by staircases which laced diagonally up past the forthright fist and forearm of the Doric pillars.

Outside, the east end is sombre and fine; receding spaces again, more subtle than inside. The tower stands sensibly on the ground and rises in a manner at once majestic and learned until, at the very top, it breaks into a little flicker of silliness. It is as if someone had tickled it.

The Budd mausoleum, away through the gravestones of the churchyard, is worth looking at for an example of the pomposity which coexisted in the Grecian movement with the frequent meanness and the occasional grandeur. It is by one Day of Camberwell.

86. ST MATTHIAS, HACKNEY
formerly Stoke Newington
MATTHIAS ROAD, N16

ID1   U: Highbury and Islington

WILLIAM
BUTTERFIELD
1849–53

Try to approach along Howard Road; from there the great saddleback tower with its bitter angle, yet also like Dürer's praying hands, stands out with tremendous force. This was an unusually cheap church, £7,000, and the workers refused to accept pay for overtime. When the present (1985) incumbent came here, there was an old woman who could remember picking watercress in the cressbeds across the road. As you walk towards the west front another strong oddity begins to take over from the tower; the traceried window has a large buttress right up the middle of it. This derives from an arrangement, already odd, at the medieval abbey church of Dorchester in Oxfordshire. Butterfield makes it much odder by a heavy

St Matthias, Hackney

St Matthias, Hackney

emphasis suggesting the chimney of some great medieval kitchen. (He has something of the same at ST ALBAN'S HOLBORN.)

The interior is at once powerful and pleasing, and the four corbels at the 'crossing' arches are things of great beauty. The church was burned out in World War II and has been correctly rebuilt, but without the decoration it had been covered with. There is no doubt this gives it a lighter feeling than at, say, ST AUGUSTINE, QUEEN'S GATE; it also shows the strength underlying the polychrome.

87. ST MICHAEL AND ALL ANGELS
BLACKHEATH PARK, GREENWICH, SE3
IF4   BR: Blackheath

GEORGE SMITH
1830

This church is one of the more extravagant and engaging of the Gothic Revival before solemnity struck, and obedience to medieval precedent. It was built as a chapel of ease to Charlton Church, but in practice it was more like a private chapel for Blackheath Park Estate, newly built on the Wricklemarsh Manor estate. While the church was 'Gothic', the villas around were Italianate. It is a homogeneous construction with the spire, sometimes known as the Devil's toothpick, at the east end. The pinnacle is used as enthusiastically as the column had been two centuries before: in the reredos, along the nave parapets and at the base of the spire. This is so high and so thin and so odd, one feels plain and dumpy looking at it. And the body of the church, approached from Blackheath, looks plain and dumpy too. The eastern tower has caused the architect difficulty inside, for while the west end is deep and suitable for a chancel, the east window just gives on to a ringing chamber. This ringing chamber has the true east window, a great portmanteau affair stretching up to light the belfry as well. A series of roof-timbers shaped like the Bridge of Sighs in Venice make the interior surprising; it is sprightly in a flimsily elegant way.

88. ST MICHAEL, CAMDEN ROAD
CAMDEN TOWN, NW1
IC2   U: Camden Town

G. F. BODLEY and
T. GARNER
1880–94

This part of Camden Town is martyr to traffic, and St Michael's (liturgical) 'west' end lies hard against the Camden Road. The entrance to the church is at the 'north-west' corner, and you pause, at the top of two short flights of steps, parted half-way by the first pier of the arcade, before stepping down into the body of the church. There is dark glass (from elsewhere, and by Pugin) in the lower windows, but light streams across the upper parts of the building and the whole effect is watery, almost submarine – an effect now enhanced by moist decay and ruinous furniture. Church life continues in a tiny tunnel-like chapel in the 'north-east' corner, where entry is now obtained. The 'Gothic' here is 'English Decorated'; inside the stone is pale; outside, stock brick does little to suggest the melancholy beauties within.

SIR CHRISTOPHER
WREN
1686–1713

89. ST MICHAEL PATERNOSTER ROYAL

COLLEGE HILL, CITY, EC4

IIE3   U: Mansion House

The 'Royal' probably comes from the fact that College Hill was full of merchants who imported Bordeaux wines from La Réole. The old church is mentioned in the 13th century, but it was rebuilt by Dick Whittington who in 1423 was buried according to his will in 'St Michael de Paternoster-church in Riola'. He founded there also a college of five priests and an almshouse; in both institutions his soul was to be prayed for. Except that he was indeed Mayor of London three times, his history bears no relation to that still acted on a hundred stages every Christmas. He

*St Michael
Paternoster Royal*

dealt wisely with the king and charitably with his fellow-citizens: cat, ship, kitchen, Dame Alice, turn again, bonds in the fire, all the rest, have been traced by scholars to myths current as far afield as Scandinavia and Persia before Whittington lived and long before they were first, about 1600, attached to his name. His body was once or twice disturbed, but is perhaps still under St Michael's. His monument was destroyed in the Great Fire.

The turret of Wren's ST MICHAEL is circular where that at ST JAMES GARLICKHYTHE is square: the effect is thus rather more baroque, though St James makes up for this by showing a scrolled pediment behind the tower. The interior, rearranged by Butterfield in 1866 but still rich in woodwork, was badly knocked about in World War II. Nothing was done for many years, but in 1958 a suggestion by the Royal Fine Arts Commission that the church should be demolished and only the tower saved was countered by the City Corporation, who insisted that all should be saved and form part of a public park alongside. By 1964 this was done, and Whittington Gardens and a Whittington Hall came into existence.

Inside, the original pulpit and reredos have been restored, and combine with furniture imported from various other churches and some made new.

The church is used as a mission to seamen. Sunday afternoon prayers are in Chinese.

---

90. NEW ST PANCRAS
St Pancras Parish Church
EUSTON ROAD, UPPER WOBURN PLACE, WC1
IIC1   U: Euston Square

WILLIAM INWOOD
and HENRY WILLIAM
INWOOD
1819–22

After the New Road was opened – that is to say, the present Marylebone, Euston and Pentonville Roads – a new kind of resident came to St Pancras. By 1816 the forces of respectability in the vestry of OLD ST PANCRAS decided the time had come for a break with the past. An Act of Parliament was procured empowering Trustees, appointed subject to a property qualification, to raise £40,000 to build a new church. Three years later the sum was doubled. The dying spirit of Old St Pancras brought the vestry to fisticuffs once or twice and sent pickpockets to the laying of the foundation stone, but before the new church was completed or the old church demoted to be a chapel of ease the age of peace and prosperity had begun.

New St Pancras cost £77,000 to build and was the most expensive church in London since St Paul's. William Inwood, a local worthy, and his son Henry William won a competition for the design, beating, luckily, Francis Bedford, and Rickman, a prolific designer of churches in the north.[1] Henry William had travelled in Greece and written on the Erechtheum, so between them father and son put up a cunning

---

[1] Thomas Rickman also systematised the familiar terminology: 'Norman', 'Early English', 'Decorated', and 'Perpendicular'.

rearrangement of it. They gave it a segmental apse instead of one of its porticoes, put the caryatid tribunes on both sides instead of only one, and put up three diminishing Towers of the Winds, one above the other, for a spire. The caryatids are terracotta and have cast iron stanchions inside; when made they were rather too tall and had to have slices taken out of their middles to fit. All the decoration is slavishly accurate, but it does not matter. The interior is slightly claustrophobic with its low, straight galleries, but the great hexastyle round the apse with its columns of scagliola, a mixture of plaster, marble chippings and glue, is impressive, and so is the original high pulpit. Both inside and out, St Pancras is rich, grand and civilised, the flower, really, of a revival which, unlike its successor, did not last long and never had a chance to inflict 'restoration' on what came before it.

Old Cape Town Cathedral, which was pulled down in 1953, was a copy of New St Pancras.

GOUGH and ROUMIEU
1848

IC2

91. OLD ST PANCRAS
PANCRAS ROAD, NW1
U: Mornington Crescent

In the Victorian Norman style with a by-pass half-timbered top to the tower: rather charming. A railway runs close beside. Fine old monuments in the graveyard, including a very grand one by the great architect Sir John Soane for himself and his wife. And yes, here is some ancient stonework exposed. Inside is a good run of 17th-century monuments: clearly an old parish church rebuilt. The railway and the flats: what have they encroached on? A cheerful village: prosperity, cow-dung, linen and lavender, turning slowly to a prosperous suburb: high principles, good food, good openings?

Let us start with Misson[1] a widely travelled man, the author about 1700 of the standard guides for the Grand Tour. St John in the Lateran at Rome, he says, is the 'Head and Mother . . . of all Christian Churches, if you except that of –' what? hazy knowledge suggests St Peter's, Santa Sophia, the Holy Sepulchre. No; 'that of St Pancrace, under Highgate near London'. Oh? Really? Let us go backwards. Norden,[2] the Elizabethan topographer, believes it is older than St Paul's, and describes it as he saw it: 'all alone as utterly forsaken, old and weather-beaten'; and then: 'Walk not there late.' One can follow a trickle of history further back, encouraged by a tradition that it may have been founded by St Augustine, but the first certain evidence of its existence dates from the second half of the 12th century.

---

[1] Maximilian Misson, *A New Voyage to Italy*, 5th edn, London 1739, vol. ii, pt. 2, p. 590.
[2] John Norden, *Speculum Britanniae. The First part. An historical and chorographical discription of Middlesex. By the travail and view of John Norden*, London 1593, p. 38.

Dedicated to the saint who was horribly martyred at 14 and became the avenger of broken oaths; St Pancras in the Fields, Pancross, Pancridge; beyond the mountain of cinders which accumulated for centuries at King's Cross and was sold to the Russian Government in 1826. One service a month. A 17th-century vicar spent some years in gaol for debt, an 18th-century vicar was run over and killed by a drunken carman. 'Thou Pankridge Parson' was a term of abuse in 1612 and Ben Jonson after a quarrel called Inigo Jones 'Pancridge Earl and Marquis of Tower Ditch'. One in a play of 1617 surprised in a compromising position says: 'We were wedded by the hand of heaven ere this work began.' 'At Pancridge, I'll lay my life on it,' is the scoffing answer. Here were buried tragic figures: Godwin and his wife, Mary Wollstonecraft, who had died giving birth to the future Mary Shelley, the author of *Frankenstein*. Indeed, Shelley first saw her here, visiting her parents' tomb; those early anarchist innocents were moved to Bournemouth in 1851 when the railway was built. No corpse stayed longer at St Pancras than it could help. Pascal Paoli, who sometimes, at the head of his Corsican brigands, drove invaders out of his native country, and sometimes dined with Reynolds and Goldsmith. He died in misery, his leonine integrity having become inconvenient to all the powers. The royalist exiles of the 1790s, the Marquis of this and the Comte et Abbé of that, who pranced disconsolately to Stowe when they could get the invitation, went to Mass at St Aloysius, Camden Town, when they could not, lived on air, and died intriguing: they were buried here, for they believed St Pancras was the last church in England at which mass was publicly said in Elizabeth's reign, or that in each church dedicated to St Pancras prayers were said for the souls of those buried in all the others. The Chevalier d'Éon, who sometimes found it convenient in carrying out Louis XV's secret missions to dress as a woman and was ordered by Louis XVI to dress as a woman for the rest of his life; who was asked whether he was not troubled by the loss of his sword and answered that he might do as much with his slipper; on whose sex bets amounting to £120,000 were laid; whom a jury charted by Lord Chief Justice Mansfield ruled to be a woman; who died of a wound got in a public demonstration of fencing in woman's clothes and who was at last found to be a man – he lies here too; then according to one story St Pancras was a bishop of Taormina.

And all points downwards; the fourth Earl Ferrers who shot his steward in cold blood and got drunk while the man was dying. He drove to be hanged at Tyburn in his own landau and lay 14 feet under the tower till he was removed. No risks taken with him. Joseph Wall, Governor of Senegal, who proposed marriage to a girl in such a way that she prosecuted him for assault and defamation, and he was convicted. Later he had a sergeant beaten to death, was arrested, escaped and gave himself up after 20 years. Tyburn; St Pancras; and the rope he was hanged with sold for a shilling an inch. Jonathan Wild, who had an organisation with an office and branch offices, a ship for export, warehouses, and a training school, all devoted to searching, at a charge, for goods he himself had caused to be stolen. He bought immunity by helping the authorities to arrest freelance criminals who did not work for him. He was hanged at last, buried at St Pancras, 'resurrected' two days later, and his skeleton was on public exhibition until 1860. A spy, hanged, drawn and quartered; a highwayman, shot in the act; a woman who had been hanged for forgery, but not well enough, and had survived for 30 years; many killed duelling at Chalk Farm, and with them a whole rout of murderers, blackmailers, pimps. With them, too, the unhappy: suicides, some of whom, knowing where they would be buried, even hanged themselves from the trees nearby to save their betters trouble; a Roman priest, who willed that his heart should be preserved in spirits at Douai; a Turkish ambassador, dead far from home, whose body was galloped all way to the churchyard at night and was buried by torchlight with Muslim rites; two 18th-century 'cellists; a man alleged to be a Jesuit earl: the last survivor of the Black Hole of Calcutta, aged ninety; 1,300 people in a pit, who died of cholera. The railways from St Pancras Station ploughed up this ancient mound of infamy and misery and a crowd of headstones was later planted thick in pairs round a tree by someone with an eye for things: they cluster there radial, lifting round the trunk, leaning, surging, like so many Paolos and Francescas in the gale. Later a coroner's court was built in a corner of the graveyard, where misery is broadly classified, intention expurgated and extenuated, and more clay returned to the thick clay it preferred.

And how shall we get on, those of us who prefer to remain above? We heard two stories when we visited St Pancras:

'Hey, son, what do you think you're playing at with that thing?'

'Football, Mister';

and then again, if you do happen to turn up a skeleton with a fine strong jaw of perfectly preserved teeth, and yours are worn out, and your dentist says it is possible, well, why not? This is the right relationship with our ancestors: with their teeth we can eat bread made of the corn their dust has nourished; with their experience we can begin to correct their mistakes.

92. ST PAUL'S, COVENT GARDEN
COVENT GARDEN, WC2
U: Covent Garden

INIGO JONES, 1633
Rebuilt by THOMAS HARDWICK THE YOUNGER 1796

IC2

An Earl of Bedford had Inigo Jones build the first square in England, the 'piazzas'[1] of Covent Garden, and in it was to be a church. A story first recorded by Horace Walpole goes that Bedford asked Jones for a simple church, little more than a barn, and that Jones promised him the handsomest barn in England. The handsome barn was built, was consecrated in 1638 as a chapel of ease to ST MARTIN-IN-THE-FIELDS, and was made a parish church in 1645.

[1] In 17th-century England 'piazza' was believed to mean arcade, or cloister: hence the plural use for Jones's square, the houses of which had ground-floor arcades.

The architectural history of this church is obscure. As it was originally built it had two walls running out from the east portico which contained rustic gateways at half-length and ended in pavilion-like houses. These, like the rest of Jones's square, have disappeared.[1] St Paul's had either one or two little bell-turrets on its vast chalet roof. A committee from ST BRIDE'S, FLEET STREET, went in 1685 to see the galleries but there were alterations made in the 17th and early 18th centuries. In 1725 Lord Burlington restored the portico at his own expense to what he thought Jones had meant. In 1788 the younger Thomas Hardwick faced part or all of the church in stone, but in 1795 it was destroyed by fire. He rebuilt it, allegedly on the same lines. In 1872 Butterfield cleared out the galleries and rearranged and decorated the inside. In 1888 a bell-turret was removed. Quite recently the west end has been rebuilt.

It is best to regard the present building with caution: it is certainly not exactly like Jones's, and may be quite unlike it. The Tuscan eastern portico with its great depth and vast pediment and eaves is probably like the original, but even here there is certainly one change; the great side-arches, admirable though they are, are not Jones's idea. Old views show that his were much narrower, like the windows behind the columns. In any case, this portico belongs squarely to the tradition which stems from Vitruvius' idea of what Etruscan temples were like.

Perhaps the present unpainted ceiling, in which the proportions of the three vast panels are excellent, bears a relation to Jones's, which was painted by Matthew Goodrich.

The church is now rather grubby and isolated; the east end dominates the refurbished Covent Garden Piazza and buskers frolic under the portico, but entry to the church involves a circuitous route round corners and through alleys. In 1975 a plan was suggested to move the altar and reopen the doors on to the Piazza, which would certainly be good for the appeal fund.

Grinling Gibbons, ironically, is buried in this simplest of churches, and Thomas Arne is commemorated. Nowadays it is actors who are memorialised here; among them, many glittering figures: Boris Karloff, Charles Cochrane, Ivor Novello, David Blair, Margaret Rutherford, Eric Portman, Noël Coward, Charlie Chaplin, Vivien Leigh, Lilian Baylis, Hattie Jacques and Edith Evans. In the little garden through which a path leads to the door at the west end, more workaday actors are recalled by a label under a bush or against a shrub.

---

[1] John Summerson, in *Architecture in Britain 1530–1830*, London 1953, p. 83, says Jones 'availed himself' of plates in Vignola for these walls and the Tuscan portico of the church in the middle.

THOMAS ARCHER
1712–30

IE4

93. ST PAUL'S, DEPTFORD
DEPTFORD HIGH STREET, SE8
BR: Deptford

Archer travelled four years on the continent, and there he developed a passionate and intelligent feeling for Italian architecture which displays itself magnificently in this church. It was one of the Fifty, and stands not far from St Nicholas, Deptford, out of which parish its own was carved. Like other large churches built in districts which have since lost their prosperity, St Paul's has little history and has been little altered, except for rearrangements of the pulpit and in the chancel. The latter, a small apse

St Paul's, Deptford

St Paul's, Deptford

with an unpierced Palladian screen, is the weakest part of the interior, perhaps because the Italian inspiration failed when confronted with the more moderate needs of the Anglican liturgy. High above the east window, now filled with pre-Raphaelitish glass, there is grisaille painting surrounded with painted red drapery. Overall, the inside is very fine: an ambiguous Greek cross, the angles filled in with large-windowed chambers on two floors, which give on to the nave with theatre-like boxes. Perhaps Archer had been in Rome and remembered those in St Peter's; perhaps he had been in Venice and remembered the ambiguous Greek cross of the sanctuary at Palladio's church of the Redentore. The magnificent ponderous mass of the ceiling is proportionate to the great Corinthian columns which support it.

Archer's triangular rectory, which faced on to the churchyard, was, alas, pulled down in 1882, but the churchyard is still a wide and proper setting for the church. Set high on a plinth, it is approached on three sides by staircases, those on the west, radial, seeming to gather support for the west portico, those on the north and south prickly and re-entrant. The plan of the plinth, which can be seen in Archer's own drawing in the King's Maps at the British Museum, is like a decorative frame. The rusticated pilasters, the huge keystones to the recessed and deeply

shadowed windows, the heavy pediments, all have a vivid rigidity which reaches thundering proportions in the great four-columned semi-circular Tuscan portico. Inside it, all is darkness; and from this rises the tower, on plan ambiguous between circular and square,[1] with pilasters two deep, and smooth urns. Above the clock stage the spire dwindles and from all aspects but the west it looks suddenly feeble. Perhaps this is again a failure of the Italian when first faced with English needs: or perhaps, as at ST JOHN'S, SMITH SQUARE, Archer's intentions were not fully carried out.

The furnishings inside are simpler than Archer had wished, having been reduced by that mean attendant on the English baroque, John James. The pulpit was cut down in 1873.

ST PETER AD VINCULA
see TOWER OF LONDON

94. ST PETER'S, WALWORTH
LIVERPOOL GROVE, SE17
ID3   U: Elephant and Castle

SIR JOHN SOANE
1823–5

The foundation stone was laid by the Archbishop of Canterbury the same day as that of Holy Trinity, Southwark; both churches stood in an area where Dissent was strong. The Waterloo Commission lent part of the £19,000 required, and might have given it outright if it had not been for the quarrels about the project in the vestry of St Mary Newington, from which the parishes were split off.

This was Soane's first church. It is very like ST JOHN ON BETHNAL GREEN and still liker HOLY TRINITY, MARYLEBONE. An Ionic portico, sunk flush in a stock-brick wall, supports a tower and an uncompromisingly narrow pepperpot. Inside, the most striking thing is the unaltered chancel, austerely rhythmical behind its big plain arch with pierced spandrels, and having still the original Grecian altar-piece, flat and angular (though no longer as Soane left it), painted to resemble Siena marble. The windows here are as they originally were at Bethnal Green, that is, tall and round-headed with a square frame inset in the bottom half. There used to be a strange transverse open loggia at the east end, which answered the vestibule under the western tower, and was reminiscent of the plan of the east end of ST ALFEGE, GREENWICH; but this has now been filled in with a Lady Chapel etc, and the whole space is more commonplace. Most

---

[1] As in the towers at Wren's St Paul's, and at Borromini's S. Agnese in Rome.

St Peter's, Walworth

remarkable of all is the undercroft. It is lit by area windows and each individual area has the earth held away by, as it were, a horizontal semi-circular arch. This prepares one for the surprise of the undercroft itself where there are barrel arches, that is, full-circle. It is like a series of intersecting tunnels, but is now very seldom visible. In this pattern of bullseye squints the poor of Walworth used to have free Christmas dinners, and in it 84 people were killed by bombs. The bombs also destroyed the glass ('after Raphael') given by Soane himself because it was the first church he built. The church has been on the whole well repaired.

WILLIAM WHITE
1865–6

ID1

95. ST SAVIOUR'S, ABERDEEN PARK
HIGHBURY, N5
U: Highbury and Islington

Here is a small, almost all brick, church neglected over the years, but sufficiently admired by its friends to receive – as well as deserve – help. It is currently being restored.

It is a very dense design, high-seeming nave and transepts clustering round its almost squat spire, which as John Betjeman saw it, 'Bulges over

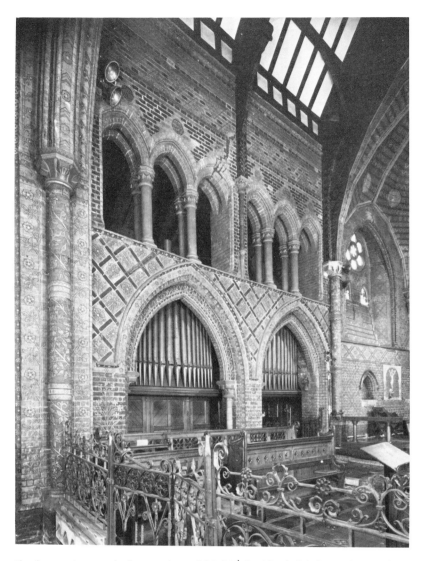

St Saviour's, Aberdeen Park

the house tops, polychromatic and high'.[1] Inside, brick in various colours is used with an almost tapestry effect to close in the carefully shaped spaces. In the chancel, over the patterns of the brick, is spread delicate stencilling of flowers and leaves. (Muslin over the tapestry.) Light through the stained glass further dapples all.

---

[1] 'St Saviour's Aberdeen Park, Highbury, London, N.', in *Collected Poems*, London 1979, pp. 154–6.

*St Saviour's,
Aberdeen Park*

S. S. TEULON
1869–76

96. ST STEPHEN'S, ROSSLYN HILL
HAMPSTEAD,NW3

IC2   U: Belsize Park

Teulon can as here be a ferociously powerful architect, singularly unsmiling. (He can smile, as at St Silas', Penton Street, Islington, where he used Kentish ragstone and rather perversely dressed it with stone-coloured brick, even to setting up a row of brick-built turrets to look like chimneys.) Mostly his work has been disliked: Pevsner refers to his 'hamfistedness', to his 'sensational display, crude, heavy, noisy', but also admits 'impressive'.[1] And so it is: St Stephen's is a great beached whale now it is disused and boarded up. There are plans for a new use and it should indeed be preserved: there is a quality here of huge and strenuous life, a kind of incandescent vigour which was very much part of the Victorian age and a respect for the logic of organic scale.

---

[1] Nikolaus Pevsner, *The Buildings of England: London, excluding the Cities of London and Westminster*, Harmondsworth 1951, p. 188.

A contemporary, Charles Eastlake, historian of 'the Revival', found its siting 'picturesque', 'the novelty of its proportions and the beauty of the materials . . . no small attraction' and its colour 'very agreeable'.[1] Such mild language after Pevsner's may surprise us. Yet that Teulon's statement may be unfamiliar, and to some unsympathetic, does not make it for either reason invalid. There were thought to be continental precedents for some of its elements, but Teulon was not an architect much interested in justifications.

St Stephen's, Rosslyn Hill

ST STEPHEN'S CHAPEL

see PALACE OF WESTMINSTER

[1] Charles Eastlake, *A History of the Gothic Revival*, 1872, 2nd edn, Leicester 1978, p. 368.

SIR CHRISTOPHER
WREN
1672–9

IIE2

97. ST STEPHEN WALBROOK
CITY, EC4
U: Bank

Twenty guineas in a silk purse, the vestry decided in February 1673, should be presented to Dr Wren or his Lady in token of its appreciation of the 'great care and extraordinary pains taken in the contriving the design of the Church'. St Stephen's has continued to be admired: by foreigners for a logic rare in English architecture, and by Londoners for the quaintness involved in a building so dull outside having such lightness and beauty within.

The first church, founded some time before 1100, was on the west bank of the Wall Brook; little is known about it except that it had a belfry from which one William le Clarke fell in 1278 and died 'by another death than his rightful death'.[1] A new church was built on the east bank in 1429. It was 120 feet long, had a cloister and an enormous number of images, including eight in the choir. Several of the windows were new-glazed with stained glass in 1614.

Wren's tower is plain and pleasant in a tweedy way and the lantern is gay and musical like those of ST MICHAEL PATERNOSTER ROYAL and ST JAMES GARLICKHYTHE, all small relations to St Paul's two western towers. The exterior of the church itself is non-committal. But when you enter from

St Stephen Walbrook

---

[1] Quoted in T. Milbourne, *London and Middlesex Archaeological Society Transactions*, vol. v, London 1881; article on the medieval churches of St Stephen Walbrook.

the street 'through a vestibule of dubious obscurity . . . a halo of dazzling
light flashes at once upon the eye; and a lovely band of Corinthian
columns, of beauteous proportions, appear in magic mazes before you . . .
On a second look, the columns slide into complete order, like a band of
young elegant dancers, at the close of a quadrille.'[1] And on a third look
and a fourth no longer the columns but the spaces they define arrange and
rearrange themselves endlessly. In all good architecture one is as much
aware of the shapes of the voids as of the shapes of the solids and here,
though the internal surfaces are thoroughly pleasing, it is space that Wren
is considering. The dome is mere wood and lead and plaster, but the

---

[1] J. Elmes, *Memoirs . . . of Sir Christopher Wren*, London 1823, p. 315.

beauty is not in the dome itself; it is in its form, its effect on light entering through its lantern, its play with the intertranspicuous cubes and cylinders of space below.

F. C. Penrose restored in the 1880s. Believing for several reasons that Wren would have preferred the church unencumbered with pews, he emptied it as far as he could. He also did sums with the measurements and discovered 'many accurate proportions in terms of low figures'.[1] For the ground plan the numbers are 4:7:10. Those who are amused by the game of considering architecture as petrified music will easily recognise in these harmonics a disposition of the dominant seventh common in the 18th century. Let us pursue. This discord can be resolved by a perfect cadence giving the harmonics 2:5:8, or by an interrupted cadence, giving the harmonics 6:9:14. A suspension in either of these cadences would hold over 7 and 10. And in fact all these numbers are to be found in the proportions of the elevation of St Stephen's.

St Stephen's was damaged during World War II but was repaired. It is now again restored. The church had been settling unevenly, so great concrete piles have been put in beneath the columns to support them. Cunningly, the piles are adjustable, so that any future settling can be more easily dealt with. A new stone floor and complete redecoration came next, but this time there was not a gilder employed, as was Wm Davis in 1679, who received 'ffor 2200 of gold roses in the said church at 16 shillings per hundred: – £17 12.0.'[2]

As we write, the propriety of installing a central altar, designed by Henry Moore, is under discussion; it is opposed by some on liturgical as well as aesthetic grounds.[3]

98. THE TEMPLE CHURCH
INNER TEMPLE LANE, CITY, EC4
U: Temple

1185
1840–1953

IID2

The Temple Church still has the ground plan of the original church of the Knights Templar; not much remains of their building (though more than that of the Knights Hospitallers, at st john's, clerkenwell). Layers of whitewash and wainscotting coming right up to the windows in the 18th century, restoration of the most violent kind in the 19th century, and bombs and rebuilding in the 20th result in a fabric almost entirely new.

The Knights Templar founded themselves in Jerusalem in 1118, just after the First Crusade, to protect Christian pilgrims in Palestine, and generally to maintain the Crusader Kingdoms in Syria, Lebanon, Palestine and Cyprus. St Bernard of Clairvaux, the great Cistercian innovator, drew up a rule for them, moderate and suitable for men of action. The Pope

[1] F. C. Penrose, *Transactions of the Royal Institute of British Architects*, New Series 6, London 1890, p. 243.
[2] *Wren Society*, vol. x, p. 122.
[3] Cf. st lawrence jewry, p. 133 and Introduction p. 25.

The Temple Church

approved the white habit with the red cross and they became a standing army in the Near East. The order owned property, was immune from every jurisdiction but that of the Pope, and only noblemen were admitted to it. Married men could join but could not wear the white habit, which signified continence. The Templars had a strong romantic appeal and prospered greatly.

It is thought that they first came to England in 1128; they certainly established themselves about then in Holborn, where Southampton Buildings now are. There they built a church in Caen stone with a Round at one end like that of the Holy Sepulchre in Jerusalem.[1] Some years later

---

[1] Of the eleven known churches in England with round naves some are connected with the military orders, but by no means all. St Sepulchre, Cambridge, and St Sepulchre, Northampton, are not. The earliest to which reference is found, one at Abingdon, was built in the mid-10th century, before the orders were formed. Mainly these churches are 11th- and 12th-century, and Little Maplestead's 14th-century fabric appears to have been built on a 12th-century plan (see W. St John Hope, *Report of the Chapter of the Order of St John of Jerusalem* for 1916).

The Temple Church

they moved to the 'New Temple' near the Thames and in 1185 the Round
of their new church was consecrated by Heraclius, Patriarch of Jerusalem.
During the same visit he consecrated the Hospitallers' round church in
Clerkenwell. Of the Templars' Round only the west door shows the original
surface; the rest of the building was, until the bombing, as like the original
as conscientious but insensitive Victorian restorers could make it. The
five-bayed rectangular choir with its two aisles of equal height was finished
in 1240, but it had probably had a smaller predecessor. There was also an
early 13th-century chapel tacked on to the south side of the Round, with a
crypt below. The crypt is still there. Another underground chamber, this
time of the 12th century, has been excavated under the south aisle of the
chancel: this is an odd little place, built before the 1240 chancel, low and
long, with a piscina, a stone bench along the north and south walls, a

staircase to the chancel and evidence suggesting an altar in the east.[1] As the Templars were always rich and had moreover the keeping of other fortunes than their own, this may have been their strong-room – doubly safe in the thickness of its walls and the holiness of its altar.

The order was entirely self-sufficient, having in it both serving brothers for the knights' physical needs and priests for their spiritual, all subordinate to the knights themselves. In England during the 12th and early 13th centuries their political power was considerable, and it did not decrease in becoming more specifically financial. Their organisation throughout Europe, their enormous riches and the safety of their convents, made them bankers to all who wished either to deposit treasure or make large-scale financial transactions. The Bishops of Ely, who were concerned under the Angevin kings with the Exchequer, had a right of lodging in the Temple.

But in 1291 the Arabs reconquered the Levant. The order returned to Cyprus and in 1306 its Grand Master was summoned to the Pope, who was then at Avignon. He was also under the thumb of King Philip IV of France who coveted the riches of the Templars. After several years the Pope's inquisitors accumulated by torture a number of confessions of blasphemy and sodomy, and in 1312 by apostolic, not ecumenical, procedure he dissolved the order. The Council of Vienne sought to transfer its property to the Knights Hospitallers, but the English barons opposed this attempt by the Church to deal in real estate, and several claimed the Templars' estates by escheat, as also did the king.

The Temple was granted by the Crown to a series of tenants, who died or were attainted until finally the Hospitallers proved their case and obtained possession in 1338. Some time during the next 50 years the apprentices of the Law, already it seems in two Societies, acquired the tenancy of it, and have occupied it since. The Temple Church has become their own church and the Societies have adopted its name.

Under the Templars there had been a prior and 13 secular chaplains; by 1540 these had dwindled to the 'Master of the Temple', as the principal priest was called, and two chaplains. Henry VIII confiscated the church from the Hospitallers in 1540, and it was again in the hands of the Crown until James I presented it to the two Societies of the Inner and Middle Temple, retaining only the appointment of the Master. During all this time the lawyers had kept the tenancy, and with it an obligation to attend divine service in the Temple Church.

Richard Hooker of the *Laws of Ecclesiastical Polity* was Master from 1585 to 1591 and had as his reader, who delivered the afternoon sermon, a Calvinist called Walter Travers. Isaak Walton quoted a common saying: 'The forenoon sermon spake Canterbury, and the afternoon Geneva'; this high-powered theological disputation filled the church with delighted barristers.

The Round seems to have been used as a kind of general waiting room by all who had business with the lawyers; the west porch was a shop with

---

[1] W. H. Godfrey, 'Recent Discoveries at the Temple', *Archaeologia*, 1953, p. 123.

chambers above, and there were also shops along the south wall. The churchyard had a tailor's shop and several shacks in it, and laundresses washed and hung up clothes there. The church itself was sometimes used as a committee room by the House of Commons.

The Round was a little damaged in the Great Fire and in 1682 Wren advised that £1,400 should be spent on repairs. They included raising the level of the floor, putting wainscotting up to the windows throughout both the Round and the chancel, and whitewashing everything else. An organ was also to be erected; the Middle Temple wished it to be made by Father Smith, the Inner Temple by Renatus Harris. Smith and Harris each made an organ and set it up; the better organ was to be chosen. Purcell and Blow played Smith's, the queen's organist played Harris's, first at alternate services and finally alternately at the same services. Harris was lent £100 by the Inner Temple for the expense of keeping a watchman on his organ. The two Societies came to no conclusion, each sticking to its original choice. Eventually, in 1685, they decided to accept the judgment of the Lord Keeper of the Great Seal, Lord Guilford, who was a lover of music and himself a performer. But Lord Guilford died without disclosing his preference and was succeeded as Lord Keeper by Lord Chief Justice Jeffreys, more famous for ferocity than for a knowledge of music. He, however, at the end of 1687, just after the Bloody Assize, decided that Smith's organ was the better and that a solatium of £200 should be given to Harris. Father Smith had provided his organ with the first 'quarter tones' to be heard in this country. They were not what we should now call quarter tones, but simply two extra keys to distinguish a true A^b from the $G\sharp$ and a true $D\sharp$ from the E^b, thus bringing four more keys within the rigid capabilities of the old unequal temperament.

Wren's whitewash and wainscotting remained until the 19th century. Some time in the 18th century buttresses and battlements had been added; these too were removed in the 19th century. Robert Smirke carried out some restorations in 1828, but it was Sidney Smirke and Decimus Burton who made such a thorough job of it in 1840–2, when 'every ancient surface was repaired away or renewed'[1] except for the vaulted ceiling of the choir. When the church was bombed and badly damaged in 1941 this ceiling survived again because the heat of the fire traversed the porous limestone quickly and evenly. The Purbeck marble columns which supported it heated slowly and unevenly, split, and had to be replaced. While this was being done the vault was carried on a temporary structure; a neat and tricky job. The new Purbeck marble piers are polished to a pearly grey which admirably shows off the caviare-like texture. The dusty electric chandeliers are cunningly exactly the same colour. The Round has been admirably repaired, and the splendid Purbeck crusaders who lay there so long and were smashed to smithereens have been wonderfully put back together and lie in peace again. The reredos of Wren's time has been brought back from the museum at Castle Barnard and new rails, seats and so on designed by Mr W. H. Godfrey, whose son was the repairing

[1] W. H. Godfrey, loc. cit.

architect, not only match but enhance. The glass, done in the late fifties by Carl Edwards, is very blue and right. The effect is now of a soaring simplicity; excellent materials have been used with appreciation and without fuss.

THE TOWER OF LONDON
99. ST JOHN IN THE WHITE TOWER
100. ST PETER AD VINCULA
TOWER HILL, EC3
U: Tower Hill

IIF3

1080–8

1305 and early 16th century

St John in the White Tower is a miniature Norman church, set high up in the White Tower, indistinguishable without from the rest of the great keep which has protected it from weather and from human onslaught. The White Tower, and St John's Chapel in it, were built in the 1080s for William the Conqueror by Gandulf, or Gandalf, Bishop of Rochester. The Celts had fortified Tower Hill, so had the Romans; the White Tower has also been known as Caesar's Tower, and St John's Chapel as Caesar's Chapel. Gandulf, conscientiously religious as well as a great builder, had spent some years in Caen as a monk and used Caen stone and Caen methods in his building. This chapel, small as it is, has that majestic Norman solidity which makes all later medieval architecture seem jazzy. The only decoration is a Tau-shaped cross on the capitals and, on the two westernmost only, a pattern reminiscent of fossilised primordial flatfish. Henry III in 1241 had the chapel painted up, had a gilded throne installed at the west end, and had some of the windows glazed (one with 'mariola tenente puerum suum' – 'a little Mary holding her boy'). Wat Tyler's rebels found Archbishop Sudbury and the Grand Prior of ST JOHN'S, CLERKENWELL at prayer before the altar and beheaded them on Tower Hill.

The chapel was burnt out in 1512, but was presumably restored, for Lady Jane Grey used it when she was queen. The Duke of Northumberland, her father-in-law, in a fruitless attempt to save his life, recanted his Protestantism there; and there also Mary Tudor married Philip II of Spain by proxy. The Stuarts seldom used it, but Wren enlarged most of the White Tower windows, including those of the chapel. In Charles II's reign the chapel was stripped and used as a store for State papers. The White Tower itself was used by the Board of Ordnance and in 1857 there was a proposal to store army clothing in the chapel. Protests led to royal intervention and, four years later, to restoration. By then the chapel was all whitewashed and panels had been inserted across the bottom of the triforium arches. But beneath this thin layer the Norman work remained intact and the restorers were not tempted to improve it. They only put some morsels of 16th- and 17th-century stained glass, including some from Strawberry Hill, into Wren's tenderly enlarged windows. So in London of all places there remains, perfect and unchanged, this small, bare, beautiful chapel built by the first King of England to have a number.

Tower of London, St John in the White Tower

St Peter ad Vincula was mainly for the garrison and prisoners. While St John's Chapel is unchanged from its building, St Peter's, like other parish churches, has assumed so many styles that it is now almost styleless. But its monuments, its associations, and its site make it a poignant place.

A Chapel of St Peter existed in 1210, which Henry III caused to be decorated and improved, at the same time as St John's Chapel, in 1241. There was a royal pew to be repaired, so it was not only for the use of the garrison; he ordered much refurbishing of images, and a marble font with marble columns. Edward I rebuilt the chapel in 1305–6, perhaps a little to the south of the other one, so that the present north wall may incorporate some of the old south wall, while the crypt remains to the north of the present building. Edward III proposed making of it some kind of collegiate church, with dean and canons, and subsequently left it sufficiently endowed to support a rector and five chaplains. Behind the church was the 'Reclusory of St Peter' where an anchorite or anchoress lived, receiving from the king's charity a penny a day. This 'living' was in the king's gift.

Henry VIII, after a general survey of the whole Tower in 1532, seems to have almost rebuilt the chapel: the present windows, arches, and timber roof are all of this time. Queen Elizabeth added a rather shack-like south door, and later generations box pews and a reredos; two nave windows

were blocked up; George II had a gallery put in over the aisle and the west end of the nave: and many local inhabitants, in and out of the Tower, set up their monuments. There was a restoration in 1876, more or less to its Henry VIII state.

Tower of London, St John in the White Tower

The church is in the corner of Tower Green. The scaffold was just in front of it, and the hopping ravens, which now croak their 'Nevermore' where it was, only partly reassure. Spies were executed in the Tower in both the wars of this century. St Peter's is a long shallow building, lidded with a heavy unpierced parapet, in flint-covered rubble. Among the flints are oyster-shells which gleam like fungus. Its tower is too thin and short to promise resurrection, and one is not surprised that Pepys found the prisoners in the Tower, although they were allowed to, not attending service there. Inside the chapel the monuments to various Lieutenants of the Tower are fine and cheerful, but beneath the pavement, as carefully arranged as a Victorian committee of seven substantial men could manage, lie the great unsuccessful. Ann Boleyn, whose little neck they pieced together again, the Countess of Rochford who had betrayed her, but who herself suffered later with her mistress, Katherine Howard; Katherine Howard; Lady Jane Grey, whose patent innocence might have saved her had her father laid aside his ambition a little longer; he lies there, too, and Northumberland, whose treason was followed by treachery to the unfortunates he used and to the religion he professed; Essex; Strafford;

Judge Jeffreys for a time; and beside him the Duke of Monmouth, whose followers Jeffreys hanged, and in whose blood handkerchiefs were dipped for luck; the kilted lords of the 'Forty-Five.

To these, and to many others who risked and lost, the outline of this squat chapel was the last sight of a world grown vengeful.

1777–8

101. WESLEY'S CHAPEL
CITY ROAD, BY BUNHILL FIELDS, EC1

IIF1

U: Old Street

In November 1739 John Wesley preached in a long-disused foundry on Windmill Hill, Finsbury. Shortly after, he bought the lease of the foundry and made it into a combination of chapel, dwelling house and school, for himself and his helpers. It also had a dispensary with a surgeon attached, a soup-kitchen, an almshouse, stables, and a sum of money for advancing to the needy – in fact, a pocket welfare state. In 1742 there was a congregation of 426; eighteen months later, of 2,200.

The lease ran out and in 1777 the new chapel and a house were built opposite Bunhill Fields. The house is much as it always was but the chapel has been so reverently and affectionately touched up and improved as to lose all flavour. The galleries began square but were made oval in the early 19th century; a porch was put up in 1891; the columns supporting the gallery were originally wood (traditionally masts from Deptford dockyard acquired by the direct permission of George III); now they are genuine pink marble. And on to everything has descended a crust of memorials to Wesleyan worthies the world over. What is original, for instance the communion table and rails and the pulpit, is carefully marked 'John Wesley's'.

APPENDIX I

WREN'S CITY CHURCHES

All Hallows, Lombard Street
demolished 1938

All Hallows the Great, Upper Thames
Street *demolished 1893–4*

All Hallows, Watling Street
demolished 1876–7

Christ Church, Newgate Street
*interior destroyed by bombing
1940*

St Alban, Wood Street *destroyed by
bombing 1940 except for tower*

St Andrew, Holborn *destroyed by
bombing 1941*

St Andrew by the Wardrobe

St Anne and St Agnes, Gresham
Street *damaged by bombing 1940*

St Antholin, Budge Row *demolished
1875*

St Augustine, Watling Street *part of
church destroyed by bombing
1941*

St Bartholomew Exchange
demolished 1840–1

St Benet, Gracechurch Street
demolished 1867–8

ST BENET, PAUL'S WHARF

St Benet Fink *demolished 1842–4*

ST BRIDE'S, FLEET STREET

St Christopher-le-Stocks
demolished 1781

St Clement, Eastcheap

St Dionis Backchurch *demolished
1878–9*

ST DUNSTAN IN THE EAST

St Edmund the King, Lombard Street
damaged by bombing 1917

St George, Botolph Lane
demolished 1903–4

ST JAMES GARLICKHYTHE

ST LAWRENCE JEWRY

ST MAGNUS THE MARTYR

ST MARGARET, LOTHBURY

St Margaret Pattens, Rood Lane

ST MARTIN LUDGATE

ST MARY ABCHURCH

ST MARY ALDERMARY

ST MARY AT HILL

St Mary Aldermanbury *interior
destroyed by bombing 1940*

St Mary Magdalen, Old Fish Street
demolished 1887

St Mary Somerset *demolished
except tower 1871*

ST MARY LE BOW

St Matthew, Friday Street
demolished 1881

St Michael Bassishaw *demolished
1899*

St Michael, Cornhill

St Michael, Crooked Lane
demolished 1831

ST MICHAEL PATERNOSTER ROYAL

St Michael, Queenhythe *demolished
1876*

St Michael, Wood Street
demolished 1897

St Mildred, Bread Street *destroyed
by bombing 1941*

St Mildred, Poultry *demolished 1872*

St Nicholas, Cole Abbey *gutted by
bombing 1941*

St Olave, Old Jewry *demolished
except tower 1888–9*

St Peter, Cornhill

St Stephen, Coleman Street
destroyed by bombing 1940

ST STEPHEN WALBROOK

St Swithin, London Stone *interior
destroyed by bombing 1941*

St Vedast, Foster Lane *damaged by
bombing 1940*

ST JAMES, PICCADILLY, is Wren's
only London Church outside
the City.

APPENDIX II

	Norman	Later Medieval	Tudor and Jacobean	Inigo Jones	Wren and his followers	The 'Fifty Churches'	Hawksmoor	18th cent.	Soane	Grecian and Regency	The 'Waterloo Churches' and till 1840	1840–70	1870–1900	Post-Victorian	City of London	Westminster	North of the Thames	South of the Thames
1. All Hallows-by-the-Tower		•													•			
2. All Hallows on the Wall								•							•			
3. All Hallows, Savernake Road													•				•	
4. All Saints, Camden Town										•							•	
5. All Saints, Chelsea Old Church		•															•	
6. All Saints, Margaret Street												•					•	
7. All Saints, Talbot Road												•					•	
8. All Souls, Langham Place										•							•	
9. Bevis Marks Synagogue					(•)										•			
10. The Brompton Oratory													•				•	
11. The Charterhouse Chapel			•												•			
12. Christ Church Spitalfields						•	•										•	
13. The Church of Christ the King												•					•	
14. Geffrye Museum, Ironmongers' Almshouses Chapel								•									•	
15. Greenwich Hospital Chapel					•					•								•
16. Guy's Hospital Chapel								•										•
17. Holy Trinity, Latimer Road													•				•	
18. Holy Trinity, Marylebone									•								•	
19. Holy Trinity, Sloane Street														•			•	
20. Lincolns Inn Chapel															•			
21. Morden College Chapel					•													•
22. Palace of Westminster, St Stephen's Chapel																•		
23. St Alban's Holborn												•					•	
24. St Alfege, Greenwich						•	•											•
25. St Anne's, Limehouse						•	•										•	
26. St Anne's, Wandsworth											•							•

	Norman	Later Medieval	Tudor and Jacobean	Inigo Jones	Wren and his followers	The 'Fifty Churches'	Hawksmoor	18th cent.	Soane	Grecian and Regency	The Waterloo Churches and till 1840	1840–70	1870–1900	Post-Victorian	City of London	Westminster	North of the Thames	South of the Thames
27. St Augustine, Kilburn													•				•	
28. St Augustine, Queen's Gate												•					•	
29. St Barnabas, Pimlico												•				•		
30. St Bartholomew the Great	•														•			
31. St Benet, Paul's Wharf					•										•			
32. St Botolph								•							•			
33. St Bride's, Fleet Street					•										•			
34. St Clement Danes					•											•		
35. St Cuthbert, Philbeach Gardens													•				•	
36. St Cyprian's, Clarence Gate														•			•	
37. St Dominic, Southampton Rd													•				•	
38. St Dunstan in the East					•										•			
39. St Dunstan, Stepney		•															•	
40. St Dunstans in the West											•				•			
41. St George's, Bloomsbury						•	•										•	
42. St George's, Hanover Square						•										•		
43. St George's in the East						•	•										•	
44. St George the Martyr, Southwark						•												•
45. St Giles, Camberwell												•						•
46. St Giles, Cripplegate			•												•			
47. St Giles-in-the-Fields						•											•	
48. St Helen's, Bishopsgate		•													•			
49. St James, Bermondsey											•							•
50. St James, Clerkenwell								•									•	
51. St James Garlickhythe					•										•			
52. St James, Piccadilly					•											•		
53. St James's Palace, The Queen's Chapel				•												•		

	Norman	Later Medieval	Tudor and Jacobean	Inigo Jones	Wren and his followers	The 'Fifty Churches'	Hawksmoor	18th cent.	Soane	Grecian and Regency	The Waterloo Churches' and till 1840	1840-70	1870-1900	Post-Victorian	City of London	Westminster	North of the Thames	South of the Thames
54. St John on Bethnal Green									•								•	
55. St John's, Clerkenwell	•							•									•	
56. St John at Hackney								•									•	
57. St John's, Hampstead								•									•	
58. St John's, Smith Square						•										•		
59. St John, Wapping								•									•	
60. St Jude on the Hill														•			•	
61. St Katherine Cree			•												•			
62. St Lawrence Jewry					•										•			
63. St Leonard's, Shoreditch						•											•	
64. St Luke's, Chelsea											•						•	
65. St Magnus the Martyr					•										•			
66. St Margaret, Lothbury					•										•			
67. St Margaret's, Westminster		•														•		
68. St Mark, Dalston													•				•	
69. St Martin, Gospel Oak												•					•	
70. St Martin-in-the-Fields						•										•		
71. St Martin Ludgate					•										•			
72. St Mary Abbots													•				•	
73. St Mary Abchurch					•										•			
74. St Mary Aldermary					•										•			
75. St Mary at Hill					•										•			
76. St Mary, Battersea								•										•
77. St Marylebone										•							•	
78. St Mary le Bow					•										•			
79. St Mary-le-Strand						•										•		
80. St Mary, Paddington								•									•	
81. St Mary's, Rotherhithe								•										•
82. St Mary Woolnoth							•								•			

	Norman	Later Medieval	Tudor and Jacobean	Inigo Jones	Wren and his followers	The 'Fifty Churches'	Hauksmoor	18th cent.	Soane	Grecian and Regency	The 'Waterloo Churches' and till 1840	1840-70	1870-1900	Post-Victorian	City of London	Westminster	North of the Thames	South of the Thames
83. St Mary Magdalene, Bermondsey			•															•
84. St Mary Magdalen, Paddington												•					•	
85. St Matthew's, Brixton										•								•
86. St Matthias, Hackney												•					•	
87. St Michael and All Angels, Blackheath Park											•							•
88. St Michael, Camden Road													•				•	
89. St Michael Paternoster Royal					•										•			
90. New St Pancras										•							•	
91. Old St Pancras		•										•					•	
92. St Paul's, Covent Garden				•												•		
93. St Paul's, Deptford						•												•
94. St Peter's, Walworth									•									•
95. St Saviour's, Aberdeen Park												•					•	
96. St Stephen's, Rosslyn Hill													•				•	
97. St Stephen Walbrook					•										•			
98. The Temple Church		•													•			
99. The Tower of London, St John in the White Tower	•														•			
100. The Tower of London, St Peter ad Vincula			•												•			
101. Wesley's Chapel								•									•	

PHOTO CREDITS

The photographs are reproduced by courtesy of the following: Birkbeck College, Univ. of London (pages 39, 65, 154); British Tourist Authority (pages 51, 81, 83, 113, 114, 135, 194); Kenneth Campbell (page 122); Conway Library (pages 31, 32, 74, 87, 175, 183); *Country Life* (page 165); André Goulancourt (pages 45, 47, 48, 61, 62, 69, 70, 71, 95, 99, 120, 174, 184, 185, 199, 200); Greater London Council (page 126); A. F. Kersting (pages 9, 11, 27, 33, 36, 40, 42, 50, 54, 58, 60, 66, 68, 76, 78, 80, 88, 98, 101, 103, 116, 124, 128, 129, 132, 133, 137, 142, 143, 151, 153, 160, 162, 167, 171, 177, 187); Philips Electronics Ltd (page 105); Royal Commission on the Historical Monuments of England (pages 26, 37, 52, 57, 59, 84, 94, 107, 111, 125, 139, 143, 145, 147, 157, 161, 167, 188, 189, 190, 191, 192, 195).

INDEX

Main entries appear in italic type.
Illustrations are asterisked.

Adelmare, Sir Julius Caesar, 108
Alberti, Leone Battista, 7
Alfune, 102
All Hallows-by-the-Tower, 7, *29–30*
All Hallows on the Wall, 17, *30–31*,
  110n
All Hallows the Great, 141
All Hallows, Savernake Road, 23, 24n,
  31–2, 31–32*
All Saints, Camden Town, *32–3*, 33*
All Saints, Chelsea Old Church, *33–4*,
  136
All Saints, Margaret Street, 23, 24n,
  35–7, 36–7*
All Saints, Newcastle upon Tyne, 120–
  21
All Saints, Talbot Road, *38*
All Souls, Langham Place, 17, *38–9*,
  39*
Allen, Godfrey, 82
Allen, Hugh, 97, 99
Andrewes, Lancelot, 30, 104
Anne, Queen of England, 12
Archer, Thomas, 7, 13, 14, 15, 124,
  183–6
Arne, Thomas, 182
Arthur, Prince, 143
Audley, Lord, 130
Augustine, Saint *see* St Augustine
Avis, Joseph, 40

Bacon, Francis, 104, 148
Bancroft, Francis, 108
Barking, Abbey of, 29
baroque, 13–14
Barry, Edward, 59
Barry, Sir Charles, 58–9
Baylis, Lilian, 182
Beckford, Lord Mayor, 156
Beckford, William, 156
Bedford, Francis, 18, 178
Bell, Alfred, 123
Bentley, J. F., 21n
Bermondsey, Abbey of, 2
Bernini, Lorenzo, 15, 169
Bernini, Pietro, 34
Best, Geoffrey, 21–2
Bethlem Hospital, 4
Betjeman, Sir John, 23, 56, 112, 145,
  187–8
Bevis Marks Synagogue, 10, 12, *40–41*,
  40*
Blackburne, E. L., 144
Blair, David, 182

Blake, William, 158
Blomfield, Bishop of London, 19–20,
  97
Blomfield, Sir Reginald, 23n, 88, 110,
  133
Boadicea, 29
Bodley, G. F., 24, 141, 176
Boleyn, Ann, 200
Bolton, Prior, 77
Bond, Martin, 108
Boniface, Archbishop of Canterbury, 75
Bonner, Bishop, 100
Boone's Chapel, 10n, 11*
Borromini, Francesco, 13, 15, 42, 186n
Bosch, Hieronymus, 43
Boullée, Etienne-Louis, 17
Brandon, John Raphael, 17, 24, 49
Brett, Tracey, ix
Brompton Oratory, the, *41–3*, 42*
Brookholding-Jones, Adrian, 43
Brooks, James, 22, 24, 31
Brown, Cecil, 133
Browne, R., 149
Browning, Robert and Elizabeth, 160
Buckler, C. A., 86
Bucknall, William, 86
Burbage, Richard, 134
Burleigh, Lord, 118
Burlington, Lord, 16, 182
Burnet, Bishop Gilbert, 12, 111
Burton, Decimus, 197
Butterfield, William, 23–4, 35, 37, 60,
  73, 169, 174, 178, 182
Buttress, Donald, 27n
Byron, George Gordon, Lord, 105

Cadwallader, 149
Canaletto, 12
Caracci, Annibale, 115
Caravaggio, Michelangelo da, 13
Carlile, Wilson, 156
Carlyle, Thomas, 49, 109
Caroe, W. D., 24
Carpenter, R. C., 23n
Carr, James, 109–10
Carr, John, 110
Castle Howard, 13n
Catherine of Aragon, 143
Catherine of Braganza, Queen, 115
Chambers, Sir William, 110, 159
Champneys, Basil, 64, 100
Chantry chapels, 5–6
Chaplin, Charlie, 182
Chapman, George, 104
Charles I, King of England, 115, 166
Charles II, King of England, 112, 115,
  148, 198

Charterhouse Chapel, the, *43–4*
Chesterfield, Lord, 125
Cheston, Chester, 144
Cheyne, Lady Jane, 34
Christ Church Spitalfields, 9, 40, *44–9*,
  45–7*, 64, 91
Christ Church, Streatham, 21n
Christian, Ewan, 46
Church Building Endowment Fund,
  the, 19
Church Building Society, the, 19
Church of Christ the King, The, 24n,
  49
Church of the Ascension, Lavender
  Hill, 31
Clairmont, Allegra, 105
Clairmont, Clare, 105
Clark, Basil, 56
Clarke, Sir John, 56
Clarke, Somers, 55
Clerkenwell Pantheon, the, 17
Cluny, Abbey of, 2
Cochrane, Charles, 182
Cockerell, F. P., 123
Commonwealth, the, 6, 8
Comper, Sir Ninian, 24, 86, 172
Counter-Reformation, 5, 19
Coward, Noël, 182
Cowper, William, 92, 167
Crosby, Lady, 108
Crosby, Sir John, 106, 108
Crosthwaite, J. C., 155
Cundy, Thomas, 74–5

d'Urfey, Thomas, 113
Dacre, Lord, of the South, 34
Dance, George (the Elder), 16, 79,
  134–6
Dance, George (the Younger), 17, 30,
  110
Davis, William, 193
de Oteswich, John, 108
de Vergara, Juan Ruyz, 119
de Worde, Wynkyn, 81
decoration, 12
Dickens, Charles, 100; *Our Mutual
  Friend*, 125
Dickinson, William, 154
Disraeli, Benjamin, 41
Dixon, Joseph, 156–7
Donne, John, 57, 93, 164
Dulwich College, 7
Duncombe, George, 140

Earp, Thomas, 172
Eastlake, Charles, 21, 23, 35, 153, 190
Ecclesiologist, The (magazine), 37